Lecture Notes in Computer Science 8350

Commenced Publication in 1973
Founding and Former Series Editors:
Gerhard Goos, Juris Hartmanis, and Jan van Leeuwen

T0211755

Erik Maehle   Kay Römer
Wolfgang Karl   Eduardo Tovar (Eds.)

Architecture of Computing Systems – ARCS 2014

27th International Conference
Lübeck, Germany, February 25-28, 2014
Proceedings

Springer

Volume Editors

Erik Maehle
Universität zu Lübeck, Institut für Technische Informatik
Lübeck, Germany
E-mail: maehle@iti.uni-luebeck.de

Kay Römer
Graz University of Technology, Institute of Technical Informatics
Graz, Austria
E-mail: roemer@tugraz.at

Wolfgang Karl
Karlsruhe Institute of Technology (KIT)
Institute of Computer Science and Computer Engineering
Karlsruhe, Germany
E-mail: karl@kit.edu

Eduardo Tovar
CISTER-ISEP, Polytechnic Institute of Porto
Porto, Portugal
E-mail: emt@isep.ipp.pt

ISSN 0302-9743   e-ISSN 1611-3349
ISBN 978-3-319-04890-1   e-ISBN 978-3-319-04891-8
DOI 10.1007/978-3-319-04891-8
Springer Cham Heidelberg New York Dordrecht London

Library of Congress Control Number: 2014930986

CR Subject Classification (1998): C.2, C.5.3, D.4, D.2.11, H.3.5, H.4, H.5.4

LNCS Sublibrary: SL 1 – Theoretical Computer Science and General Issues

Typesetting: Camera-ready by author, data conversion by Scientific Publishing Services, Chennai, India

Printed on acid-free paper

Springer is part of Springer Science+Business Media (www.springer.com)

Preface

The 27th International Conference on Architecture of Computing Systems (ARCS 2014) was hosted by the Institute of Computer Engineering at the University of Luebeck, Germany, from February 25 to 28, 2014 and continued the long-standing ARCS tradition of reporting top-notch results in computer architecture and related areas. It was organized by the special interest group on Architecture of Computing Systems of the GI (Gesellschaft für Informatik e.V.) and ITG (Informationstechnische Gesellschaft im VDE), where the latter held the organizational and financial responsibility for the 2014 edition. The conference was also supported by IFIP (International Federation of Information Processing), Working Group 10.3 on Concurrent Systems.

The special focus of ARCS 2014 was on connecting computing with the physical world. This reflects the fact that more and more computing systems are deeply embedded into the real world, closely interacting with their physical environment as well as with human users, forming large and dynamic distributed embedded systems. These cyber-physical systems provide new opportunities and challenges for computer and systems architecture, such as ultra-low power consumption, while at the same time meeting real-time constraints and dependability requirements. Novel concepts for self-organization and adaptation are required to address highly dynamic environments, networks, and changing user requirements. Traditional topics of computer architecture, in particular in the area of parallel and high performance computing, are also advancing rapidly, driven mainly by new multi/many-core systems and accelerators.

The conference attracted 44 submissions from 23 countries. Each paper was assigned to at least three Program Committee members for reviewing. The Committee selected 20 submissions for publication with authors from 14 countries. These papers were organized in six sessions covering topics like parallelization methods, self-organization and trust, system design, sensor systems, virtualization or dependability aspects. Three invited talks on "Control of Cyber-physical Systems" by Karl H. Johansson, KTH Royal Institute of Technology, Sweden; "Approximate Computing" by Ravi Nair, IBM Thomas J. Watson Research Center, Yorktown Heights, USA; and "High Performance Computers for Earth System Science" by Thomas Ludwig, German Climate Computing Centre, Hamburg, Germany, completed the strong technical program. Four workshops focusing on specific sub-topics of ARCS were organized in conjunction with the main conference, one on dependability and fault tolerance, one on multi-objective many-core design, one on parallel systems and algorithms, as well as one on self-optimization in organic and autonomic computing systems.

We would like to thank the many individuals who contributed to the success of the conference, in particular the members of the Program Committee as well as the additional external reviewers, for the time and effort they put into reviewing the submissions carefully and selecting a high-quality program. Many thanks also to all authors for submitting their work. The workshops were organized and coordinated by Walter Stechele and Thomas Wild, the proceedings were compiled by Thilo Pionteck, and the financial issues managed by Karl-Erwin Großpietsch. The local arrangements were coordinated by Christian Renner, and the website was maintained by Steffen Prehn. Our gratitude goes to all of them as well as all of the other people, in particular the ITG office team, who helped in the organization of ARCS 2014.

December 2013

Erik Maehle
Kay Römer
Wolfgang Karl
Eduardo Tovar

Organization

General Co-chairs

Erik Maehle   Universität zu Lübeck, Germany
Kay Römer   Graz University of Technology, Austria

Program Co-chairs

Wolfgang Karl   Karlsruhe Institute of Technology, Germany
Eduardo Tovar   ISEP-IPP Porto, Portugal

Workshop and Tutorial Co-chairs

Walter Stechele   Technische Universität München, Germany
Thomas Wild   Technische Universität München, Germany

Publication Chair

Thilo Pionteck   Hamburg University of Technology, Germany

Finance Chair

Karl-Erwin Großpietsch   St. Augustin, Germany

Local Organization

Christian Renner   Universität zu Lübeck, Germany

Program Committee

Michael Beigl   Karlsruhe Institute of Technology, Germany
Mladen Berekovic   Technische Universität Braunschweig, Germany
Koen Bertels   Delft University of Technology, The Netherlands

Erol Koser
Björn Lisper
Jörg Mische
Julian Oppermann
Johny Paul
Sebastian Schlingmann
Matthias Sommer
Ericles Sousa
Volker Wenzel
Xinhai Zhang

Tilman Küstner
Pedro Miguens
Nuno Neves
Ahsan Qamar
Rafael Rosales
Nuno Sebastião
Henning Spiegelberg
Florian Stock
Ioannis Zgeras

Invited Talks

Karl Hendrik Johansson, KTH Royal Institute of Technology, Sweden

Control of Cyber-physical Systems: Fundamental Challenges and Applications to Transportation Networks

Cyber-physical systems are engineered systems whose operations are monitored, coordinated, controlled, and integrated by computing and communication cores interacting with humans and the physical environment. In this talk, we will discuss some recent developments on control architectures for cyber-physical systems. Motivated by application projects in goods transportation, we will consider the influence of local and partial plant state and model information on the synthesis problem. Some fundamental bounds relating global system performance with local information exchange and physical interactions will be introduced. Details will be given on an emerging goods transportation system based on fleets of platooning heavy-duty vehicles utilizing vehicle-to-vehicle and vehicle-to-infrastructure communications. Some preliminary results from a large-scale evaluation currently being performed on the highway road network in Northern Europe will be discussed, showing the fuel saving and transport efficiency potentials of the system but also some of the challenges with humans in the loop and technology transfer. The presentation will be based on joint work with collaborators at KTH and at Scania.

Ravi Nair, IBM Thomas J. Watson Research Center, Yorktown Heights, NY, USA

Approximate Computing

There is an unprecedented amount of data being produced in the world today. Yet, cost and energy considerations are limiting a corresponding growth in the compute capability needed to process and analyze this data in a conventional manner. The adoption of computing devices by a wider segment of the world's population is leading to computing of the sort where the results are often ephemeral, and where there is a greater acceptance of approximate results. In addition though, approximate results are acceptable even in enterprise computing where, in comparison to traditional activities like accounting and inventory control, new activities such as decision support, search and data-mining are consuming increasingly greater cycles and are frequently performed on input data that may be unreliable. It is becoming evident that there are significant computational and energy efficiencies to be gained by relaxing the expectation of preciseness in today's computational models and moving to a more approximate computing model. This talk will examine the implications of this notion of approximate computing on the exploitation of new technology and on the design of future systems.

Thomas Ludwig, DKRZ Deutsches Klimarechenzentrum GmbH, Germany

High Performance Computers for Earth System Science

Earth system science has a long tradition in using high performance computers. The process of gaining new insight heavily depends on the available compute power. For decades we observe an exponential increase in this compute power. With the advent of Exascale architectures we are faced with new challenges for this research community. The talk will highlight options for new types of research as well as risks to be able to conduct specific investigations.

Table of Contents

System Design II and Sensor Systems

Virtualization: I/O, Memory, Cloud

Dependability: Safety, Security, and Reliability Aspects

Resource-Aware Harris Corner Detection Based on Adaptive Pruning*

Johny Paul[1], Walter Stechele[1], Manfred Kröhnert[2],
Tamim Asfour[2], Benjamin Oechslein[3], Christoph Erhardt[3],
Jens Schedel[3], Daniel Lohmann[3], and Wolfgang Schröder-Preikschat[3]

[1] Technical University of Munich, Germany
[2] Karlsruhe Institute of Technology, Germany
[3] Friedrich-Alexander University Erlangen-Nuremberg, Germany
{johny.paul,walter.stechele}@tum.de,
{manfred.kroehnert,asfour}@kit.edu,
{oechslein,erhardt,schedel,lohmann,wosch}@cs.fau.de

Abstract. Corner-detection techniques are being widely used in computer vision – for example in object recognition to find suitable candidate points for feature registration and matching. Most computer-vision applications have to operate on real-time video sequences, hence maintaining a consistent throughput and high accuracy are important constrains that ensure high-quality object recognition. A high throughput can be achieved by exploiting the inherent parallelism within the algorithm on massively parallel architectures like many-core processors. However, accelerating such algorithms on many-core CPUs offers several challenges as the achieved speedup depends on the instantaneous load on the processing elements. In this work, we present a new resource-aware Harris corner-detection algorithm for many-core processors. The novel algorithm can adapt itself to the dynamically varying load on a many-core processor to process the frame within a predefined time interval. The results show a 19% improvement in throughput and an 18% improvement in accuracy.

Keywords: Harris corner detection, resource-aware programming, invasive computing, adaptive pruning.

1 Introduction

Corner detection is used within computer-vision algorithms like motion detection, image registration, video tracking, feature descriptors for object recognition etc. to infer the contents of an image. Several corner detectors exist today in the literature and comparative evaluations have shown that the Harris [9] corner detectors achieve some of the best results. Recent evaluations in real-time applications such as video tracking [7], visual SLAM [8] and robotic navigation [19] have demonstrated that the preferred way to detect features in a scene is the use of a Harris detector in combination with more complex feature descriptors. Harris detectors are also used in the humanoid robot

---

* This work was supported by the German Research Foundation (DFG) as part of the Transregional Collaborative Research Centre "Invasive Computing" (SFB/TR 89).

E. Maehle et al. (Eds.): ARCS 2014, LNCS 8350, pp. 1–12, 2014.

ARMAR-III [2] for recognizing and tracking textured objects [3]. A humanoid robot like ARMAR has to handle various tasks like vision, motion planning, speech recognition, etc. with the workload spread across multiple industrial PCs. The data from various sensors flows into the processing system, each dedicated for a different task like computer vision, motion control, speech processing, etc. Similarly, the humanoid robot Asimo uses two PCs, a control and planning processor plus an additional digital signal processor (DSP) for sound processing [18]. Two processor boards were also used in the humanoid robots HRP-2 [11] and HRP-4C [12]. The Hand Arm System from DLR [10] has three layers of computing hierarchy consisting of COTS PCs for control applications, an auxiliary Linux workstation for user interfaces and a composition layer constituted by FPGAs for hardware-accelerated tasks.

The use of multiple PCs results in high power consumption, low interconnect bandwidth and occupies a large amount of space on the robot. The use of many-core processors can mitigate some of the above mentioned problems on account of their immense computational power assembled in a compact design. However, the available resources on a many-core chip (processing elements (PEs), memories, interconnects, etc.) have to be shared among various applications running concurrently, which leads to unpredictable execution time or frame drops for vision applications. Our work focuses on analyzing the effect of sharing resources on a conventional Harris detector and propose a new resource-aware Harris detector to resolve the issues. Evaluations shows that the newly proposed Harris detector is capable of adapting to varying load conditions on the many-core processor and delivers better results in terms of throughput, accuracy and latency. This work also describes how to distribute the workload on the massively parallel PEs for best results, avoiding frame drops, even under varying load conditions.

This paper is organized as follows. Section 2 describes the state-of-the-art algorithms used for corner detection and different schemes using for accelerating the algorithm. Section 3 provides a brief overview of the conventional Harris detector and describes some of the challenges with implementing a conventional Harris detector on many-core processors. Section 4 starts with a brief description of various pruning techniques to accelerate corner detection. This is followed by the description of the resource-aware corner detector using an enhanced pruning technique. Section 5 provides an overview of the many-core system used for evaluation and Section 6 describes the implementation and results, followed by Section 7, which concludes the paper.

2   State of the Art

Several techniques exist today to detect corners in an image. These include Harris corner detection [9], SUSAN [20], FAST [17], etc. Independent of the technique used, corner detection is a compute-intensive task and two main techniques have been used to speed it up. The first approach focuses on algorithmic techniques to reduce the computational complexity, while the second employs hardware accelerators or graphics processing units (GPUs) to accelerate the conventional algorithm. Independent of the technique used, they all pose a challenge to the programmer; how to control the worst-case execution time and avoid frame drops when the resources on the processor are shared across multiple applications. High throughput can be guaranteed using hardware accelerators based on field-programmable gate arrays (FPGAs). However, the flexibility offered by FPGAs is quite low and requires very high effort in terms of design, implementation and verification. On the other hand, GPUs are very powerful and provide significant acceleration over small multi-core processors due to their massively parallel architecture. However, they consume very high power, are less flexible, difficult to debug and require data transfers between processor and the hardware accelerator, which increases the overall latency.

The use of many-core processors can overcome many of the above mentioned hurdles as they offer higher computing power necessary to accelerate the algorithms, while at the same time retaining the simplicity in programming and debugging. Today it is possible to put onto a single chip a large number of general-purpose cores, certainly tens of highly complex cores as on Intel's Single-Chip Cloud Computer [15] or Tilera's 64-core processor [4]. A major challenge associated with todays many-core systems is the question of how to program such systems to make best use of their computing power. In order to address these issues, [14] propose a new resource-aware operating system (ROS) for many-core hardware, with direct support for parallel applications and a scalable kernel. ROS offers a resource-management scheme based on resource provisioning which enables system-wide, efficient accounting and utilization of resources. Resources such as cores and memory are explicitly granted to the applications and revoked. The kernel exposes information about a process's current resource allocation and the system's utilization, and allows the application programs to make requests based on this information.

The demand for more stringent (OS-supported) resource awareness was also proposed in [21], put forward by a new programming methodology called *Invasive Computing*. The main idea and novelty of Invasive Computing is that it extends resource-aware programming support to various layers in the many-core system like resource-aware OS, communication interfaces like Network-on-Chip (NoC), and PEs. Programs running on this system get the ability to explore and dynamically spread their computations to neighboring processors and execute portions of code with a high degree of parallelism in parallel based on the availability of resources. Once the program terminates or if the degree of parallelism is expected to be lower again, the program may enter a *retreat* phase. At this point, the resources can be deallocated and execution resumed, for example, sequentially on a single processor. In this work, a resource-aware Harris corner-detection algorithm is evaluated using the Invasive Computing methodology. However, the concepts demonstrated in this work are platform-independent and can be demonstrated on any resource-aware platform including ROS.

3 Harris Corner Detection

This section provides a brief overview of the conventional Harris corner-detection algorithm. The calculation is based on the local auto-correlation function that is approximated by a matrix M over a small window w for each pixel $p(x, y)$:

$$M = \begin{bmatrix} \sum_w W(x)I_x^2 & \sum_w W(x)I_xI_y \\ \sum_w W(x)I_xI_y & \sum_w W(x)I_y^2 \end{bmatrix} = \begin{bmatrix} a & b \\ c & d \end{bmatrix} \tag{1}$$

where I_x and I_y are horizontal and vertical intensity gradients, respectively, and $W(x)$ is an averaging filter that can be a box or a Gaussian filter. The eigenvalues λ_1 and λ_2 (where $\lambda_1 \geq \lambda_2$) indicate the type of intensity change in the window w around $p(x, y)$. If both λ_1 and λ_2 are small, $p(x, y)$ is a point in a flat region. If λ_1 is large and λ_2 is small, $p(x, y)$ is an edge point and if both λ_1 and λ_2 are large, $p(x, y)$ represents a corner point. Harris combines the eigenvalues into a single corner measure R as shown in (2) (k is an empirical constant with value 0.04 to 0.06). Once the corner measure is computed for every pixel, a threshold is applied on the corner measures to discard the obvious non-corners.

$$R = \lambda_1\lambda_2 - k \cdot (\lambda_1 + \lambda_2)^2 = (ac - b^2) - k \cdot (a + c)^2 \qquad (2)$$

Corner detection is often employed as the first step in computer-vision applications with real-time video input. Hence, the application has to maintain a steady throughput and good response time to ensure quality results. However, the presence of other high-priority tasks may alter the behavior of the corner-detection algorithm. To evaluate such a dynamically changing situation, we analyzed the behavior of the conventional Harris detector on a many-core processor with 32 PEs. Fig. 1 shows resource-allocation schemes (left) along with the execution-time profiles (right). A video input with 640×480 pixels at 10 frames per second was used, with the test running for 20 seconds. To evaluate the impact of other applications running concurrently on the many-core system, applications like audio processing, motor control, etc. were used. These applications create dynamically changing load on the processor based on what the robot is doing at that point in time. For instance, the speech-recognition application is activated when the user speaks to the robot. The conventional OS scheduler schedules the threads of the applications based on the overall system load. Sharing of available resources resulted in the execution-time profile shown in Fig. 1. It can be seen that the execution time varies from 0 to 430 milliseconds, based on the load condition. A lack of sufficient resources leads to very high processing intervals or frame drops (a processing interval of zero represents a frame drop). The number of frames dropped during this evaluation is as high as **20%** and the worst-case latency increased by 4.3x (100 milliseconds to 430 milliseconds). Frame drops reduce the quality of the results and the robot may lose track of the object if too many consecutive frames are dropped. In order to overcome these challenges, we present a modified Harris detector for many-core processors capable of allocating resources based on the current workload. The algorithm can also adapt the workload based on the currently available resources. The following

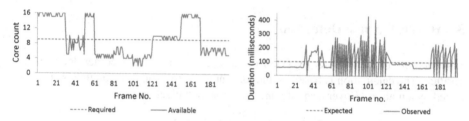

Fig. 1. Variation in processing interval based on available resources

sections demonstrate how the resources are claimed and how the processing interval can be constrained to guarantee consistent throughput and processing intervals.

4   Pruning Techniques

A pruning technique to reduce the computational complexity of the conventional Harris detector is described in [22]. This technique relies on the fact that in most situations, the obvious non-corners constitute a large majority of the image. Hence the Harris detectors incur a lot of redundant computations as they evaluate the entire image for a high corner response. From (2), R is most influenced by the term $(ac - b^2)$ as the two $(a + c)$ terms cancel out. For a good corner, R needs to be a large value. Hence maximizing $(ac-b^2)$ can select good corners without explicit eigenvalue computation. However, this technique cannot demonstrate a noticeable speedup on platforms with FPU as the pixels are pruned away in the final step, just before eigenvalue computation. The limitations in [22] can be resolved using the multi-stage pruning technique described in [1]. The main difference between these techniques is that the second one can prune away pixels at a very early stage. A corner response (CR) is defined as:

$$CR = min\left(|I_x|, |I_y|\right), \tag{3}$$

where I_x and I_y are the horizontal and vertical pixel-intensity derivatives. If CR is greater than a predefined gradient threshold, the pixel is a corner candidate and should be retained for processing in the subsequent steps. This technique ensures that the non-corner pixels are removed prior to more intensive processing. All candidate corners from the previous steps are further assessed by computing the eigenvalues as in the conventional Harris detector (2). Finally a non-maxima suppression is applied to suppress the corners that are close to each other. Some of the challenges posed by the conventional Harris detector on a many-core system can be resolved using the pruning techniques described above. In situations where the system is under-utilized, the threshold can be reduced, thereby processing more pixels and achieving a higher accuracy, whereas increasing the threshold can prune away more pixels when the processing system is heavily loaded by other high-priority tasks. Fig. 3 shows the relation between the threshold and the processing interval. The results were captured by applying the pruning technique to six different video sequences whose snapshots are shown in Fig. 2 (each video sequence consists of 200 frames). In order to evaluate the impact of pruning on the accuracy of detected corners, we use the metrics named *precision* and *recall* as proposed in [13]. The value of recall measures the number of correct matches out of

| Bricks | kitchen | Corridor | Window | Bunny | Cereal |

Fig. 2. Snapshot of the video-sequences used for evaluation

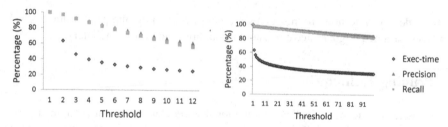

Fig. 3. Multi-stage pruning technique   **Fig. 4.** Resource-aware pruning

the total number of possible matches, and the value of precision measures the number of correct matches out of all matches returned by the algorithm. From Fig. 3 it can be seen that the application performs well for a threshold below four. However, increasing the threshold further results in a drastic decrease in precision and recall rates (as low as 60% for a threshold of 12). Values beyond this point are not plotted in the graph as the corners with an accuracy below 60% are not suitable for practical use. The second drawback of this algorithm is that it offers only few candidate points for adaptations within an acceptable accuracy range.

In order to overcome the challenges with the multi-stage pruning technique, we present an enhanced pruning technique with better flexibility and higher accuracy compared to the conventional pruning technique presented in Section 4. Our algorithm uses a new threshold model as described in (4), where product of vertical and horizontal difference in pixel intensities is used and the candidates with low CR values are pruned away.

$$CR = (|I_x \cdot I_y|) \tag{4}$$

This new model results in significantly more selection points as shown in Fig. 4, offering a higher flexibility to the resource-aware algorithm whenever adaptations are necessary. In addition to this, there is a significant improvement in both precision and recall rates. For example, precision is improved from 84.0% to 90.8% and recall is improved from 82.3% to 89.2% for the same speedup value of 35%. The new model shows a consistent improvement in precision and recall for the entire range and higher values are obtained as the threshold is increased. A more detailed analysis on the video sequences shows that the effects of pruning vary based on the scene. For example, the speedup achieved (using the same threshold) is low for cluttered scenes like *Bricks* while the majority of the pixels can be pruned away for scenes with plain backgrounds. Fig. 5 shows the relation between speedup and accuracy for all six video sequences. This means that the amount of computing resources required to perform the corner detection will vary from one scene to another based on the nature of the foreground, background, etc. and therefore the resources have to be allocated on a frame-to-frame basis, based on the scene captured. A resource-aware many-core platform meeting the above requirements, is presented in Section 5 with emphasis on how to allocate and release resources in real-time based on application requirements.

5   Evaluation Platform

As described in Section 2, our work focuses on exploring the benefits of resource-aware Harris corner detection. Therefore, we implemented our algorithms on top of OctoPOS

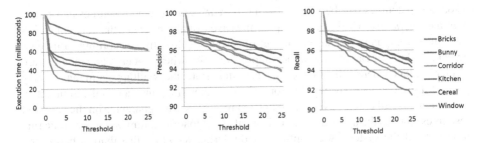

Fig. 5. Effects of pruning on processing time, precision and accuracy

[16], a resource-aware operating system for Invasive Computing. OctoPOS shares the same view with ROS [14] as far as application-directed resource management of many-core processors is concerned. Also, both approaches resort to an event-based kernel architecture and largely benefit from asynchronous and non-blocking system calls. The main difference, however, is in the execution model of OctoPOS that was specifically designed to support invasive-parallel applications.

5.1 System Programming Interface

At the OctoPOS interface, resource-aware programming maps to three fundamental system calls: `invade()`, `infect()` and `retreat()`. The typical usage of these calls in the course of an application programm are depicted in Fig. 6. First, the application's

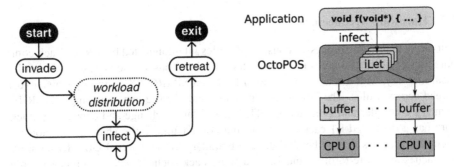

Fig. 6. Structure of an invasive program   Fig. 7. Execution model of applications in Octo-POS

resource demand has to be expressed to the system. We call this the *invade* phase. It yields a set of resources in the form of a *claim*, the central data structure in the system for representing the resources associated with an application (processors, memory, etc.). Depending on the structure of the *claim*, the application has to distribute its workload accordingly. For example, it can tune its algorithms towards the number of processors present in the claim. Actual computation is then performed using the *infect* call. After execution finishes, another computation phase can be started on the same set of resources, resources can be released using *retreat*, or additional resources can be acquired using *invade*. The basic concept of Invasive Computing states that an application dynamically expands and shrinks its set of resources at runtime according to its own demand and that it can react to undersupply situations where not enough resources are available. Hence, depending on the current system state, the resulting claim may or may not fulfill the demands specified before. On the other side, once an application gets a claim, it gains full control over the associated resources. This guarantee on the acquired resources enables the application to balance its workload according to the dynamic runtime state of the system. Assumptions made during workload distribution before the *infect* phase hold until the application itself changes its resource allocation following the *infect* phase.

The main building blocks of applications in OctoPOS are so-called *i*-lets: Fragments of a program potentially executed in parallel with mostly run-to-completion semantics. These are represented by function and data pointers and thus are very lightweight entities. An *i*-let is like a Cilk procedure [5], but allows for the blocking of its executing thread by creating a "featherweight" continuation when actually releasing a PE. An application can create an arbitrary number of *i*-lets to be executed – potentially in parallel – using the *infect* system call. As depicted in Fig. 7, OctoPOS forwards *i*-lets to processor-local buffer queues for execution. Overall, this leads to an efficient implementation of *i*-let creation and dispatching. Moreover, with a tiled hardware architecture as described in Section 5.2, the buffering scheme is a possible candidate for hardware acceleration: To execute *i*-lets on distant tiles without obstructing the processors in the tile, the buffers can be maintained in hardware and accessed directly through the NoC. This leads to a very scalable system architecture especially suitable for many-core systems.

5.2 Hardware Architecture

Our target many-core processor consists of 9 tiles interconnected by a NoC. Each compute tiles consists of 4 cores interconnected by a local bus and some fast, on-chip tile-local memory, with a total of 32 cores (LEON3, a SPARC V8 design by Gaisler [6]) spread across 8 tiles. The 9th tile is a memory and I/O tile encompassing a DDR-III memory controller and Ethernet, UART, etc. for data exchange and debugging. Each core has a dedicated L1 cache while all the cores within a tile share a common L2 cache for accesses that go beyond the tile boundary to the external DDR-III memory. L1 caches are write-through and L2 is a write-back cache. Cache coherency is only maintained within the tile boundary to eliminate a possible scalability bottleneck when scaling to higher core counts. Therefore, data consistency has to be handled by the programmer through proper programming techniques that are built on top of hardware features to provide consistent data access and exchange between the different cache-coherency domains. This scheme is somewhat similar to the Intel SCC.

6 Implementation and Results

The first step in the resource-aware Harris detector is to allocate sufficient resources to perform corner detection within the interval specified by the user. The number of PEs required is calculated based on the input-image resolution, the processing interval, the nature of the scene, etc. The analysis starts with the generation of a differential image, where each pixel is computed using (4). In order to speed up the pruning logic within the algorithm, an integral histogram is computed from the differential image as described in Algorithms 1 and 2, where n is the total number of pixels to be processed, I_{diff} is the differential image, $limit$ is the maximum possible value generated by (4) and H is the integral histogram computed from differential image. Once the integral histogram is computed, the values in the bin represent the number of pixels to be processed by the algorithm when the threshold is set to histogram-bin-index. The number of PEs (N_{pe}) is calculated using (5).

$$N_{pe} \geq \frac{n \cdot T_{prn} + P_{pix}(th) \cdot T_{hcd}}{T_{exe} \cdot \eta(N_{pe})} \tag{5}$$

where n is the total number of pixels, T_{prn} is the processing time per pixel until the generation of integral histogram, P_{pix} is the number of pixels to be processed as computed by the pruning algorithm (a function of the threshold value th), T_{hcd} is the time to compute R for pixels with CR above threshold, T_{exe} is the processing interval and $\eta(N_{pe})$ represents the algorithm's efficiency as a function of degree-of-parallelism or available resources (N_{pe}). Including an efficiency factor is important as every additional i-let created by the algorithm also creates additional load on the external memory and shared communication interfaces, limiting the overall scalability. For the best results, the threshold value th can be set to zero so that the algorithm will attempt to process all pixels in the image. It should be noted that T_{prn} and T_{hcd} may vary based on the actual implementation and processor architecture. Hence these values are estimated by profiling the application on the target platform. Fig. 8 shows the change in efficiency against degree of parallelism, on the target HW. It can be seen clearly that when the number of i-lets is doubled from 1 to 2, the execution time does not halve, but is reduced by a factor of 1.96, which means an efficiency of 98%. In the next step, an invade request (for N_{pe}) is raised and the OS makes a final decision on the number of PEs considering the current system load. The PE count may vary from zero (if the system is too heavily loaded and no further resources can be allocated at that point in time) to the total number of PEs requested (provided that a sufficient number of idle PEs exist in the system and the current power mode offers sufficient power budget to enable the

Algorithm 1. Differential image

```
1: i ← 0
2: h ← 0
3: while i < n do
4:    I_diff(i) ← |dx(i) · dy(i)|
5:    h(I_diff(i)) ← h(I_diff(i)) + 1
6:    i ← i + 1
7: end while
```

Algorithm 2. Integral histogram

```
1: i ← 0
2: H ← 0
3: while i < limit do
4:    k ← i
5:    while k < limit do
6:       H(i) ← H(i) + h(k)
7:       k ← k + 1
8:    end while
9:    i ← i + 1
10: end while
```

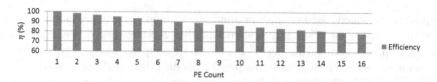

Fig. 8. Efficiency map for Harris detector on target hardware

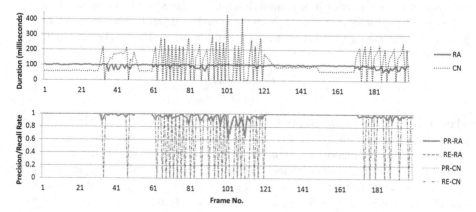

Fig. 9. Comparison between conventional and resource-aware model (RA = resource-aware-model, CN = conventional-model, PR = precision, RE = recall)

selected PEs). This means that under numerous circumstances the application has to adapt to the limited resources offered by the runtime system by increasing the threshold value th until the condition in (6) is satisfied.

$$P_{pix}(th) \leq \frac{N_{pe} \cdot T_{exe} \cdot \eta(N_{pe}) - n \cdot T_{prn}}{T_{hcd}} \tag{6}$$

The new workload is processed by the allocated PEs and the resources can be released at the end of the processing interval or a new invade request can be raised if more PEs are required for the next frame due to a change in the scene. The behavior of the new resource-aware Harris detector is depicted in Fig. 9. The resource-allocation scheme remains same as described in Fig. 1. The execution-time profile in Fig. 9 shows that the resource-aware Harris detector can constrain the execution time per frame to the specified value of 100 milliseconds. The use of the conventional algorithm resulted in very high latencies under circumstances where sufficient resources are not available, and dropped frames occasionally. The values of precision and recall drops slightly in the region where the application has to adapt by pruning pixels. However, this helps to avoid overshoot in execution time and eliminate frame drops, so that results are consistently available within the predefined intervals. An overall comparison between the two scenarios is shown in Table 1. The use of the conventional algorithm leads to a very high worst-case execution time(WCET) and frame drops. The precision and recall values are low for the conventional algorithm as a frame drop leads to zero precision and recall for that particular frame. In brief, the resource-aware Harris detector can operate

Table 1. Comparison between conventional and resource-aware Harris detectors

	Throughput	WCET	Precision	Recall
Conventional	**81%**	4.31x	0.82	0.81
Resource-aware	100%	1.04x	**0.98**	**0.98**

very well under dynamically changing conditions by adapting the workload, avoiding frame drops and regulating the WCET, leading to high precision and recall rates.

7 Conclusion

This paper presented a resource-aware Harris corner detector and demonstrated how to estimate the resources required for corner detection based on the scene, the resolution of the input image and the user-specified time interval. The application is aware of available resources on the many-core processor and can adapt the workload if sufficient resources are not available. The enhanced corner detector can generate results within the specified search interval and avoid frame drops. Our experiments show that incorporating resource awareness into the conventional Harris detector can significantly improve the quality of the algorithm. A detailed evaluation was conducted on an FPGA-based hardware prototype to ensure the validity of the results. The results show up to 19% improvement in throughput and 18% improvement in accuracy as described in Section6. Though the evaluations were conducted using the OS and hardware explained under Section 5, the benefits are expected to be visible on any resource-aware platform including ROS [14]. The resource allocation and release happens once per frame and the additional overhead in execution time is negligible when compared to the time taken by the detector to process millions of pixels in every frame.

References

1. Alkaabi, S., Deravi, F.: Candidate pruning for fast corner detection. Electronics Letters 40(1), 18–19 (2004)
2. Asfour, T., Azad, P., et al.: ARMAR-III: An integrated humanoid platform for sensory-motor control. In: 6th IEEE-RAS International Conference on Humanoid Robots. IEEE (2006)
3. Azad, P., Asfour, T., Dillmann, R.: Combining harris interest points and the sift descriptor for fast scale-invariant object recognition. In: Intelligent Robots and Systems, IROS 2009. IEEE (2009)
4. Bell, S., Edwards, B., et al.: Tile64-processor: A 64-core soc with mesh interconnect. In: Solid-State Circuits Conference, 2008. Digest of Technical Papers, pp. 88–598. IEEE (2008)
5. Blumofe, R.D., Joerg, C.F., et al.: Cilk: An efficient multithreaded runtime system. In: Proceedings of the Fifth ACM SIGPLAN Symposium on Principles and Practice of Parallel Programming, PPoPP 1995 (1995)
6. Gaisler, J., Catovic, E.: Multi-core processor based on leon3-ft ip core (leon3-ft-mp). In: DASIA 2006-Data Systems in Aerospace, vol. 630, p. 76 (2006)
7. Gauglitz, S., Höllerer, T., et al.: Evaluation of interest point detectors and feature descriptors for visual tracking. International Journal of Computer Vision 94(3), 335–360 (2011)

8. Gil, A., Mozos, O.M., Ballesta, M., Reinoso, O.: A comparative evaluation of interest point detectors and local descriptors for visual slam. Machine Vision and Applications 21(6), 905–920 (2010)

9. Harris, C., Stephens, M.: A combined corner and edge detector. In: Alvey Vision Conference, Manchester, UK, vol. 15, p. 50 (1988)

10. Jorg, S., Nickl, M., Nothhelfer, A., et al.: The computing and communication architecture of the dlr hand arm system. In: 2011 IEEE/RSJ International Conference on Intelligent Robots and Systems (IROS), pp. 1055–1062. IEEE (2011)

11. Kaneko, K., Kanehiro, F., Kajita, S., Hirukawa, H., et al.: Humanoid robot HRP-2. In: Proceedings of the 2004 IEEE International Conference on Robotics and Automation, ICRA 2004, vol. 2, pp. 1083–1090 (May 2004)

12. Kaneko, K., Kanehiro, F., Morisawa, M., Miura, K., Nakaoka, S., Kajita, S.: Cybernetic human HRP-4C. In: 9th IEEE-RAS International Conference on Humanoid Robots, Humanoids 2009, pp. 7–14 (December 2009)

13. Klippenstein, J., Zhang, H.: Quantitative evaluation of feature extractors for visual slam. In: Fourth Canadian Conference on Computer and Robot Vision, CRV 2007, pp. 157–164. IEEE (2007)

14. Klues, K., Rhoden, B., Zhu, Y., Waterman, A., Brewer, E.: Processes and resource management in a scalable many-core os. In: HotPar 2010, Berkeley, CA (2010)

15. Mattson, T., Riepen, M., et al.: The 48-core scc processor: the programmer's view. In: Proceedings of the 2010 ACM/IEEE International Conference for High Performance Computing, Networking, Storage and Analysis, pp. 1–11. IEEE Computer Society (2010)

16. Oechslein, B., Schedel, J., Henkel, J., Lohmann, D., Schröder-Preikschat, W., et al.: Octopos: A parallel operating system for invasive computing. In: Proceedings of the International Workshop on Systems for Future Multi-Core Architectures (SFMA). EuroSys (2011)

17. Rosten, E., Drummond, T.: Machine learning for high-speed corner detection. In: Leonardis, A., Bischof, H., Pinz, A. (eds.) ECCV 2006, Part I. LNCS, vol. 3951, pp. 430–443. Springer, Heidelberg (2006)

18. Sakagami, Y., Watanabe, R., Aoyama, C., Matsunaga, S., et al.: The intelligent ASIMO: system overview and integration. In: IEEE/RSJ International Conference on Intelligent Robots and Systems, vol. 3, pp. 2478–2483 (2002)

19. Schmidt, A., Kraft, M., Kasiński, A.: An evaluation of image feature detectors and descriptors for robot navigation. In: Bolc, L., Tadeusiewicz, R., Chmielewski, L.J., Wojciechowski, K. (eds.) ICCVG 2010, Part II. LNCS, vol. 6375, pp. 251–259. Springer, Heidelberg (2010)

20. Smith, S.M., Brady, J.M.: Susan—a new approach to low level image processing. International Journal of Computer Vision 23(1), 45–78 (1997)

21. Teich, J., Henkel, J., Herkersdorf, A., Schröder-Preikschat, W., et al.: Invasive Computing: An Overview. In: Hübner, M., Becker, J. (eds.) Multiprocessor System-on-Chip – Hardware Design and ToolIntegration, pp. 241–268. Springer, Heidelberg (2011)

22. Wu, M., Ramakrishnan, N., Lam, S.-K., Srikanthan, T.: Low-complexity pruning for accelerating corner detection. In: 2012 IEEE International Symposium on Circuits and Systems (ISCAS), pp. 1684–1687. IEEE (2012)

Victim Selection Policies for Intel TBB: Overheads and Energy Footprint

Alexandru C. Iordan, Magnus Jahre, and Lasse Natvig

Norwegian University of Science and Technology, Trondheim, Norway
{iordan,jahre,lasse}@idi.ntnu.no

Abstract. With the wide adoption of Chip Multiprocessors (CMPs), software developers need to switch to parallel programming to reach the performance potential of CMPs and maximize their energy efficiency. Management overheads due to parallelization can cause sub-linear speed-ups and increase the energy consumption of parallel programs. In this paper, we investigate the parallelization overheads of Intel TBB with a particular focus on its victim selection policy. We implement an "all knowing" oracle victim selection scheme as well as a pseudo-random scheme and compare them against TBB's default random selection policy. We also break down TBB's parallelization overheads and report how basic operations like task spawning, task stealing and task de-queuing impact the energy footprint. Our experiments show that failed task stealing is by far the highest energy consumer. In fact, the oracle victim selection policy can reduce the application energy footprint by 13.6% compared to TBB's default policy.

Keywords: Intel TBB, victim selection, energy efficiency.

1 Introduction

Energy consumption has become the main challenge for almost all systems in the information world, from HPC to embedded devices. Architects and developers are trying to find solutions for problems ranging from reducing the high cost of operation of data centers to maximizing the battery life of mobile and embedded systems. For over 20 years, techniques like transistor-speed scaling, pipelining, out-of-order execution and speculation have increased CPU performance at a rate of 50% per year [1]. However, diminishing returns from transistor scaling and power budget limitations has almost removed the single-core performance improvement trend.

The introduction of Chip Multiprocessors (CMPs) enabled the mitigation of development constraints like the *power wall* and the *ILP wall*. CMPs allow chip designers to utilize the increasing transistor count available with each new generation without increasing the power budget [2]. However, to fully take advantage of this architecture, parallel software is required since the performance potential of CMPs lies in exploiting thread level parallelism. This places a new burden on the software developers because there is no widely adopted programming

E. Maehle et al. (Eds.): ARCS 2014, LNCS 8350, pp. 13–24, 2014.

model that facilitates easy parallelization. In this work, we focus on *Task Based Programming* (TBP) which is a parallel programming model that has received significant attention recently [3–6].

To reduce the impact of parallelization overheads, a necessary first step is to identify the root cause of such overheads. To this end, we investigate the extra instructions added by parallelization management and the energy consumption of these instructions which we refer to as the *energy footprint*. More precisely, the energy footprint is the energy spent for executing the given application or section of code in the context of the test system.

In our experiments, we utilize Intel's Thread Building Blocks (TBB) [6] library for parallelization. TBB is a C++ template library designed to help programmers create portable, parallel applications using task parallelism. It was designed to avoid the low level programming inherent in the direct use of threading packages such as pthreads [6].

To allow for extensive and noninvasive measurements, we use a performance simulator and a power estimation tool in our study. We implement two victim selection policies in addition to TBB's random policy and report the performance and energy overheads of 5 PARSEC benchmarks [7]. We also break down TBB's overheads and look into basic TBP operations like task spawning, task stealing and task de-queuing. In our results, failed steals are the highest contributor to the overheads' energy footprint. With more accurate victim selection, the energy footprint of the application can be reduced by up to 13.6%.

2 Intel TBB

The concept of parallel programming is almost as old as the computer itself. Over the years, many parallel languages have been developed and a multitude of research was done in an effort to improve raw performance and maximize hardware utilization [8]. With the majority of those approaches, one factor was often overlooked: the composability of the resulting solution. Composability of an applications refers to its ability to run efficiently side by side with other applications and being able to cope with the fact that it does not have exclusive access to the hardware resources [9]. In today's *multi-core era*, if parallel applications are not developed to dynamically scale and take advantage of all the resources that are available to them, the overall efficiency of the system suffers. In this work we focus on Intel's TBB version 4.1.1., which was design to ensure a high degree of composability.

TBB allows parallelism to be annotated both explicitly, by calling the *spawn()* method, and implicitly, through some templates like *parallel_for* or *parallel_reduce*. Tasks get created by the *spawn()* method and then added to the calling thread's task queue inside the arena (see Fig. 1). From the arena the task is available for execution by its owner thread or by other workers through stealing. A task can instantiate and spawn other tasks resulting a hierarchical task tree.

When an application thread instantiates the *tbb::task_scheduler_init* object, that thread becomes a TBB master thread (MT). All threads created by TBB to

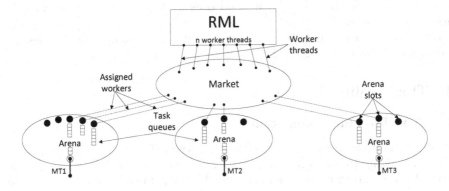

Fig. 1. Components of TBB's task scheduler

help complete the work of the MT are called *worker threads*. The *Resource Management Layer* (RML) is the component that hosts the pool of worker threads and gets instantiated first (see Fig. 1). No worker threads are created at this point, this being postponed until the first task is spawned.

Next a *Market* component is instantiated. This component was added in version 3.0 of TBB to ensure the composability of the framework. It guarantees that the work (the tasks) of one MT are isolated from other MTs that may be executing on the same machine. The role of the market is to assign workers to the arenas of each MT. The limit of the total number of workers available is set to 1 less than the maximum of the argument of the *tbb::task_scheduler_init* constructor and the total number of logical CPUs on the executing system.

Finally, the *Arena* associated with calling MT gets allocated. An arena encapsulates all the tasks and the execution resources (worker threads) available to a MT. Each arena is assigned a number of slots representing the number of workers the arena requires to perform its parallel tasks. This is defined as 1 less than the minimum of the argument of the *tbb::task_scheduler_init* constructor and the total number of workers available (limit set by the market). Because several MTs can coexist, the total number of workers requested by all arenas can be greater than the number of workers available in the RML's pool. In this situation, the market will allot workers proportionally to each MT's request.

All these components and limits are created only once, during the first instance of the *tbb::task_scheduler_init* object in the current execution. If an MT is not the first one to call the task scheduler, it will only create a new arena that will comply with the limitation imposed by the market. Upon creation or destruction of an arena, the worker threads can migrate between the active arenas.

After they are created, each worker thread runs a scheduling procedure called *wait_for_all()* consisting of 3 nested loops. The inner loop is executing the current task by calling its *execute()* method. TBB is a continuation-passing style library which means that the completion of this task returns a pointer to the next task that needs to be executed. If a new task is not referenced, the inner loop exits.

In the middle loop the *get_task()* method tries to dequeue the local task queue using a LIFO order. If successful, the inner loop is called again. If unsuccessful because the queue is empty, the middle loop exits and the outer loop invokes the stealing mechanism by calling the *receive_or_steal_task()* method.

3   The Stealing Mechanism

3.1   The TBB Implementation

Stealing is part of the *receive_or_steal_task()* method. This method includes some other techniques to find a new task to execute than just stealing: mailing tasks via task-to-thread affinity mechanism, reload offloaded non-priority tasks, reload tasks abandoned by other workers. *Receive_or_steal_task()* method runs an infinite loop and calls each of the above mentioned mechanisms, stealing being the last one. Before a steal is attempted, a victim thread is selected randomly from the current arena. If the attempt is successful, the method returns and the scheduler re-enters the inner loop. If unsuccessful, a failure counter is incremented and the execution pauses before looping back. Also, if the failure counter surpasses a given threshold (default value is 100), the current worker thread is freed and returns to the RML.

The first step when a steal is performed is to use the *lock_task_pool()* method and try to get a lock on the victim. If the *lock_task_pool()* fails, the worker thread goes through a 5 steps exponential backoff. After 5 fails, the current thread yields its resources and waits for its next time slot to try again locking the same victim. This locking mechanism assures the high composability of TBB we discussed in Section 2. However, since we simulate 1 thread / hardware core, the yielding function returns immediately and the thief thread will continue to try to lock its victim.

A stealing attempt can fail for several reasons. The most common situation is selecting from a victim with an empty task queue. Applications with an unbalanced workload distribution face this problem often.

Race contention is also a common situation for failure. When 2 or more threads are trying to get exclusive access to the same task queue by calling the *lock_task_pool()*, only one can succeed. A thief can return from the *lock_task_pool()* only if it either succeeds or the victim's task queue has been depleted.

A special situation is when a thief thread is competing for access with the owner thread of that task queue. If there are more than 1 task in the queue, there is no race contention because the thief will steal at one end while the owner will dequeue the other. However, if there is only 1 task in the queue, the owner thread will have priority and the thief will backoff even if it already acquired the lock.

3.2   The Oracle Selection Scheme

In an attempt to set an upper bound for the performance gain, we first implemented an "all knowing" scheme we call oracle selection. This method leverages on the fact that we use a simulator and not a real machine and it provides TBB with information that would be otherwise very "expensive" to obtain. We created a data structure to store the occupancy of all tasks queues in the arena as well as the level of congestion for each queue (the number of workers trying to steal from this queue). This structure is stored outside the simulated memory space in our simulator and is updated by the application through specialized instructions called markers. Since we do all this computation outside the simulated environment, our TBB application sees the victim selection as an extremely fast procedure. The queue with available tasks for stealing and with the lowest congestion level is selected as victim. This oracle scheme provides very fast and accurate results, but it is not optimal. There are still situations when updates to our structure do not propagate fast enough and the selected victim ends up creating conflicts.

3.3 The Pseudo-random Selection Scheme

The second selection method we implemented is a pseudo-random scheme inspired by the Wool library [5]. For the first stealing attempt, we randomly select a task queue. If stealing from this victim fails, we then start a loop and sequentially scan the other active task queues, excluding the one of the current thread. In this way we will first try to steal from all possible queues before looping back in the *receive_or_steal_task()* and selecting a new random victim. Also, we removed the call to the yielding function from the *lock_task_pool()* and forced the method to return after the 5 steps exponential backoff. This approach eliminates the conflicts caused by the immediate return of the yielding function, but it will also make the stealing mechanism a bit more aggressive since it allows it to select new victims faster. It is worth mentioning that by doing this, we did not eliminate TBB's composability feature since yielding is implemented in more than one place.

4 Methodology

4.1 Simulation Tools

We performed our experiments using a parallel, x86 computer architecture simulator called Sniper [10]. Sniper uses the interval core model [11] and Graphite simulation infrastructure [12] to provide fast and accurate simulations. Our model is based on a Nehalem-based Xeon 5500-series multi-core CPU (code name Gainestown) with a clock frequency of 2.66 GHz and 3 levels of cache. Table 1 lists the main characteristics of the modeled processor.

The performance results from Sniper are fed into a power estimation tool called McPAT [13]. An important characteristic of McPAT is its ability to model dynamic, static and short-circuit power. Because we use only one CPU model, for a given core count the static power is a constant value. This is why for all our experiments we computed the energy footprint using only the dynamic power.

Table 1. Main characteristics of modeled processor

Core		Cache		Main mem.	
#cores	1-,2-,4-, 8-,16-cores		Size	Assoc.	
Clock frequency	2.66 GHz	L1 i/dCache	#cores x 32KB	4/8	Size 2/4/8/ 16/32 GB
Instruction set	x86-64	L2 Cache	#cores x 256KB	8	
Dispatch width	4	L3 Cache	2/4/8/ 16/32 MB	16	
Window size	128				

4.2 Benchmarks

For our experiments, we used the default TBB implementations of *Blacksc-holes*, *Bodytrack*, *Fluidanimate*, *Streamcluster* and *Swaptions* benchmarks with the medium input set from the PARSEC suite [7]. Collectively, these benchmarks express parallelism both explicitly as well as through some templates like *parallel_for*, *parallel_reduce* and pipelines. They also employ some special TBB constructs like cache affinity partitioners and cache allocators. All these provide a wide test base for our study.

Parallelization was done using TBB version 4.1.1. which we customized in order to isolate and measure the overheads introduced by task spawning, task de-queuing and task stealing. We added special instructions called *markers* in the beginning and at the end of each function of interest to allow us to make measurements on the enclosed region of code.

To ensure statistically stable results, we performed 10 simulations of each benchmark for every core count. We averaged the performance results before estimating the power requirements. We computed the standard deviation (σ) of the execution time for each 10 simulation set as a percentage out of the average value for the set. Our results show a σ that ranges between 0.09% and 14.1% with no outliers (an outlier is a value that is above or bellow $3\sigma\pm$average value).

5 Results

Parallelization overheads often account for the sub-linear speedups of parallel implementation. While this still means that the work gets done faster, the energy required to complete the parallel execution is often equal or greater than the serial one. In Section 5.1 we quantify these overheads as the difference in number of executed instructions between parallel and serial executions. We also break down the the overheads and see how task spawning, task de-queuing and task stealing impact the parallel execution and its energy footprint. For better visualization Fig. 3 is plotted with logarithmic scale on the vertical axis. Finally, in Section 5.2 we look into what performance and energy efficiency gains we can achieve by modifying the victim selection policy.

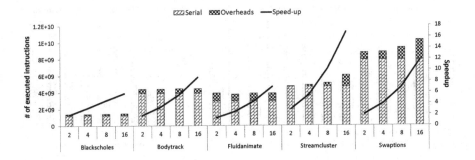

Fig. 2. Executed number of instructions and speedup

5.1 Parallel Overheads

Blackscholes employs TBB's *parallel_for* template for all the options in the input portfolio. Tasks are created by dividing these options on to the thread workers. This benchmark uses an *auto partitioning* algorithm to control the granularity of the tasks in order to handle work imbalance as well as possible. In Fig. 2 you can see that the overheads are almost constant across the core count. This shows how small the parallel section is compared to the serial one and also why we see only a 5.8 speedup on the 16 core execution. Fig. 3 breaks down the overheads and shows the energy footprint of the task spawning, task de-queuing and task stealing. Because we kept the input set constant across all core counts, our total number of tasks increases as we scale up the number of execution threads, but tasks also become finer. This has two consequences: the energy footprint for spawning increases from 2 to 16 cores (see Fig. 3) and the overhead to useful work ratio per task increases with the core count. Fig. 3 shows the same trend for the *get_task()* method. Second, we have the high number of stealing attempts. The energy footprint for failed steals is highest among what we measured and the trend is: more cores means more conflicts which leads to more failed attempts. Successful stealing has a smaller footprint but the same trend.

Bodytrack uses a 2 stage TBB pipeline construct to process the input images. In each stage *parallel_for* templates are used to divide the workload into parallel tasks. The difference compared to Blackscholes is that a special parameter of the *parallel_for* template, the *grain size*, is used to ensure a minimum size for each task. Similar with Blackscholes, Fig. 2 shows a low parallel/sequential ratio as well as a sub-linear speedup. Because Bodytrack has larger sequential regions throughout the execution, the average number of threads that are active during the execution is lower than for the other benchmarks. This means that the worker threads return to RML (see Fig. 1) because of work starvation more times. However, before returning, they attempt to steal 100 times each and fail which drives up the energy footprint (see Fig. 3).

Fluidanimate computes the interactions between the particles of an incompressible fluid. Its input set, a matrix describing the positions of the particles,

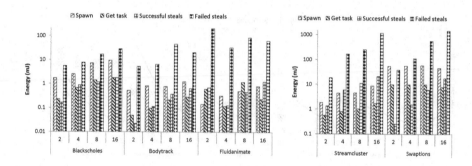

Fig. 3. Energy footprint for task management operations

is divided into a grid of size N*M = the number of threads. For 2 threads we have a 1*2 grid, for 4 threads we have a 2*2 grid, for 8 threads we have 2*4 grid and for 16 threads we have a 4*4 grid. For each particle in the grid, the interactions with all its neighbors on the 8 surrounding directions are computed. When parallelized, this translates into larger lists of tasks that can be spawned for a square grid compared to a rectangular one. For this reason, our 4- and 16-cores simulations show fewer calls to the *get_task()* method and considerable less attempts to steal when compared to the 2- and 8-cores respectively (see Fig. 3).

The Streamcluster results are the best in terms of speedup when comparing the parallel version to the serial one (see Fig 2). This happens because the input set does not fit into the cache hierarchy and there is a lot of access to main memory when executed sequentially. The parallel tasks use much smaller blocks of data with higher spacial locality. Coupled with the use of TBB's cache allocators, this results in almost no misses for the L3 cache. Spawning and *get_task()* follow the same trend as those of Bodytrack because of the same reason: the *parallel_for* as well as the *parallel_reduce* templates are used together with the *grain size* parameter. Again, failed steals have the largest energy footprint among what we measured for this benchmark (see Fig. 3).

Swaptions spawns over 600000 tasks, the largest number among all of our test applications. Like Bodytrack and Streamcluster, the *parallel_for* templates are prevented from dividing the workload too thin. In Fig. 2 we can see that overheads grow with the core count which shows a higher parallel/sequential ratio than for the first 3 benchmarks. In Fig. 3 we can see how failed stealing footprint grows significantly as the number of conflicts grows with the core count.

5.2 Improving Task Stealing

TBB uses a random victim selection policy. While fast and easy to implement, this approach is not fair: the same victim can be selected several times even if it is not the best candidate [14]. Because we account part of the failed stealing attempts in our experiments to this exact scenario, we looked into changing the selection policy in order to improve performance and energy efficiency.

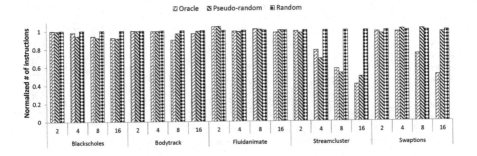

Fig. 4. Victim selection policies - comparison of overheads

Fig. 4 shows an overall decrease in the number of executed instructions for our oracle scheme. The results for both our victim selection methods in Fig. 4 are normalized against TBB's random results. Benchmarks that have a small number of total tasks like Blackscholes, Bodytrack and Fluidanimate see only a marginal improvement in both Fig. 4 and Fig. 5. There are numerous phases during the execution of these benchmarks when all queues are empty. However, these phases are don't last enough to retire the workers meaning that they just waste energy trying to steal. Both Streamcluster and Swaptions show better results with the oracle selection in both Fig. 4 and Fig. 5.

Our results with the pseudo-random victim selection are also mixed. Overall we recorded an increase with all "bad" metrics like the number of failed stealing attempts, the number of conflicts and backoffs. However, the sequential scanning for victims is "cheaper" in terms of executed instructions than the default method which can be seen in Fig. 4. Again, in terms of energy footprint Blackscholes, Bodytrack and Fluidanimate performed only marginally better or even worse than the default random selection. Streamcluster is the only benchmarked that showed improvements in all our test (see Fig. 5). It is also worth mentioning that for 16-cores we recorded in average 2.14 times more failed stealing attempts than the default method. For Swaption, Fig. 5 shows improvements for 2- to 8-cores but not for the 16-cores execution, where we recorded in average 4.27 times more failed stealing attempts than the default method. This shows that our pseudo-random implementation can be a bit too aggressive.

6   Related Work

The energy efficiency of parallel systems and the overheads parallelization brings have been the subject of many studies. Reducing the power requirements of multi-core CPUs, improving the energy efficiency of big parallel systems or reducing the overheads of parallel implementations have been explored by many researchers and plenty of solutions have been found. However, to the best of our knowledge, none of them tries to quantify the energy consumption of parallel overheads.

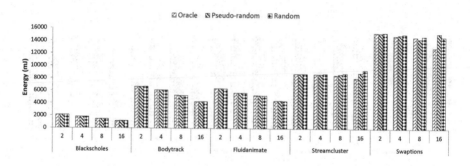

Fig. 5. Victim selection policies - comparison of total energy footprint

Li and Martinez studied the power-performance implications of running parallel applications on CMPs [15]. Using both an analytical model and detailed simulations, the authors show that parallel computing can bring significant power savings through judiciously selections of the granularity and voltage/frequency levels.

Contreras and Martonosi study and characterize some of the overheads of Intel's TBB [14]. They concluded that task management operation can have a detrimental effect on the performance of parallel execution. The authors also note that random stealing fails to scale with increasing core counts and that alternative policies can improve performance.

Bhattacharjee and Martonosi propose a thread criticality predictor which they build using memory hierarchy statistics [16]. The authors implement this predictor in two different applications. First, they implement it into TBB's task scheduler and show that task stealing can be improved over the original random approach. Second, they use the predictor to guide DVFS and to reduce dynamic energy in barrier-based applications. The authors conclude that the thread criticality predictor offers good accuracy at very low hardware overhead.

Podobas et al. do a performance comparative study of several TBP libraries, including TBB [17]. They use both micro-benchmarks and a subset of the BOTS suite to characterize application performance and the costs for task creation and stealing. The study concludes that Wool has the lowest overhead for task spawning and task stealing. However, our previous study showed Wool to be far more aggressive when stealing than TBB which means that as we scale up the core number, Wool will perform worse [18].

The *direct task stack* is a TBP algorithm for extremely fine grained parallel applications [19]. Its implementation in the Wool library shows very low overheads for task creation and task stealing. The experimental result show that Wool significantly outperforms other implementations like Cilk++, TBB or OpenMP for extremely fine grained parallel applications (tens of cycles/task).

Vandierendonck et al. advocate the use of TBP models with nested task spawning for writing general-purpose programs [20]. The authors developed a Cilk-like language to express parallel pipelines and extended a Cilk-like scheduler to recognize and enforce argument dependency types on task spawns. This programming model enhances the ease of programming parallel pipelines.

Chen et al. do a study to evaluate TBB's scalability against Pthreads implementations and to measure some of TBB's overheads [21]. Their results show possible bottlenecks that limit the scalability of TBB. They also show that TBB runtime overheads increase with core counts and in the current implementation will become the main performance bottleneck when scaling to tens of cores.

Ami Marowka introduces TBBench, a micro-benchmark suite designed for Intel's TBB [22]. TBBench is designed to measure the overheads associated with *parallel_for* and *parallel_reduce* constructs and mutual exclusion mechanisms like *Mutex*, *Spin_mutex* and *Queuing_mutex*. The experimental results show that TBB's mutual exclusion mechanisms and scheduler exhibit less overheads than the equivalent OpenMP constructs.

7 Conclusion

Intel's TBB is a runtime library designed to encourage programmers to create portable, parallel applications using task parallelism. TBB was developed to dynamically scale on the existing resources, employing task stealing to deal with workload imbalance. Recently, the ICT sector is facing concerns about energy consumption and TBB has the potential of addressing these issues.

In the current study, we quantified the management overheads involved in parallelizing an application using TBB. We experimented with three victim selection policies. Using the "all knowing" oracle selection method, we saw a reduction of up to 60% in the number of executed instructions which translates into a 13% reduction in energy consumption compared to random victim selection. The pseudo-random also showed overall better results than the random scheme, with up to a 5% reduction in the energy footprint. We also looked at individual TBB operations like task spawning, task stealing and task de-queuing. Among these, we observed that the task stealing mechanism scales worst with core count and creates the highest energy footprint.

The results in this work suggest that there is a potential for improving the energy efficiency of victim selection policies. However, it is still unclear how to reach this potential with a practical implementation. We plan to investigate this and other issues in future work.

References

1. Borkar, S., Chien, A.A.: The Future of Microprocessors. Commun. ACM 54(5) (May 2011)
2. Fuller, S., Millett, L.: Computing Performance: Game Over or Next Level? Computer 44(1) (2011)
3. Cilk++: A quick, easy and reliable way to improve threaded performance, http://software.intel.com/en-us/articles/intel-cilk-plus/ (accessed September 15, 2013)
4. Leijen, D., Schulte, W., Burckhardt, S.: The Design of a Task Parallel Library. In: Proc. of the 24th Conf. on Object Oriented Programming, Systems Languages and Applications (2009)

5. Faxén, K.F.: Wool - A Work Stealing Library. SIGARCH Computer Architecture News 36(5) (2008)
6. Intel Corporation. Intel Threading Building Blocks Reference Manual, http://threadingbuildingblocks.org/ (accessed September 15, 2013)
7. Bienia, C.: Benchmarking Modern Multiprocessors. PhD thesis, Princeton University (January 2011)
8. Patterson, D.: The Trouble With Multicore. IEEE Spectrum 47(7) (2010)
9. Pan, H., Hindman, B., Asanović, K.: Composing Parallel Software Efficiently with Lithe. In: Proc. of the ACM SIGPLAN Conf. on Programming Language Design and Implementation (2010)
10. Carlson, T.E., Heirman, W., Eeckhout, L.: Sniper: Exploring the Level of Abstraction for Scalable and Accurate Parallel Multi-Core Simulations. In: Int'l Conf. for High Performance Computing, Networking, Storage and Analysis (2011)
11. Genbrugge, D., Eyerman, S., Eeckhout, L.: Interval Simulation: Raising the Level of Abstraction in Architectural Simulation. In: Proc. of the IEEE 16th Int'l Symp. on High Performance Computer Architecture (2010)
12. Miller, J., Kasture, H., Kurian, G., Gruenwald, C., Beckmann, N., Celio, C., Eastep, J., Agarwal, A.: Graphite: A Distributed Parallel Simulator for Multicores. In: Proc. of the IEEE 16th Int'l Symp. on High Performance Computer Architecture (2010)
13. Li, S., Ahn, J., Strong, R., Brockman, J., Tullsen, D., Jouppi, N.: McPAT: An Integrated Power, Area, and Timing Modeling Framework for Multi-Core and Many-Core Architectures. In: Proc. of the 42nd Annual IEEE/ACM International Symp. on Microarchitecture (2009)
14. Contreras, G., Martonosi, M.: Characterizing and Improving the Performance of Intel Threading Building Blocks. In: IEEE Int'l Symp. on Workload Characterization (2008)
15. Li, J., Martínez, J.: Power-Performance Considerations of Parallel Computing on Chip Multiprocessors. ACM Trans. Archit. Code Optim. 2 (2005)
16. Bhattacharjee, A., Martonosi, M.: Thread Criticality Predictors for Dynamic Performance, Power, and Resource Management in Chip Multiprocessors. In: Proc. of the 36th Annual Int'l Symp. on Computer Architecture (2009)
17. Podobas, A., Brorsson, M., Faxén, K.F.: A Comparison of Some Recent Task-based Parallel Programming Models. In: Third Workshop on Programmability Issues for Multi-Core Computers (2009)
18. Iordan, A.C., Jahre, M., Natvig, L.: On the Energy Footprint of Task Based Parallel Applications. In: Proc. of the Int'l Conf. on High Performance Computing & Simulation (2013)
19. Faxén, K.F.: Efficient Work Stealing for Fine Grained Parallelism. In: 39th Int'l Conf. on Parallel Processing (2010)
20. Vandierendonck, H., Pratikakis, P., Nikolopoulos, D.S.: Parallel Programming of General-Purpose Programs Using Task-Based Programming Models. In: Proc. of the 3rd USENIX Conference on Hot Topic in Parallelism, HotPar 2011 (2011)
21. Chen, X., Chen, W., Li, J., Zheng, Z., Shen, L., Wang, Z.: Characterizing Fine-Grain Parallelism on Modern Multicore Platform. In: IEEE 17th Int'l Conf. on Parallel and Distributed Systems (2011)
22. Marowka, A.: TBBench: A Micro-Benchmark Suite for Intel Threading Building Blocks. JIPS 8(2) (2012)

Non-preemptive Scheduling
of Real-Time Software Transactional Memory

António Barros and Luís Miguel Pinho

CISTER/INESC-TEC
School of Engineering of the Polytechnic Institute of Porto
Porto, Portugal
{amb,lmp}@isep.ipp.pt

Abstract. Recent embedded processor architectures containing multiple heterogeneous cores and non-coherent caches, bring renewed attention to the use of Software Transactional Memory (STM) as a building block for developing parallel applications. STM promises to ease concurrent and parallel software development, but relies on the possibility of abort conflicting transactions to maintain data consistency, which affects the execution time of tasks carrying transactions. Thus, execution time overheads resulting from aborts must be limited, otherwise the timing behaviour of the task set will not be predictable. In this paper we formalise a FIFO-based algorithm to order the sequence of commits of concurrent transactions. Furthermore, we propose and evaluate two non-preemptive scheduling strategies, in order to avoid transaction starvation.

1 Introduction

The current trend to increase processing power by manufacturing chips including multiple processor cores provided the ability to execute concurrent software in parallel. This tendency for even larger number of processor cores will further impact the way systems are developed. Some recently proposed architectures for embedded systems, like the STMicroelectronics P2012 [4] (prototypes are available with 69 cores), Kalray's MPPA [10] (up to 1024 cores; current version is 256 cores) allow both to concentrate multiple applications into the same processor, maximizing the hardware utilisation, and reducing cost, size, weight, and power requirements, and also to improve application performance by exploiting parallelism at the application level.

Nevertheless, integrating a high number of cores in a chip raises several problems, due to core interconnection and memory hierarchy. Cache coherency is being challenged [7] although some solutions can scale to dozens of cores [13], and some chips still provide (software-based) solutions. Buses do not to scale and the paradigm is shifting to networks-on-chip (NoC). Furthermore, platforms can be homogeneous, with either symmetric multiprocessing or asymmetric multiprocessing, or heterogeneous, with different core types. This influences substantially in the way applications share data.

E. Maehle et al. (Eds.): ARCS 2014, LNCS 8350, pp. 25–36, 2014.

Caches can be private to the cluster/tile, being coherent at that level, globally coherent in the chip, or not made coherent at all (*e.g.* [4] and [10]). As the number of cores increases, traditional solutions, such as buses or caches may become bottlenecks due to the contention on simultaneous accesses.

These challenging architectures introduce more complexity for sharing data between parallel threads. Lock-based synchronisation solutions are seldom used to avoid race conditions, but in multiprocessor systems, coarse-grained locks serialise non-conflicting operations that could progress in parallel, causing an impact on the system throughput, while fine-grained locks increase the complexity of system development, causing an impact on composability.

Alternatively, non-blocking approaches present strong conceptual advantages [19] and have been shown in several cases to perform better than lock-based ones [6]. The software transactional memory (STM) [18], is a concept in which a critical section – the *transaction* – executes in isolation, without blocking, regardless of other simultaneous transactions. An optimistic concurrency control mechanism is responsible to serialise concurrent transactions, maintaining the consistency of shared data objects. Conflicts are solved applying a contention policy that selects the transaction that will commit, while the contender will most likely abort and repeat. Solutions must be devised that reduce contention.

The time overhead resulting from aborts affects the worst-case execution time (WCET) of a task that executes a transaction. Therefore, the timing behaviour of a task can only be predictable if the transaction overhead is bounded, allowing to determine the WCET and the utilisation of the task. Additionally, minimising the number of aborts reduces wasted execution time.

In this paper, we formalise a FIFO-based contention management algorithm and two non-preemptive scheduling strategies that provide predictability and prevent transaction starvation. We evaluate the behaviour of these strategies by simulation, analysing the introduced overhead and consequent impact in schedulability.

The paper is structured as follows. Section 2 describes the problem of guaranteeing timing requirements when using STM in embedded real-time systems based on parallel architectures, and presents relevant published work in this field. Section 3 sets the system model in which the assumptions of this work are valid. We then formalise a decentralised algorithm to manage conflicts between concurrent transactions (Section 4). This contention management policy is more effective if transactions are not preempted, as we show in Section 5. The results from simulations that compare the performance of the contention management algorithm, under the two proposed scheduling strategies against pure partitioned EDF (P-EDF) are presented in section 6. This paper terminates with the conclusions and perspectives for further work in Section 7.

2   Background and Related Work

Transactional memory promises to ease concurrent programming: the programmer must indicate which code that forms the *transaction*, and relies an underlying mechanism that maintains the consistency of shared data objects located at the *transactional memory*. Multiple transactions can be executed optimistically in parallel; however, when conflicting concurrent object accesses occurs (either a *read-write* or a *write-write* conflict) a contention policy is applied to guarantee the serialisation of the concurrent schedules, usually allowing one transaction to complete and aborting (and, consequently, repeat) the contenders. This approach has proved to scale well with multiprocessors [8], delivers higher throughput than coarse-grained locks and does not increase design complexity as fine-grained locks do [16].

STM achieves better performances when contention is low, causing low transaction abort ratio. Thus, STM behaves very well in systems exhibiting the following characteristics [11]: a predominance of read-only transactions, short-running transactions and a low ratio of context switching during the execution of a transaction. Some transactions may present characteristics (*e.g.* long-running, low priority) that can potentially expose them to starvation. In parallel systems literature, the main concern about STM is on system throughput, and the contention management policy has often the role to prevent livelock (a pair of transactions indefinitely aborting each other) and starvation (one transaction being constantly aborted by the contenders), so that each transaction will eventually conclude and the system will progress as a whole.

In real-time systems, the guarantee that a transaction will *eventually* conclude is not sufficient to assure the timing requirements that are critical to such type of systems: it must be known *how long* it will take to conclude. The verification of the schedulability of the task set requires that the WCET of each task is known, which can only be calculated if the maximum time used to commit the included transaction is known. As such, STM can be used in real-time systems as long as the employed contention management policy provides guarantees on the maximum number of retries each transaction is subject to.

Although the concept of STM is not new and numerous works have been published, only a few works dealt with it in the context of real-time systems. In [12], a data access mechanism is proposed for uniprocessor platforms – the Preemptible Atomic Regions – together with an analysis to bound the response time of jobs. An atomic region is guaranteed to be free from other tasks' interference because any transaction preempted by a higher-priority task is immediately aborted, and its effects undone. As no concurrent transactions are allowed in the system, it is impractical in multiprocessor systems. However, this policy matches with the *Abort-and-Restart* model [15].

In [2], and based on previous work on lock-free objects, Anderson *et al.* establish scheduling conditions for lock-free transactions under Earliest Deadline First (EDF) and Deadline Monotonic (DM), exclusively for uniprocessor systems. A different approach to support transactions in multiprocessor systems is provided in [1]: a wait-free mechanism relies on a helping scheme that provides an upper bound on the transaction execution time. In this approach, an arriving transaction must help pending transactions before being able to proceed, even if no conflicts would occur, so the upper bound is likely to increase with the number of processors in the system.

In [9], Fahmy *et al.* describe an algorithm to calculate an upper-bound on the worst-case response time of tasks on a multiprocessor system using STM. Tasks are scheduled with the Pfair approach. Each task can have multiple atomic regions, and concurrent transactions can interfere with each other. Conflicts are detected and solved during the commit phase. This analysis is limited for small atomic regions, assuming that any transaction will execute in, at most, two quanta.

Sarni *et al.* propose real-time scheduling of concurrent transactions for soft real-time systems in [17]. The authors adapted a practical STM to run on a real-time kernel, and modified the contention manager to apply their proposed policy. In this model, transactions are characterised by scheduling parameters, which are taken into account whenever solving a detected conflict between transactions. Conflicting transactions are serialised based exclusively on their absolute deadlines, which may have a negative effect on transactions with further deadlines.

In [3], we defend a FIFO-based approach to serialise concurrent transactions as a means to predict the time required to commit, but only provide a sketch of the decision algorithm. However, this paper does not take into account the considerable effect of preempting transaction on the predictability of the time required to commit.

These works provide already some perspectives on how to deal with STM in real-time systems. However, it is clear that there are many issues pending, and further research is necessary to take advantage of future parallel architectures. Therefore, this paper proposes new approaches to manage contention between conflicting transactions, using on-line information, with the purpose of reducing the overall number of retries, increasing responsiveness and reducing useless processor utilisation, while assuring deadlines are met.

3   System Model

We assume that jobs are released by a set of periodic tasks $\tau = \{\tau_1, \ldots, \tau_n\}$, and scheduled on m identical processors denoted $P = \{P_1, \ldots, P_m\}$, under partitioned EDF (each task is statically assigned to a processor and each processor schedules its set of tasks under classical EDF). Each task τ_i is characterised by the period of job arrivals T_i, the worst-case execution time C_i, and the relative deadline D_i. The jth job of task τ_i, hence forward denominated $\tau_{i,j}$, is characterised by the time the job arrives r_{ij}, and the absolute deadline of the job d_{ij}, defined as

$$d_{ij} = r_{ij} + D_i. \tag{1}$$

For the sake of simplicity, we assume that each task τ_i performs at most one transaction, ω_i. Nevertheless, the results of this paper are extensible to tasks executing multiple non-nested transactions. Each transaction is characterised by:

- C_{Ti} – the maximum execution time required to execute the sequential code once and try to commit,

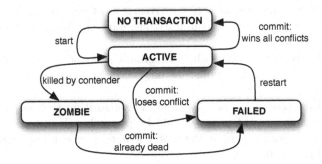

Fig. 1. State diagram of a transaction

- $DataSet_i$ – the data set, a collection of shared objects accessed by the transaction, which is divided into
- $ReadSet_i$ – the read set, the collection of objects that are accessed solely for reading, and
- $WriteSet_i$ – the write set, a collection of objects that are modified during the execution of the transaction.

A collection of STM objects $O = \{o_1, \ldots, o_p\}$ are assumed to be located at shared memory, being globally accessible to tasks, independently of the processor in which transactions are executing. We assume multiple simultaneous transactions are supported, and for each object there is a chronologically ordered list that contains records of all transactions currently accessing the object.

Each instance of a transaction has a life cycle that follows the states represented in Figure 1. Once a transaction arrives, it executes the transaction code and then tries to commit; if no conflicts are detected, the transaction commits, otherwise it may be aborted, retrying immediately. A transaction may be aborted multiple times until successfully commit. *Transaction overhead* is the execution time wasted executing aborted attempts. Transaction overhead of task τ_i is given considering the maximum number of failed attempts experienced by any of its jobs, $aborts_i$ before the transaction commits:

$$overhead_i = aborts_i \cdot C_{Ti}. \tag{2}$$

The WCET of a task that executes a transaction is then given by the time required to execute the code of the task without aborts C_i', with the maximum transaction overhead:

$$C_i = C_i' + overhead_i. \tag{3}$$

The utilisation of this task is expressed by

$$U_i = C_i/T_i. \tag{4}$$

4   Contention Management

A STM contention management policy oriented for real-time systems must tackle three issues.

- *Predictability.* When a transaction arrives, it must be assured that it will not exceed a determined time to commit (thus, imposing an upper bound on the number of aborts).
- *Starvation avoidance.* The ability to commit must be distributed fairly between contending transactions, so no task will have an excessive abort overhead.
- *Decentralised contention management.* The algorithm that implements the contention management policy should be preferably decentralised and executed by each transaction at the moment it tries to commit, and not on a dedicated processor.

In [3], we advanced that these issues are covered by a policy that sequences contending transactions by their chronological order of arrival, i.e. by the moment a transaction starts executing its first attempt. The algorithm we now formalise considers only static parameters, such as time of arrivals and core ids, so it is simple to reach a decentralised consensus. The time until commit should depend solely on the ongoing transactions at the moment the transaction starts, and independent of future arrivals of other transactions.

In algorithm 1 we detail the operations executed by every transaction when trying to commit. If the transaction was not previously turned in to *zombie*, it will take ownership of the objects in its data set. A transaction will have to wait that an object is released before taking ownership of it. For every object in its write set, the transaction determines if it wins against all contenders. In order to preserve work, the transaction just considers the contenders that are currently *active* and *running* (i.e. the host job is not preempted). If it fails on one object, then it immediately releases all owned objects, aborts and repeats. If all conflicts are won, it can immediately release the objects in the read set, commit updates, and mark the contenders in the write set as *zombies*, before releasing the objects.

Unlike locking solutions, the shared objects are just owned during the process of commit, and not during the whole critical section, which improves parallelism. Furthermore, the ownership process is controlled by the STM and should be transparent to the programmer, which improves composability.

However, if we consider preemptions during the execution of transactions, this behaviour can be seriously undermined, as we demonstrate in the next section.

5 Scheduling Transactions

The way tasks are scheduled on multiple cores can affect the contention management behaviour and influence the success rate and predictability of transactions. Our algorithm permits that a transaction overtakes a preempted transaction: this avoids deadlock between conflicting transactions executing in the same core, and preserves work of running transactions ready to commit. However, this reduces the probability of committing transactions that are prone to be preempted (e.g. long transaction, or low-priority job). Furthermore, a frequently preempted

---

Algorithm 1. STM contention management algorithm proposed for real-time systems

---

Require: Current job of task τ_i has finished executing transaction ω_i.
Ensure: Transaction ω_i commits if and only if it wins all conflicts.

1. **if** ω_i status is ACTIVE **then**
2.   **for all** $o_k \in DataSet_i$ **do**
3.   **if** ω_i status is ACTIVE **then**
4.   Take ownership of o_k
5.   **for all** ω_j contending with ω_i on o_k **do**
6.   **if** ω_j status is ACTIVE **then**
7.   **if** τ_j status is RUNNING **then**
8.   **if** arrival(ω_i) > arrival(ω_j) **then**
9.   Set ω_i status as FAILED
10.   **else if** arrival(ω_i) = arrival(ω_j) **and** Core(τ_i) > Core(τ_j) **then**
11.   Set ω_i status as FAILED
12.   **else**
13.   Stop checking further objects
14.   **if** ω_i status is ACTIVE **then**
15.   **for all** $o_k \in ReadSet_i$ **do**
16.   Remove ω_i entry from list
17.   Release o_k
18.   Commit updates
19.   **for all** $o_k \in WriteSet_i$ **do**
20.   Remove ω_i entry from list
21.   **for all** ω_j accessing o_k **do**
22.   Set ω_j status as ZOMBIE
23.   Release o_k
24.   **else**
25.   Release all currently owned objects
26.   Abort and repeat ω_i
27. **else**
28.   Abort and repeat ω_i

---

transaction may fail to commit for contending transactions that are more recent but are allowed to commit while the transaction is preempted, inverting artificially the intended behaviour of the system.

Cancelling temporarily preemptions, during the execution of a transaction, solves the problems of long transaction starvation and unpredictability stated above. If a transaction is guaranteed that it will not be preempted, then the success of transaction will depend solely on the contention management policy.

This solution can be compared with priority boosting [14]: raising the priority of a job to the highest level during a critical section cancels effectively preemptions. The Flexible Multiprocessor Locking Protocol (FMLP) [5] follows a similar approach to the one presented in this paper, executing critical sections non-preemptively, by their order of arrival. However, FMLP can serialise critical sections with non-intersecting datasets but accessing objects in the same group; STM allows such transactions to proceed and commit in parallel.

In this paper, we consider two non-preemptive approaches:

- *Non-preemptible until commit (NPUC).*
  In this approach, the job is assured to be scheduled from the moment the transaction arrives until it successfully commits.
- *Non-preemptible during attempt (NPDA).*
  In this approach, the task is non-preemptible during the transaction, but has preemption points between attempts. Any higher-priority job can be scheduled at any of these points.

5.1 Non-preemptible Until Commit

Under NPUC, each transaction will take-over the core in which it is executing, and will fail until all active direct contenders (transactions whose data accesses will conflict with the accesses of the transaction in consideration) that arrived earlier have committed and finished.

NPUC is totally predictable, as the time required for the transaction to successfully commit depends solely on the transactions that are already executing when the transaction arrives. Since direct contenders (transactions that have, at least, one conflict with the write set) will also wait for their own earlier direct contenders to finish, contention is propagated in chain. So, in the worst case, a transaction will have to wait for $(m - 1)$ transactions to complete, assuming that every other core is already executing one transaction.

The predictability given by NPUC comes with a cost: higher priority tasks will have their responsiveness reduced due to lower-priority blocking.

5.2 Non-preemptible during Attempt

Under NPDA, preemptions are limited during a transaction to preemption points inserted between attempts. This policy assures that the success of each attempt depends only on the running transactions, and reduces lower-priority blocking as compared with NPUC, improving responsiveness of higher-priority tasks.

Since jobs can be preempted between transaction attempts, one core can hold more than one ongoing transaction at any given time. This means that the number of earlier conflicting transactions for a given transaction is not limited to the number of remaining cores $(m - 1)$, as in NPUC. So, although NPDA increases responsiveness of higher priority jobs, it is less predictable than NPUC.

6 Simulation Results

We developed a simulation environment to test the proposed contention management algorithm under different scheduling policies – pure P-EDF, P-EDF with NPUC and P-EDF with NPDA – in systems containing from 2 to 64 cores.

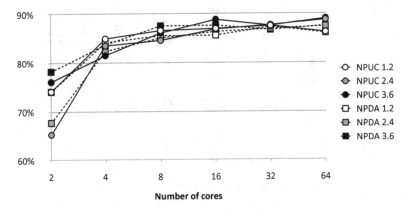

Fig. 2. Maximum aborts per transaction, normalised to P-EDF

For each system we generated randomly 20 synchronous task sets for three degrees of contention. The degree of contention is characterised by the ratio of the sum of all dataset sizes and the number of TM objects. In the experiments, we used 1.2, 2.4 and 3.6 ratios. All task sets demand each core a maximum ideal utilisation (not considering abort overhead) of 0.75.

In each task set, all tasks executed one transaction, and 50% were update transactions. The sequential execution time of each transaction C_T was 20% of the ideal WCET (without abort overhead) of the task. Each transaction could access, at most, 5 shared TM objects.

In each simulation, we recorded for each task the maximum number of aborts experienced in a job, the total number of aborts, the number of deadlines missed and the total execution time. For every task set, we simulated 10^6 time units under P-EDF, NPUC and NPDA.

First, we wanted to know how cancelling preemptions would affect the maximum number aborts experienced in a job of a task. We normalised the maximum number of aborts experienced in a job in NPUC and NPDA simulations to the values recorded in P-EDF simulations. Figure 2 presents the averages of these normalised results, indicating that cancelling preemptions tends to reduce the maximum number of aborts.

Next, we wanted to observe how the execution time would increase, due to aborts. Figure 3 shows the increase in execution time due to transaction overhead. We can observe that the amount of execution time with aborted transactions increases with contention density, as expected. The non-preemptive approaches also present very similar overheads (they overlap in this chart), and are lower than P-EDF, which means that they tend to produce less aborts, at the overall system perspective.

Table 1 reveals the total number of missed deadlines for each set of 20 simulations. Deadline misses are practically due to a very limited number of tasks with very high ideal utilisations, close to 0.75, and small periods. Inspection of simulation logs reveals that such tasks have laxities that are barely sufficient

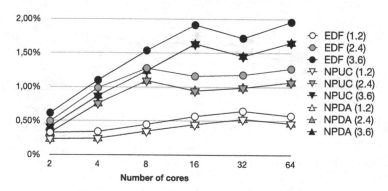

Fig. 3. System overall transaction overhead

Table 1. Total deadlines missed (20 simulations)

Cores	1.2			2.4			3.6		
	EDF	NPUC	NPDA	EDF	NPUC	NPDA	EDF	NPUC	NPDA
2	0	0	0	0	1	0	0	0	0
4	0	0	37	0	35	1	21	1	1
8	0	77	0	657	520	540	964	959	954
16	6	60	49	154	256	220	1939	1897	1687
32	33	204	147	483	723	589	1768	2317	1884
64	246	450	310	1400	1923	1424	4843	4757	4389

to accommodate transactions from concurrent tasks on the same core (in low contention scenarios), or accommodate multiple aborts (in higher contention scenarios). These characteristics do not fit non-preemptive approaches.

These results suggest that STM can naturally adapt to systems in which cores are grouped in tiles of 8 or 16 cores, and STM is isolated inside each partition (tile). Note that this maps well with cluster based many-core architectures which are emerging, where dozens or hundreds of processors are grouped into 8 or 16 core shared memory partitions, being the clusters interconnected by NoC.

7   Conclusions and Further Work

In this paper we propose a decentralised contention management algorithm for Software Transactional Memory (STM), for multi-core real-time systems, in which conflicting transactions are serialised by their chronological order of arrival. This algorithm is fair and avoids starvation across transactions. However, preempting a transaction reduces the probability of successfully commit, and so we propose two approaches to limit preemptions: non-preemptive until commit (NPUC) and non-preemptive during attempt (NPDA). NPUC is more predictable, while NPDA improves responsiveness of more urgent tasks.

Simulation results show that non-preemptive approaches can reduce transaction overhead. However, judicious processor allocation is required for tasks that have small laxity to accommodate transaction retries.

Acknowledgement. We would like to thank the anonymous reviewers for their suggestions and comments. This work was partially supported by National Funds through FCT (Portuguese Foundation for Science and Technology) and by ERDF (European Regional Development Fund) through COMPETE (Operational Programme 'Thematic Factors of Competitiveness'), within projects FCOMP-01-0124-FEDER-015006 (VIPCORE) and FCOMP-01-0124-FEDER-037281 (CISTER); by FCT and EU ARTEMIS JU, within project ARTEMIS/0003/2012, JU grant nr. 333053 (CONCERTO).

References

1. Anderson, J.H., Jain, R., Ramamurthy, S.: Implementing hard real-time transactions on multiprocessors. In: Real-Time Database and Information Systems: Research Advances, pp. 247–260. Kluwer Academic Publishers, Norwell (1997)
2. Anderson, J.H., Ramamurthy, S., Moir, M., Jeffay, K.: Lock-free transactions for real-time systems. In: Real-Time Database Systems: Issues and Applications, pp. 215–234. Kluwer Academic Publishers, Norwell (1997)
3. Barros, A., Pinho, L.M.: Software transactional memory as a building block for parallel embedded real-time systems. In: Proceedings of the 37th EUROMICRO Conference on Software Engineering and Advanced Applications (SEAA 2011), Oulu, Finland (August 2011)
4. Benini, L., Flamand, E., Fuin, D., Melpignano, D.: P2012: Building an ecosystem for a scalable, modular and high-efficiency embedded computing accelerator. In: Proceedings of the Conference & Exhibition Design, Automation Test in Europe (DATE 2012), pp. 983–987 (March 2012)
5. Block, A., Leontyev, H., Brandenburg, B.B., Anderson, J.H.: A Flexible Real-Time Locking Protocol for Multiprocessors. In: Proceedings of the 13th IEEE International Conference on Embedded and Real-Time Computing Systems and Applications (RTCSA 2007), Daegu, South Korea, pp. 47–56 (August 2007)
6. Brandenburg, B.B., Calandrino, J.M., Block, A., Leontyev, H., Anderson, J.H.: Real-Time Synchronization on Multiprocessors: To Block or Not to Block, to Suspend or Spin? In: Proceedings of the 14th IEEE Real-Time and Embedded Technology and Applications Symposium (RTAS 2008), pp. 342–353 (April 2008)
7. Choi, B., Komuravelli, R., Sung, H., Smolinski, R., Honarmand, N., Adve, S., Adve, V., Carter, N., Chou, C.-T.: Denovo: Rethinking the memory hierarchy for disciplined parallelism. In: Proceedings of the International Conference on Parallel Architectures and Compilation Techniques (PACT), pp. 155–166 (October 2011)
8. Dragojević, A., Felber, P., Gramoli, V., Guerraoui, R.: Why STM can be more than a research toy. Communications of the ACM 54(4), 70–77 (2011)
9. Fahmy, S.F., Ravindran, B., Jensen, E.D.: On Bounding Response Times under Software Transactional Memory in Distributed Multiprocessor Real-Time Systems. In: Proceedings of the Design, Automation & Test in Europe Conference & Exhibition (DATE 2009), pp. 688–693 (April 2009)
10. Kalray: MPPA 256 – Many-core processors (2012), http://www.kalray.eu/products/mppa-manycore/mppa-256/

11. Maldonado, W., Marlier, P., Felber, P., Suissa, A., Hendler, D., Fedorova, A., Lawall, J.L., Muller, G.: Scheduling support for transactional memory contention management. In: Proceedings of the 15th ACM SIGPLAN Symposium on Principles and Practice of Parallel Programming (PPoPP 2010), pp. 79–90 (January 2010)
12. Manson, J., Baker, J., Cunei, A., Jagannathan, S., Prochazka, M., Xin, B., Vitek, J.: Preemptible Atomic Regions for Real-Time Java. In: Proceedings of the 26th IEEE International Real-Time Systems Symposium (RTSS 2005), Miami, FL, pp. 62–71 (December 2005)
13. Martin, M.M.K., Hill, M.D., Sorin, D.J.: Why on-chip cache coherence is here to stay. Communications of the ACM 55(7), 78–89 (2012)
14. Rajkumar, R.: Real-time synchronization protocols for shared memory multiprocessors. In: Proceedings of the 10th International Conference on Distributed Computing Systems, pp. 116–123 (1990)
15. Ras, J., Cheng, A.M.K.: Response time analysis for the Abort-and-Restart event handlers of the Priority-Based Functional Reactive Programming (P-FRP) paradigm. In: Proceedings of the 15th IEEE International Conference on Embedded and Real-Time Computing Systems and Applications (RTCSA), pp. 305–314 (2009)
16. Rossbach, C.J., Hofmann, O.S., Witchel, E.: Is transactional programming actually easier? In: Proceedings of the 15th ACM SIGPLAN Symposium on Principles and Practice of Parallel Programming (PPoPP 2010), pp. 47–56 (January 2010)
17. Sarni, T., Queudet, A., Valduriez, P.: Real-Time Support for Software Transactional Memory. In: Proceedings of the 15th IEEE International Conference on Embedded and Real-Time Computing Systems and Applications (RTCSA 2009), pp. 477–485 (August 2009)
18. Shavit, N., Touitou, D.: Software transactional memory. In: Proceedings of the 14th Annual ACM Symposium on Principles of Distributed Computing (PODC 1995), pp. 204–213 (August 1995)
19. Tsigas, P., Zhang, Y.: Non-blocking data sharing in multiprocessor real-time systems. In: Proceedings of the 6th IEEE International Conference on Real-Time Computing Systems and Applications (RTCSA 1999), pp. 247–254 (December 1999)

Trust-Enhanced Self-configuration for Organic Computing Systems

Nizar Msadek, Rolf Kiefhaber, Bernhard Fechner, and Theo Ungerer

Institute of Computer Science
University of Augsburg
86135 Augsburg, Germany
{Msadek,Kiefhaber,Fechner,Ungerer}@informatik.uni-augsburg.de

Abstract. Organic Computing (OC) enhances computer systems by postulating life-like properties to enable a system to self-configure, self-heal, self-optimize and self-protect. It is a solution to reduce the complexity of systems but is based on a benevolence assumption that all parts of the system are reliable and interested to further the system goal. In open and heterogeneous systems, the benevolence assumption is unrealistic, since uncertainties about the participants' behavior have to be regarded. We propose trust as a concept to cope with these uncertainties.

This paper presents a trust enhancement of the self-configuration algorithm based on the well-known Contract Net Protocol. This baseline algorithm can be used in a distributed system, i.e., multi-agent system, cloud computing or grid system, to equally distribute the load of services on the nodes. However, the trust enhancement of self-configuration assigns services with different importance levels to nodes so that more important services are assigned to more reliable nodes. Evaluations have been conducted to rate the effectiveness of the algorithm when nodes are failing, i.e., the reduction of failures of important services. The results show that our self-configuration algorithm increases the availability of important services by more than 12%. To our knowledge this is the first trust integrated self-configuration process that proposes to build reliable and robust heterogeneous distributed systems in a decentralized way.

Keywords: Organic Computing, Self-Configuration, Trust, Contract Net Protocol.

1   Introduction

The Organic Computing Initiative [1] has become an important research area for future information processing systems. This initiative consists of developing computer systems capable of so-called self-x properties (like self-configuration, self-optimization, self-healing and self-protection) to cope with the rapidly growing complexity of computing systems and to reduce the barriers that complexity poses to further growth. These properties are achieved by constantly observing the system and initiating autonomous reconfiguration if necessary. An essential aspect that becomes particularly prominent in these systems is trust. In this

E. Maehle et al. (Eds.): ARCS 2014, LNCS 8350, pp. 37–48, 2014.

paper we adopt the definition of trust [2] of the research unit OC-Trust of the German Research Foundation (DFG). In their research, trust covers different facets, as, for example, safety, reliability, credibility and usability. Our investigation focuses on the reliability aspect. In this paper, when we speak of trust we mean always reliability. Furthermore, it is assumed that a node can not realistically assess its own trust value because it trusts itself fully. Therefore, the calculation of the trust value for the trust-enhanced self-configuration must be done with the following trust metrics.

- **Direct Trust [3]** is based on the experiences a node has made directly with an interaction partner node. Typically, trust values are calculated by taking the mean or weighted mean of past experiences.
- **Reputation [4]** is based on the trust values of others that had experiences with the interaction partner. Reputation is typically collected if not enough or outdated experiences exist.
- **Confidence [5]** Before both values, direct trust and reputation, can be aggregated to a total trust value, the reliability of one's own trust value has to be determined, the so-called confidence. If a node does have a direct trust value but is not confident about its accuracy, it needs to include reputation data as well.

When all the aforementioned values are obtained, a total trust value based on the direct trust and reputation values can be calculated using confidence to weight both parts against each other. This value can then be used to improve the self-configuration.

Our objective is to enhance the self-configuration process with trust capabilities to enable building a reliable system from unreliable components. This is achieved by improving the availability of important services.

The remainder of this paper is structured as follows. Section 2 presents related work on self-configuration including a comparison with our work. Our metrics for enabling a node to host a specific service are presented in section 3 together with the self-configuration process. The results of the evaluations are shown in section 4. The paper closes with a conclusion and future work in section 5.

2   Related Work

There are many sophisticated approaches to deal with the allocation problem of services on nodes, either to achieve good load balancing or to minimize energy consumption.

An approach that has become a standard by FIPA[1] is the Contract Net Protocol [6]. It consists of finding an agent that is the most suitable to provide a service. This approach is often adapted and applied in many application domains, for example, manufacturing systems [7], resource allocation in grids and

---

[1] FIPA: Interaction Protocol Specifications - [Accessed: Sept 03, 2013]
  http://www.fipa.org/specs/fipa00029/

sensor web environments [8] [9], as well as in hospitals [10], electronic market-places [11], power distribution network restoration [12], etc. Our model is based on the Contract Net Protocol, extended by trust. In this context, trust serves as a mean to give nodes a clue about with which nodes to cooperate.

Bittencourt et al. [13] presented an approach to schedule processes composed of dependent services onto a grid. This approach is implemented in the Xavantes grid middleware and arranges the services in groups. It has the drawback of a central service distribution instance and therefore a single point of failure can occur. Trumler et al. [14] described a scheduling algorithm for distributing services onto nodes based on social behavior. It is implemented in the OCµ middleware. In their model, nodes can calculate a QoS for the services to decide which service is assigned to which node. In this case only resource constraints are used to describe cases when a service should be hosted depending on a specific hardware. In contrast to our approach, this algorithm does not include reliability constraints.

In [15], Topcuoglu et al. presented an approach to consider the priorities of tasks. They try to select tasks in order of their priorities and to schedule them to the best machine that minimize their finish time in an insertion based manner. This approach has been shown to significantly improve the schedule computation time. However, a disadvantage is that important tasks might run on unreliable nodes and are prone to fail. Later, in [16], reliability constraints were considered to find a homogeneous allocation of the instances of services. Contrary to this work, our approach is able to work with heterogeneous systems.

3   Trust-Enhanced Self-configuration

The approach of trust-enhanced self-configuration is a crucial part for developing dependable and robust systems using self-x properties. This consists mainly of finding a robust distribution of services by including trust. The services are cat-egorized into important services with a high required trust, and non important services with a low required trust. Important services are those, which are nec-essary for the functionality of the entire system. E.g., Bernard et al. [17] present a computing grid to solve computationally intensive problems. In their model, trust is incorporated to enable nodes to form Trusted Communities (TCs). The manager, that administrates these TCs is an example for an important service, since its failure deteriorates the entire TC.

The goal is to maximize the availability of important services. Therefore, it is necessary to assign important services to more reliable nodes. Reliability in this context is expressed by a trust value based on previously developed trust metrics [3] [4] [5]. In addition to the reliability, resource requirements (e.g., like CPU and memory) should also be considered to balance the load of the nodes.

3.1   Metrics

The self-configuration focuses on assigning services with different required trust levels to nodes which have different reliability levels so that more important services are assigned to more reliable nodes. Furthermore, the overall utilization of resources in the network should be well-balanced. Therefore, a metric is defined to calculate a Quality of Service (QoS_{total}), i.e., the suitability of node to host a specific service.

$$QoS_{total} = (1 - \alpha) \cdot QoS_{trust} + \alpha \cdot QoS_{workload}. \tag{1}$$

The relationship between trust and workload can be set through $\alpha \in [0, 1]$. If $\alpha = 1$, the QoS_{total} is only obtained by the current value $QoS_{workload}$, i.e., the suitability of a node to host a specific service with regard to its workload. If $\alpha = 0$, the QoS_{total} is decided only by the actual QoS_{trust} value, i.e., the suitability of a node to host a specific service with regard to its reliability. A higher value α favors $QoS_{workload}$ over QoS_{trust}.

– **QoS_{trust}** indicates how well the reliability of a node fulfilled the required reliability of a service. Figure 1 visualizes formula 2 to calculate the QoS_{trust}.

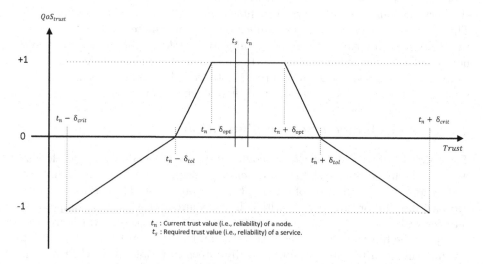

Fig. 1. QoS_{trust} based on the difference between the reliability t_n of node n compared to the required reliability t_s of service s

t_n represents the current trust value of a node n based on the trust metrics [3] [4] [5]. In this work, it is assumed that t_n is constant at a certain point in time. However, t_n is likely to change over time. This issue is work in progress and will be addressed in a subsequent publication of self-optimization. t_s represents the required trust value of service s defined by the user. If both values are close enough then n has fulfilled the required trust value of a service s. Close enough is defined by the threshold δ_{opt} (optimal area). If the difference between t_n and t_s is more than δ_{opt}, then QoS_{trust} will be gradually decreased until it reaches 0 at $t_n \pm \delta_{tol}$ (tolerance area).

If t_s is even beyond $t_n \pm \delta_{tol}$ then the QoS_{trust} will drop below 0(critical area). In the case that the divergence between t_n and t_s is more than δ_{crit}, the QoS_{trust} remains constant at -1. This is expressed by the formula 2, with $t_s, t_n \in [0, 1]$ and $0 < \delta_{opt} < \delta_{tol} < \delta_{crit}$.

$$QoS_{trust}(t_s) = \begin{cases} 1 & \text{if } 0 \leq |t_n - t_s| \leq \delta_{opt} \\ \frac{-|t_s - t_n| + \delta_{tol}}{\delta_{tol} - \delta_{opt}} & \text{if } \delta_{opt} < |t_n - t_s| \leq \delta_{tol} \\ \frac{-|t_s - t_n| + \delta_{tol}}{\delta_{crit} - \delta_{tol}} & \text{if } \delta_{tol} < |t_n - t_s| \leq \delta_{crit} \\ -1 & \text{otherwise} \end{cases} \tag{2}$$

– **QoS_workload** gives an estimation of the workload of a node. As long as the load of a node is lower than two times its maximum capacity, the quality of service (QoS) decreases linearly, otherwise it remains constant at -1. We assume that the capacity of a node has not a hard limit (e.g., swapping data from RAM to hard drive provides extra memory at the cost of runtime). The QoS regarding only one resource i is calculated as follows :

$$workload_i(V_{req_i}) = \begin{cases} \frac{V_{av_i} - V_{req_i}}{V_{max_i}} & \text{if } V_{req_i} \leq V_{av_i} + V_{max_i} \\ -1 & \text{otherwise} \end{cases} \tag{3}$$

with $V_{max_i} > 0$, $V_{req_i} > 0$, and $V_{av_i} \leq V_{max_i}$.
It is to note that V_{req_i} means the required resource i of a service. The available resource amount of a node is denoted by V_{av_i} and its maximum resource amount by V_{max_i}. However, every node can have multiple resources n. Therefore the $QoS_{workload}$ is calculated by the average sum of all resource values.

$$QoS_{workload} = \frac{1}{n} \sum_{i=1}^{n} workload_i(V_{req_i}) \tag{4}$$

3.2   Self-configuration Process

This section discusses the methodology for distributing services. This consists of a collection of services with different importance levels which should run on nodes with different reliability. It is known to be a NP-hard problem to find an optimal solution for the distribution of the services on the nodes, so that the quality of service is optimal [18]. Furthermore, there is no known algorithm which can, for a given solution, in a polynomial time identify whether it is optimal. The aim behind self-configuration is to find a distributed and robust but not necessarily optimal yet good enough solution.

The quality of service metric presented in 3.1 is used to evaluate the distribution phase which is based on the Contract Net Protocol [6]. During the distribution phase, every node in the network can act as a manager or contractor. A *manager* is responsible for assigning services. A *contractor* is responsible for the actual execution of the service. The manager is determined by the user. Figure 2 visualizes a step-by-step example on how the negotiation process is run between nodes.

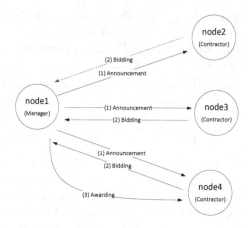

Fig. 2. Elementary representation of the distribution phase

1. **Announcement:** The manager (e.g., node1) that wants to distribute a service, initiates contract negotiation by advertising the existence of that service to the other contractors (e.g., node2, node3 and node4) with a service announcement message. A service announcement can be transmitted to a single contractor in the network (unicast), to a specific set of contractors (multicast) or to all contractors (broadcast).
2. **Bidding:** Every contractor that receives the announcement calculates the $QoS_{workload}$ for the given service based on its own available resources and then submits its bid in form of $QoS_{workload}$ to the manager. Note that the service announcement is ignored if the service cannot be hosted due to missing resources.
3. **Awarding:** When the expiration time (i.e., the deadline for receiving bids) has passed, the manager that sent the service announcement must calculate QoS_{trust} for every contractor in order to build the QoS_{total} and decides who to award the contract to. In the basic Contract Net Protocol the manager selects among the received bids the contractor with the highest $QoS_{workload}$. Our enhancement improves the Awarding phase by including trust (QoS_{trust}) so that more reliable contractors always have a higher chance to receive the service than less reliable contractors. The result of this process will be then communicated to the contractors that submitted a bid. It is to note that the expiration time is defined by the user.

3.3   Conflict Resolution

During the self-configuration process, several nodes could be ranked with the same QoS_{total}. This might lead to a conflict for the manager to decide to whom to award the service. To avoid this a conflict resolution mechanism is used which does not need any further messages. The conflict resolution mechanism consists of three stages which might be used in the following chronological order:

1. **Minimum latency:** The node with the lowest latency will get the service.
2. **Minimum amount of already assigned services:** The node with the least amount of already assigned services will get the service, assuming that a lower amount of services will produce less load (e.g., process or thread switching produces additional load).
3. **Node ID:** It is unlikely but not impossible that all of the former values were equal. In this case the node with the lowest id will be used to find a solution to the conflict because every node has a unique id.

4 Evaluation

In this section an evaluation for the introduced self-configuration approach is provided. For the purpose of evaluating and testing, an evaluator based on TEM [19] has been implemented which is able to simulate the distributed self-configuration process. The evaluation network consists of 50 nodes, where all nodes are able to communicate with each other using message passing. Experiments with more nodes were tested and yielded similar results, but with 50 nodes more observable effects were seen. Each node has a limited resource capacity (e.g., CPU and memory) and is judged by an individual trust value (reliability) without any central knowledge. Notice that the reliability will always range between 0 and 1. The value of 0 means that the node is not reliable at all while a value of 1 stands for whole reliability. Four type of nodes are defined with different reliability and resources (see Table 1).

Table 1. Mixture of heterogeneous nodes

Node Type	CPU (MHz)	Memory (MB)	Reliability	Amount (%)
Embedded	200-800	500-1000	0.7-0.9	10
Smartphone	500-1500	500-1500	0.3-0.6	50
Laptop	1500-2000	2000-4000	0.4-0.8	30
Workstation	2000-3000	4000-8000	0.4-0.9	10

Then 150 services, 75 of them important and 75 unimportant (50/50 ratio), with random resources (CPU $\in [0, 800]$ and RAM $\in [0, 1000]$ are generated so that all nodes are loaded on average to 60%. Without additional information important services might run on unreliable nodes and are prone to fail. Such situations can be avoided. With the use of the trust metrics [3] [4] [5], the reliability of a node can be measured and taken into consideration for the service distribution. Hence, the goal is to maximize the availability of important services. Therefore, it is necessary to assign the more important services to more reliable nodes. In the following the results of the conducted evaluations are presented.

4.1 Quality of Distribution

To evaluate the distribution of important services with regard to trust, the mapping between the reliability of the node and the required reliability of the service is compared using different values for α. If $\alpha = 1$, the service distribution is only obtained by considering the resource utilization as in a typical load balancing scenario. Figure 3 shows the results of this experiment with $\alpha = 1$, whereas the values on the x-axis represent nodes together with services and their reliability is depicted on the y-axis. The dotted line represents the expected reliability of important services sorted in descending order. However, the rectangular points show the reliability of nodes on which an important service is running. In the majority of cases, the divergence between both values, i.e., the current reliability of a node and the required reliability of the service is very important. This explains why the majority of important services are hosted on unreliable nodes.

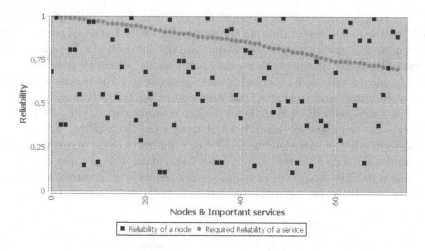

Fig. 3. Quality of distribution without trust ($\alpha = 1$)

To overcome this issue, trust has been taken into consideration. Figure 4 illustrates exactly the same information as Figure 3, but with $\alpha = 1/2$ to provide a better assigning of important services on reliable nodes.

Please note that the allocation of services is referred to as the trust-workload trade-off problem in which it is impossible to make any trust distribution better without making at least the load balancing distribution worse. This trade-off depends on the specific assortment of α. It is therefore imperative in future work to focus on learning the optimal trade-off α between trust and workload.

4.2   Permanent Node Failures

The improved self-configuration algorithm should assure beside load balancing that the majority of important services runs on reliable nodes. This can be shown by letting unreliable nodes fail and comparing the amount of unavailable important services of the baseline algorithm (i.e., load balancing distribution using Contact Net Protocol) with the trust-enhanced version. However, it should be noted that in a real life situation it is unlikely that all of the unreliable

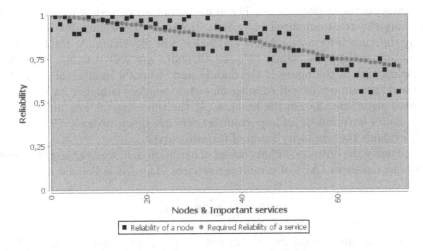

Fig. 4. Quality of distribution with trust ($\alpha = 1/2$)

nodes fail at once. For this purpose we adopt a more realistic approach using a selection metric to decide which node fails at each time step. This selection metric is based on a roulette wheel selection, where nodes with lower trust values (unreliable nodes) have a higher chance to fail than other nodes with a higher trust values (reliable nodes). Our goal is to evaluate the cumulated amount of unavailable important services for the trust-enhanced and baseline algorithm. Figure 5 shows the results of this experiment, whereas the values on the x-axis stand for the trust-enhanced and baseline algorithm and their cumulative amount of unavailable important services are depicted on the y-axis. The dotted

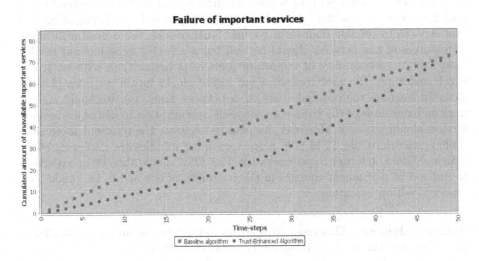

Fig. 5. Failure of important services

line represents the cumulated number of important services that failed per time step using the trust-enhanced algorithm. However, the square line illustrates exactly the same information but with the baseline algorithm. At the first step, the two curves look the same, because all nodes are still running. The most interesting part in the figure is the middle part, where a number of nodes has failed and the number of still running important services is higher for the trust-enhanced algorithm than in the baseline. At the time step 50, i.e., in that case, all the nodes have failed, all important services are down (exactly 75 services), which explains the similarity again of the two curves.

To quantify the obtained enhancement of our approach, we calculate the availability enhancement (AE) of important services. The AE is defined as follows:

$$AE = \frac{1}{ts} \sum_{i=1}^{ts} (c_i - t_i) \tag{5}$$

where ts means the number of time steps. c_i is the amount of unavailable services at time step i calculated with the baseline algorithm. However, t_i is the amount of unavailable services at time step i calculated with the trust-enhanced algorithm.

Concluding, the evaluation shows that with trust the availability of important services is better than without trust. In addition, we did not observe any simulation[2] with the trust metric that showed a bad mapping between reliability of nodes and required reliability of services. The use of trust leads to positive impact on the QoS metric because an availability enhancement (AE) of more than 12% was achieved with $\alpha = \frac{1}{2}$.

5   Summary and Outlook

In this paper, a new design of a self-configuration algorithm for organic computing systems is presented. Its main task is to improve the assigning of important services to reliable nodes using trust. Furthermore, the overall utilization of resources in the network should be well balanced. Our experimental results show that the availability of important services is better than without trust, which underlines the effectiveness of our approach. In future work we plan to focus on learning the optimal trade-off α between trust and workload and to work on extensions of the trust-enhanced self-configuration to distribute several services simultaneously. Moreover, we plan to integrate the trust-enhanced self-configuration into the TEM [19], a trust enabling middleware implemented in Java and based on a peer to peer network. The TEM should then be in a position to respond to permanent changes in the reliability of the nodes, i.e., under the aspect of self-optimization.

Acknowledgment. This research is sponsored by the research unit OC-Trust (FOR 1085) of the German Research Foundation (DFG).

---

[2] In total, about 10000 runs were evaluated.

References

1. Müller-Schloer, C.: Organic Computing - On the Feasibility of Controlled Emergence. In: International Conference on Hardware/Software Codesign and System Synthesis, CODES + ISSS 2004, vol. 2-5 (2004)
2. Steghöfer, J.-P., Kiefhaber, R., Leichtenstern, K., Bernard, Y., Klejnowski, L., Reif, W., Ungerer, T., André, E., Hähner, J., Müller-Schloer, C.: Trustworthy Organic Computing Systems: Challenges and Perspectives. In: Xie, B., Branke, J., Sadjadi, S.M., Zhang, D., Zhou, X. (eds.) ATC 2010. LNCS, vol. 6407, pp. 62–76. Springer, Heidelberg (2010)
3. Kiefhaber, R., Satzger, B., Schmitt, J., Roth, M., Ungerer, T.: Trust measurement methods in organic computing systems by direct observation. In: The 8th IEEE/IFIP International Conference on Embedded and Ubiquitous Computing (EUC 2010), pp. 105–111 (December 2010)
4. Kiefhaber, R., Hammer, S., Savs, B., Schmitt, J., Roth, M., Kluge, F., André, E., Ungerer, T.: The neighbor-trust metric to measure reputation in organic computing systems. In: The 5th IEEE Conference on Self-Adaptive and Self-Organizing Systems Workshops (SASOW 2011), pp. 41–46 (October 2011)
5. Kiefhaber, R., Anders, G., Siefert, F., Ungerer, T., Reif, W.: Confidence as a means to assess the accuracy of trust values. In: The 11th IEEE International Conference on Trust, Security and Privacy in Computing and Communications, TrustCom 2012 (September 2012)
6. Smith, R.G.: The Contract Net Protocol: High-Level Communication and Control in a Distributed Problem Solver. In: Defence Research Establishment Atlantic, IEEE Transactions on Computers, pp. 1–10 (1980)
7. Hsieh, F.-S., Chiang, C.Y.: Workflow planning in holonic manufacturing systems with extended contract net protocol. In: Chien, B.-C., Hong, T.-P., Chen, S.-M., Ali, M. (eds.) IEA/AIE 2009. LNCS, vol. 5579, pp. 701–710. Springer, Heidelberg (2009)
8. Kinnebrew, J.S., Biswas, G.: Efficient allocation of hierarchically-decomposable tasks in a sensor web contract net. In: Conference on Web Intelligence and Intelligent Agent Technology, vol. 2, pp. 225–232 (2009)
9. Goswami, K., Gupta, A.: Resource selection in grids using contract net. In: 16th Euromicro Conference on Parallel, Distributed and Network-Based Processing, pp. 105–109 (2008)
10. Deshpande, U., Gupta, A., Basu, A.: Performance improvement of the contract net protocol using instance based learning. In: 5th International Workshop - Distributed Computing (2003)
11. Dellarocas, C., Klein, M., Rodriguez-Aguilar, J.A.: An exception-handling architecture for open electronic marketplaces of contract net software agents. In: Proceedings of the 2nd ACM Conference on Electronic Commerce (2000)
12. Kodama, J., Hamagami, T., Shinji, H., Tanabe, T., Funabashi, T., Hirata, H.: Multi-agent-based autonomous power distribution network restoration using contract net protocol. Electrical Engineering in Japan 166 (2009)
13. Bittencourt, L., Madeira, E.R.M., Cicerre, F.R.L., Buzato, L.E.: A path clustering heuristic for scheduling task graphs onto a grid. In: 3rd International Workshop on Middleware for Grid Computing, MGC 2005 (2005)
14. Trumler, W., Klaus, R., Ungerer, T.: Self-configuration Via Cooperative Social Behavior. In: Yang, L.T., Jin, H., Ma, J., Ungerer, T. (eds.) ATC 2006. LNCS, vol. 4158, pp. 90–99. Springer, Heidelberg (2006)

15. Topcuoglu, H., Hariri, S., Wu, M.Y.: Performance-effective and low-complexity task scheduling for heterogeneous computing. IEEE Transactions on Parallel and Distributed Systems 13(3), 260–274 (2002)
16. Beaumont, O., Eyraud-Dubois, L., Larchevêque, H.: Reliable service allocation in clouds. In: 27th IEEE International Parallel & Distributed Processing Symposium (2013)
17. Bernard, Y., Klejnowski, L., Hähner, J., Christian, M.S.: Towards trust in desktop grid systems. In: 10th IEEE/ACM International Conference on Cluster, Cloud and Grid Computing (2010)
18. Reischuk, K.R.: Komplexitätstheorie: Band 1. Teubner Verlag (1999)
19. Anders, G., Siefert, F., Msadek, N., Kiefhaber, R., Kosak, O., Reif, W., Ungerer, T.: TEMAS - A Trust-Enabling Multi-Agent System for Open Environments. Technical report, Universität Augsburg (2013)

Estimation of Reward and Decision Making for Trust-Adaptive Agents in Normative Environments

Jan Kantert, Yvonne Bernard, Lukas Klejnowski, and Christian Müller-Schloer

Institute of Systems Engineering, Leibniz Universität Hannover, Germany

Abstract. In an open trusted Desktop Grid system with a normative environment incentives and sanctions may change during runtime. Every agent in the system computes work for other agents and also submits jobs to other agents. It has to decide for which agents it wants to work and to which agent it wants to give its jobs. We introduced a trust metric to isolate misbehaving agents. After getting a job processed by another agent it will get a reward. When processing a job for another agent it will get a positive trust-rating, but no direct reward. To come to a decision when accepting or rejecting jobs we need to be able to estimate the reward. Since the environment may change at runtime and to overcome delayed reward issues we use a neural network to estimate the reward based on the environment and trust level.

1 Introduction

The Organic Computing Initiative [1] concentrates on developing new solutions to manage the complexity of today's computing systems. As embedded devices, smart phones, other mobile devices and further PCs become more and more cheap and powerful, system designers need to ensure that systems consisting of several devices are both efficient and robust. Maintaining the openness of such complex systems is the main challenge we regard here: Agents (representing e.g. devices, PCs) can join and leave the system at any time. Moreover, if we regard systems distributed over the Internet, these agents are from different administrative domains. System designers cannot know whether the agents are benevolent, uncooperative or even malicious. This leads to an information uncertainty which agents who act within the systems need to cope with: They cannot know whether or not another agent is cooperative.

Therefore, we introduce trust as a computational concept to model the expected future behaviour of agents. Adding trust information to cooperation decisions leads to performance improvement, especially in systems with misbehaving agents [2]. So far, we have realised agents with a local trust-adaptive decision mechanism. But there are system states where local knowledge alone does not suffice to overcome the undesired situation. One example of such a global state is the *trust breakdown*: the emergent global shutdown of trust relations, which is the result of local *trust crises* as defined in [3]. In order to overcome these

E. Maehle et al. (Eds.): ARCS 2014, LNCS 8350, pp. 49–59, 2014.

undesired global system states, we add a hierarchical component, which detects such global situations and legislates norms to bring the system back into target space [4].

In an environment with changing norms an agent cannot have a static decision mechanism, because incentives and sanctions are not known at design time. Agents need to evaluate and rate all actions during runtime. Unfortunately, they are only partially able to predict the reward of all available actions. We evaluated different learning algorithms to learn job acceptance thresholds in previous papers [5], but since the reward is delayed when jobs are submitted it is hard to correlate actions to reward. This delayed reward makes it impossible for the agent to learn the outcome of a specific action. To overcome those problems we introduce a reward estimation component. It will be used in the worker to rate all actions based on the environment. When reward is received by the submitter, the estimation will be updated based on the environment parameters.

2   Application Scenario

Our application scenario is an open distributed trusted desktop grid with agents representing client machines and making decisions on behalf of their users (especially about resource selection). The system is distributed without central control. The applications regarded produce bag-of-task jobs, i. e. tasks that are independent of each other. A system like this is suited for scenarios where most clients run applications that produce grid jobs and thus are in high demand of computing resources, e.g. video rendering.

According to the taxonomy of [6], we classify the agents of this Desktop Grid System as: egoistic, volatile, distributed over the Internet, dynamic, faulty and heterogeneous. Agents can join and leave the system at any time. They take part in the system to get their jobs calculated faster than they could do on their own. Every agent will distribute jobs at some point and will calculate the speedup:

$$speedup = \frac{time_{own}}{time_{distributed}} \tag{1}$$

An agent also needs to work for other agents. To prevent abuse and increase robustness we introduced a trust metric to our system, which is based on ratings for all performed actions. Those ratings are based on the current valid norms in the system, which may change during runtime. All agents have a submitter and a worker component, which have to take the following decision:

- Worker - For which agents will I work?
- Submitter - To which agent will I give my jobs?

In Figure 1 we model the worker as event-driven process chain. When the worker receives a job offer it needs to decide whether it wants to accept the job. Based on the current normative environment both actions will influence the trust level of agent. Our hypothesis is that this will directly influence the success of the submitter, because other agents will base their actions on trust.

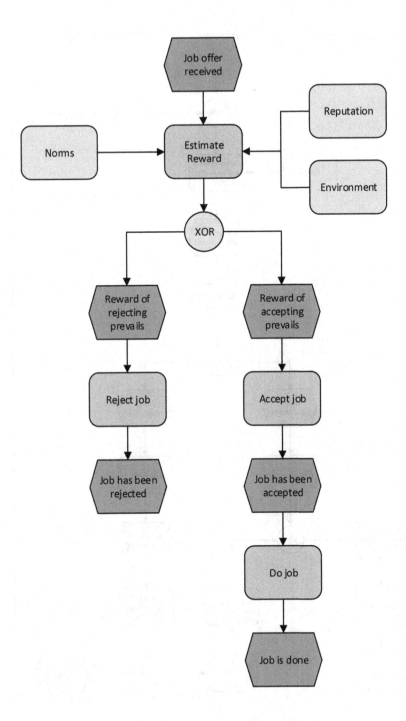

Fig. 1. Event-driven process chain for worker

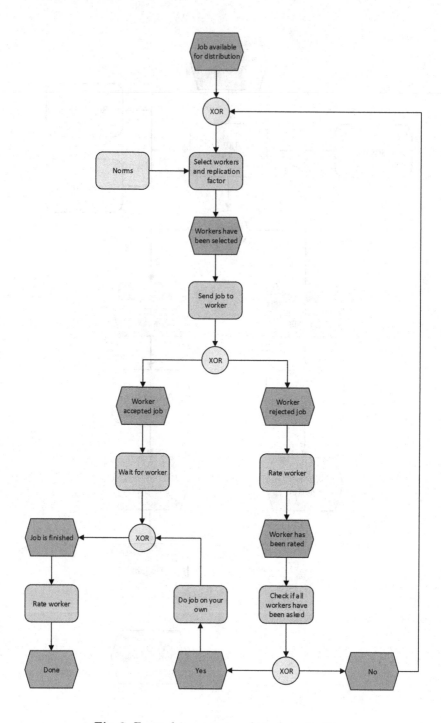

Fig. 2. Event-driven process chain for submitter

In Figure 2 the submitter is modelled as an event-driven process chain. Once the agent has work to distribute it has to decide which agent the job should be given to. Based on the trust levels of the selected agents it may decide to replicate the job one or multiple times. Next step is to ask the desired workers to accept the work unit. Depending on the normative environment there will be sanctions and incentives for rejecting or accepting a job. If the worker accepts, the submitter will wait until the job is done and rate the worker afterwards. If the worker rejects, the rating will be issued immediately. If no worker can be found or no worker accepts the job the agent will do the job on its own.

3   Previous and Related Work

We regard an open Desktop Grid, therefore, agents have to cope with malicious agents, which might refuse to accept work units for computation or deliver no, delayed, incomplete or wrong computational results for the work units they accept. Such a behaviour leads to improved personal benefits of the malicious agents but harms the efficiency of the system as it leads to resubmissions and waste. Therefore, agents need to cope with uncertainty how other agents will behave. Usually, replication and majority voting as mechanism to validate results are common techniques to cope with incomplete information about other agents' cooperativity. But replication of a work unit largely increases the system's workload and thus leads to low system performance. Therefore, in [2], we introduce a trust-based approach to cope with information uncertainty in such open systems: Agents rate each interaction they have with other agents. A rating is given each time an agent has rejected, delayed or successfully computed a work unit. We here do not rate agent rewards received by a sum of interactions (e.g. Scheduling success rate), but rather rate atomic agent interactions. These ratings are both stored locally as direct experience and globally as reputation values. A reputation value is an aggregation of other agent's rated experiences with an agent A_j. Using his own experience and reputation, agent A_i computes an aggregated trust value $aggTL_{i,j}$ which depends on the number of experiences the agent has had with A_i in the past [2]. The fewer own experiences it has, the more the globally aggregated reputation is used. This aggregated trust value defines an expectation how the agent is going to behave in the future (e.g. if it is asked to compute a work unit). Agents use a trust threshold plane defining whether to cooperate with an agent based on this trust information. So far, the trust threshold plane was predefined by the designer.

This threshold plane can also be coarsely represented by a table mapping the workload of the agents (WL_{total}) and the own reputation (Rep_i) of the agent A_i itself into three intervals [7]. This TT^{acc} trust decision table is shown in Table 1. The agent tries to keep its reputation to a level, where it can best submit work units itself. If its reputation is low, it is more likely to work for others in order to build up reputation which will increase its performance in submitter role. For each interval combination, the agent defines a trust threshold (TT^{acc}). If $aggTL_{i,j}$ is larger than TT^{acc}, agent A_i accepts and computes the work unit offered by agent A_j. If agents use trust information in submitter role, they are more likely to find a fast and reliable interaction partner. In worker role, agents use trust information in order to build self-organised implicit Trusted Communities [7]: Misbehaving agents are marked as outsiders and forced to either leave the system or change their behaviour to a more cooperative one in order to get their work units accepted in the future. Nonetheless, a sampling of the situation in three values in each dimension (low, medium, high reputation and low, medium, high workload) might not be optimal to define such a decision plane defined by $TT^{acc} = f(Rep_i, WL_{total})$. Therefore, we are interested in the optimal situation sampling and whether there is room for performance improvement by using a more fine-grained sampling for Rep_i and WL_{total}. Thus, we want to reach an enhanced version of the agents' trust decision (Table 1) by using a learning technique to improve $TT^{acc} = f(Rep_i, WL_{total})$ at runtime. As in our current trust threshold (Table 1) function currently used in the Controller, the learning agent A_i will accept a work unit from agent A_j if $aggTL_{i,j} \geq TT^{acc}$.

Table 1. Decision table: trust-adaptive agent in worker role

WL_{total}	Rep_i **low**	Rep_i **medium**	Rep_i **high**
low	TT^{acc} low	TT^{acc} high	TT^{acc} high
medium	TT^{acc} low	TT^{acc} medium	TT^{acc} high
high	TT^{acc} low	TT^{acc} medium	TT^{acc} medium

In [5], we have shown that our implementation of learning algorithms led to a slight performance improvement, but we think that there is room for further improvement with the mechanism presented in this paper. Therefore, we analyse the delayed reward problem and propose a better solution. Additionally, we want agents to learn their behaviour from scratch and therefore we will not add the designer-given rules (see threshold Table 1) to the solution space of the learning mechanism. In this paper, we introduce a new learning mechanism with focuses on the delayed reward problem.

4   Delayed Reward

In previous work all decisions were based on thresholds, which have been learned by learning algorithms. This worked well for a static environment and non-colluding attacks to the system. If we consider colluding attacks or a changing normative environment those algorithms fail to predict reasonable actions. As seen in Figure 3 all previous actions in the worker will get their reward after the submitter received the results of its previous actions. Typically, an agent will produce one job with multiple work units every 10k time units. However, it will receive a request whether to work for another agent almost once per time unit. Every decision to accept or reject a job will influence reputation and trust level of the agent. Nevertheless, the agent will only be rewarded after submitting its

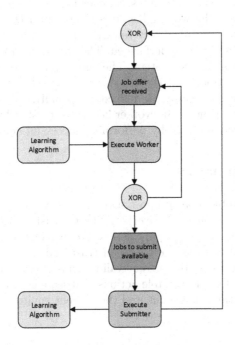

Fig. 3. Event-driven process chain of the learning process with worker and submitter

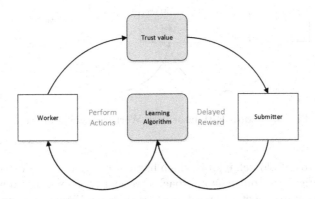

Fig. 4. Block diagramm of the learning process with worker and submitter

own jobs and getting back the results. To correlate specific actions taken in the worker to the reward received in the submitter is nearly impossible.

As seen in Figure 4 the worker bases its decision on the learned threshold. Since it does not receive any direct reward there will be no feedback or improvement after the action was performed. The worker is only able to affect the trust level of the agent in the system. The submitter, however, will receive rewards, based on its actions, but the success of those actions is mostly based on trust which the agent itself cannot influence. Eventually, we got two components which depend on each other. The worker generates trust, which is leveraged by the submitter to receive reward by performing successful actions.

5   Reward Estimator

To overcome this problem we propose a reward estimator to forecast the outcome of a potential action in the worker. The forecast is based on the agent's trust and observed environment parameters. We expect better results with this approach, because all actions are based on trust and we have a self-referential fitness landscape [8]. Based on current valid norms the agent can calculate his resulting trust value for all available actions. Subsequently, the agent estimates its reward based on this trust value and the current environment.

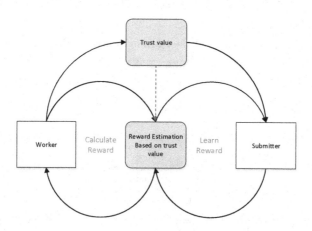

Fig. 5. Reward Estimator with Worker and Submitter

In contrast to the old behaviour, which has caused issues with delayed rewards (as shown in Figure 4), our new approach is to learn the expected reward based on the current environment and trust level (as shown in Figure 5), which allows to select more favorable actions. As long as the hypothesis that reward is directly coupled to the trust value in the current environment holds, we can directly estimate the reward of our actions.

Our estimator is implemented as a neural network using WEKA [9]. As environment we use the current average workload and current average trust level in the system. When submitting a work unit (see Figure 2) we will remember the values of those environment variables. After the job has been completed we use the saved environment values and the received reward to improve the estimation by training the neural network. In the worker (see Figure 1) we will select the best actions based on the expected reward. When accepting or rejecting jobs in the worker we will estimate each reward based on the current environment and the current trust-level using the neural network.

6   Evaluation

We evaluated our new reward-based approach against our previous implementation with decision thresholds in a changing environment. Our scenario is a situation with very high load, where it is important to maintain a sufficient trust level to always find a cooperation partner. To maintain trust, preventing negative ratings, which might occur if an agent rejects a job, is important. In normal situations it would be allright to reject jobs of agents with a low trust value, but it will get the agent into trouble under high load. Our previous implementation was not able to adapt to these changes in the environment. Figure 6 shows the average speedup for the previous implementation on the left and our new implementation on the right. Speedup of the previous implementation is about 1, which means that the agent should preferably process the job on its own. Our new implementation with reward estimation did perform significantly better and was able to maintain good collaboration in this scenario.

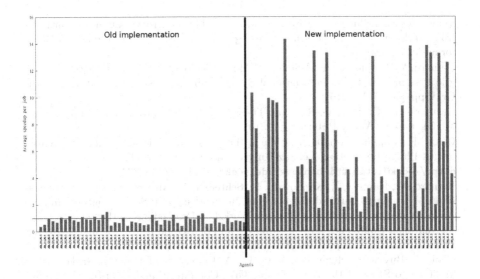

Fig. 6. Speedup of agents with decision table (ADA) and norm adaptive agent (NAA)

All norm-adaptive agents achieved a speedup higher than 1, which means they gained an advantage by participating in the system. However, some agents performed better than others. Only a few agents got near the theoretical maximal speedup of 16. We found some indications that agents with lower speedup did get stuck in some local optimal in their reward function and assume that this behaviour may be improved by better exploration of the reward function.

7   Conclusion and Future Work

With our new approach we were able to improve the adaptivity of our agents in changing environments. This is an important step towards a normative system, where incentives and sanctions may change during runtime. We showed that our implementation works well for high load situations. Also we did some initial experiments with changing incentives and got promising results.

In future work we want to change norms during runtime to improve behaviour of our system in extreme situations like very high load. To achieve this we observe the system from "above" and try to recognize abnormal behaviour pattern. In case of discovering anomalous behaviour, we will try to mitigate the situation by changing norms.

Acknowledgements. This research is funded by the research unit "OC-Trust" (FOR 1085) of the German Research Foundation (DFG).

References

1. Tomforde, S., Hähner, J., Müller-Schloer, C.: The multi-level observer/controller framework for learning and self-optimising systems. Int. J. Data Mining and Bioinformatics (2012)
2. Bernard, Y., Klejnowski, L., Hähner, J., Müller-Schloer, C.: Towards trust in desktop grid systems. In: IEEE International Symposium on Cluster Computing and the Grid, pp. 637–642 (2010)
3. Castelfranchi, C., Falcone, R.: Trust Theory: A Socio-Cognitive and Computational Model, 1st edn. Wiley Publishing (2010)
4. Cakar, E.: Population-based runtime optimisation in static and dynamic environments. Ph.D. dissertation, Leibniz Universität Hannover (2011),
   http://edok01.tib.uni-hannover.de/edoks/e01dh11/668667427.pdf
5. Bernard, Y., Kantert, J., Klejnowski, L., Schreiber, N., Müller-Schloer, C.: Application of learning to trust-adaptive agents. In: Workshop on Social Concepts in Self-Adaptive and Self-Organising Systems, Workshop Proceedings of the Seventh IEEE International Conference on Self-Adaptive and Self-Organizing Systems (SASOW), Philadelphia, USA, September 9-13 (2013)
6. Choi, S., Buyya, R., Kim, H., Byun, E.: A Taxonomy of Desktop Grids and its Mapping to State of the Art Systems. Grid Computing and Distributed Systems Laboratory, The University of Melbourne, Tech. Rep. (2008)

7. Bernard, Y., Klejnowski, L., Cakar, E., Hahner, J., Müller-Schloer, C.: Efficiency and robustness using trusted communities in a trusted desktop grid. In: 2011 Fifth IEEE Conference on Self-Adaptive and Self-Organizing Systems Workshops, SASOW (2011)
8. Cakar, E., Müller-Schloer, C.: Self-organising interaction patterns of homogeneous and heterogeneous multi-agent populations. In: Third IEEE International Conference on Self-Adaptive and Self-Organizing Systems, SASO 2009, pp. 165–174 (2009)
9. Hall, M., Frank, E., Holmes, G., Pfahringer, B., Reutemann, P., Witten, I.H.: The weka data mining software: an update. SIGKDD Explor. Newsl. 11(1), 10–18 (2009), http://doi.acm.org/10.1145/1656274.1656278

An Adaptive
Personal Learning Environment Architecture

Alexander Kiy, Ulrike Lucke, and Dietmar Zoerner

Institute of Computer Science, University of Potsdam, Germany
firstname.lastname@uni-potsdam.de

Abstract. Institutions are facing the challenge to integrate legacy systems with steadily growing new ones, using different technologies and interaction patterns. With the demand of offering the best potential of all systems, several not matching systems including their functions have to be aggregated and offered in a useable way. This paper presents an adaptive, generalizable and self-organized Personal Learning Environment (PLE) framework with the potential to integrate several heterogeneous services using a service-oriented architecture. First, a general overview over the field is given, followed by the description of the core components of the PLE framework. A prototypical implementation is presented. Finally, it's shown how the PLE framework can be dynamically adapted to a changing system environment, reflecting experiences from first user studies.

Keywords: Service-oriented architecture (SOA), University Service Bus (USB), Personal Learning Environment (PLE).

1   Introduction

The IT infrastructure of universities usually consists of heterogeneous, historically developed systems and software environments which have to meet the university-specific requirements for research, teaching and administration. While more and more new technologies are introduced and existing ones continue being operated we are facing an increasing complexity in design, development and maintenance of complex networked application systems [1].

Service-oriented architectures (SOA) offer some potential in such fields. With their weak coupling, they break up rigid connections between single systems and make them more generalizable and thus reusable for other contexts or services. The late binding of a SOA additionally offers an opportunity to substitute semantically similar service providers at runtime. The adaptivity to connect different systems with each other and to provide a homogenous view is usually achieved by means of an Enterprise Service Bus (ESB) as a middleware component of an overall system architecture. Adapted to the needs of the university we will call this specific implementation of an ESB a University Service Bus (USB).

But the simplifications related to an ESB are only one side of the coin. The user is not able to interact with the ESB in a direct and user-friendly way. To make use of an ESB all services have to get their representation in the graphical user interface,

E. Maehle et al. (Eds.): ARCS 2014, LNCS 8350, pp. 60–71, 2014.

forming a mashup of existing and new interface components. Only in this way, Quality of Service and Quality of Experience can be brought together [2].

Narrowing the academic context to educational issues, a Personal Learning Environment (PLE) is a current concept of how learners organize themselves by making use of "a collection of tools brought together under the conceptual notion of openness, interoperability and learner control" [3]. Moreover, there exists the notion of an institutional PLE (iPLE) as an environment that provides a personalized interface to university data and services and provides the opportunity to expose that data and services to a student's personal tools [4]. However, the concept of personalized and personal learning environments has to break through the institutional barriers to meet the requirements of life-long learning. On the one hand a university member must be enabled to use common web 2.0 tools in everyday context. On the other hand after graduation he/she must be able to continue learning using the preferred and familiar learning environment. Furthermore, the special needs of teachers and tutors (e.g. simplified application procedures and communication flows to students, customized tools for improving courses and teaching quality) have to be considered.

It is a complex task to offer personalized institutional services to institutional and non-institutional members by taking heterogeneous systems and different user requirements into account. Following a review on existing approaches in section 1.1, the detailed challenges will be considered in section 1.2. This is followed by a detailed description of the PLE framework. The paper concludes with some gained experiences and an outlook on further work.

1.1   Related Work

The approach to use a service-oriented architecture to solve complex integration problems to support cross-system processes where all systems are equipped with a service interface is not new. The resulting web services encapsulate generalized, cross-system core functions, which enables not only the flexible composition of systems, but also interoperability across heterogeneous environments.

Good experiences could be collected with the use of service-oriented architecture in several domains, e.g. integration of e-learning services into the university infrastructure [5] as well as developing adaptive ESB frameworks to handle problems of a changing environment [1].

In the field of Personal Learning Environments several projects [6][8][12][13] were started over the time, but none attempted to combine institutional elements of an iPLE with the concept of a generalizable PLE. Either it was tried to imitate the iGoogle concept with the aim to create an own PLE, or the approach was to improve an existing learning management system (LMS) with some functionalities to realize an iPLE. All of this work was only focused on one side although the goal has to be to integrate the institutional functions of an iPLE into a PLE.

The ROLE-Project (Responsive Open Learning Environments), for instance, is based on the theory of self-regulated learning and therefore assumes the learner is capable to create his own PLE with a set of widgets offered over a marketplace. The whole system is cloud-based and thus operated as Software as a Service (SaaS). They don't make use of a pre-delivered orchestration of learning goals, tools, services or content [6] and also work without a set of institutional widgets offering specific information about the LMS and other usual daily used services. Unsurprisingly, for many users it's pointless to invest the effort of designing their PLE. Moreover, there is a lack of transparency for the users; several tools of quite different providers are used, each with different terms of use and privacy policies[1]. Undoubtedly, the use of web 2.0 tools including the existing resources offers a great potential for the users. However, it can't be neglected that they are still working, teaching and learning in an institutional context from which they obtain their major information.

More work deals with making conventional LMS more adaptable by focusing on the connection, interaction and enrichment of conventional LMS with the resulting PLE over an ESB [7], but these solutions establish only another static point-to-point connection without any chance to substitute the LMS or to transfer this concept into another institution using another LMS.

The GRAPPLE project [8] goes a different way by providing learners an environment that guides them and can be adapted e.g. to personal preferences, competences or personal and social contexts called Adaptive Learning Environment (ALE). It is connected over a service-oriented framework using an event bus with the used learning management systems. The resulting system may solve some core challenges but is not capable of adapting to a changing environmental behavior or generalizable for other contexts of use. All presented system developments have in common that they offer the user a more or less personalized view with a subset of tools he might need for his daily working and learning process, each with its own layout and interaction patterns. None of the systems combine the aspects of an iPLE with those of a PLE with web 2.0 tools, or even offers an generic framework which is reusable for other institutions with other service systems (e.g. other LMS, Campus Management Systems (CaMS), and so on). Furthermore, most described solutions are based on proprietary system connections which can't be substituted easily. This problem is tackled by the framework presented in this article.

1.2 Challenges of an Adaptive PLE Framework

The conception of a generic and extendable architecture for a personal learning environment framework leads to several problems which have to be solved.

Infrastructure that has grown over the years mostly consists of different distributed software systems, which have been developed with a variety of different technologies and programming languages. When designing and developing a PLE framework, several problems from different domains have to be considered (e.g. technical, pedagogical, social, privacy and many more). In the following, the focus shall be on the technical dimension whose problems inter alia can be solved with the resulting PLE framework. The most relevant challenges are:

- distributed diverse content scattered over several systems (transcripts in LMS, grades in CaMS, e-papers in publisher portals, videos & recordings in streaming platform etc.)
- large amount of point-to-point connections between single software components (inter alia LMS and CaMS, LMS and library for digital copies)

---

[1] https://support.google.com/websearch/answer/2492212

— only a few standards to support interoperability of systems
— lack of system interfaces or web service endpoints
— complex workflows involving several systems to achieve relatively simple goals (e.g. request a course for the semester and prepare it with the necessary services)
— in worst case different usernames and passwords for every used system
— lack of integration for third-party providers' services like iGoogle widgets, Dropbox and common web 2.0 tools for cooperation and communication
— high expense when substituting a service including adjusting the specific interfaces of legacy systems
— guest students and guest lectures want to continue using their profiles, credentials, documents and meta information's "hidden" in several varying systems after leaving the university
— every systems has its own rights and role management (sometimes permissions are missing to achieve a certain workflow)
— every system holds different user profiles, user settings and many more information (some of them should be consistent in all systems and manageable over a common interface)
— a possibility is missing to transfer existing profile information to new systems without providing the same details for each system separately, or to change the information (see Multiple-Sign-In of Google), the ability to use different profiles in one system
— several heterogeneous graphical user interfaces with quite different use concepts and layouts may confuse the users

In the next sections, an architecture and prototypical implementation will be presented that go beyond existing solutions and adequately solve these problems.

2   System Architecture of a PLE Framework

To solve the addressed challenges a scalable service-oriented architecture is used as a basis for the whole framework on which all relevant systems can exchange their services independent of the specific software implementation.

The system architecture consists of two main layers – the *Public Layer* and the *University Layer*, as depicted in figure 1. The *Public Layer* represents every service or request existing outside the specific institutional infrastructure, e.g. cloud services, distributed institutional services or federated services as well as domain specific requests from members, federated members or externals. In turn, the *University Layer* consists of internal services, organized in a *Public Gateway Layer* and a *Private Service Layer*. The main components of both layers are the university service buses (USB) [9] as a special realization of an Enterprise Service Bus (ESB). The Public USB handles all requests coming from the Public Layer, e.g. requests for the University API Place. If necessary, it passes them to the private USB in the Private Service Layer. The Public Gateway Layer also provides the portal server and other specific graphical user interfaces like web applications or native mobile apps to the user. The portal server aggregates all services that are available for the user in a consistent, comprehensive and unified view.

The Private Service Layer contains on the one hand all major service providers (e.g. the CaMS, the LMS or other e-learning tools) as well as the process engine which itself is a special service provider. On the other hand, it comprises the Identity and Access Management (IAM). The providers offer different services via diverse interfaces, like for instance SOAP (Simple Object Access Protocol), REST (Representational state transfer), XML-Sides, AMF (Action Message Format), SRU (Search/Retrieve via URL), RPC (Remote Procedure Call) and many more. The task of the IAM is to handle all permission and identity requests of users who want to access special service providers.

In the following sections, the adaptivity of the USB's, the process engine and the Identity and Access Management will be examined more closely.

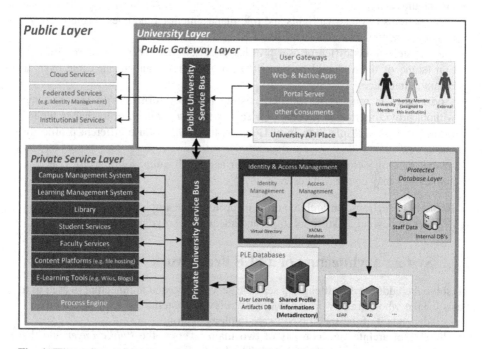

Fig. 1. The system architecture of the presented PLE framework separates public and private services by means of a gateway layer, where two independent service buses cooperate

2.1   University Service Buses

The two University Service Buses are working as an integration layer between the service providers and the service consumers. The service providers are e.g. the campus management system, the library, student services or external federated services. The main service consumers can be other service providers, the *User Gateways* like the portal server or other graphical user interfaces and the *University API Place*. The University API Place offers a generic web service interface with available services which can be used in other contexts, e.g. by independently developed applications, from other universities or everyone else. (This can be compared to the concept of Amazon Web Services.) It includes a documentation of the services and their endpoints for different protocols in order to simplify their use.

The distinction of the Public and the Private USB are used to ensure on the one hand security and performance of the overall architecture and to have the full flexibility on the other hand of logically subdividing users and services which are only relevant to the University API Place. So it is even possible to throttle the access regarding special services without causing side effects to the processes of the *Private Service Layer*.The Public USB consumes services, for instance from external cloud services or federated services, and passes them to the Private USB. Vice versa, it provides services from the Private USB to the University API Place or the graphical user interfaces. Furthermore, only the Private Layer is enclosed by a firewall, and only the Private USB deals with the issue of granting or prohibiting the access to services with the help of the IAM. Both USB's take care of tasks like data and protocol transformation, data and service security, load balancing or routing.

The adaptivity of the USB's is reached by the use of a well-defined generic web service interface. If an existing system will be replaced by another, for instance the LMS, then only once the specific service provider interface has to be adapted to the generic web service interface definition and finally connected to the USB. No other systems have to be touched. Other LMS can also be attached to the ESB by providing the generic LMS interface description. For every connected system such a generic service provider description is used to make it possible to either connect semantically similar systems to the USB or to exchange existing systems at runtime without the need of touching other system components. Such an interface description is mostly provided as a WSDL file and can be transformed with XSD to match other system specifications.

2.2   Process Engine

To implement an efficient Personal Learning Environment, not only all corresponding systems have to be connected with each other over an University Service Bus. Moreover, respective processes have to be designed, developed and established to offer the best support for daily working and learning. To achieve this, a process engine is used to choreography the complex processes involving different service providers. Whereas basic as well as composed services can be connected to the USB, the process engine handles only the orchestration of services and thus it includes all composed services of the PLE-framework. When designing a process which interacts with multiple applications and systems it is first decomposed into elementary steps. This can be achieved by accessing the interfaces of existing service providers connected to the USB, which can be either basic or already composed services. These interfaces are used to assemble the overall process. For this purpose, different forms of description like Business Process Model and Notation or the Business Process Execution Language can be used. This process is then connected as a new service to the Private USB and can be reused by other services. Accordingly, it can be offered through the graphical user interfaces.

The process engine controls and executes the previously defined workflows. Also, the process engine is able to handle lengthy processes, which are based on rules and whose procedure should be monitored. In the PLE framework the process engine aggregates all major cross-system processes for the institution. Important composed processes are, for example:

— synchronization of user profiles   (defined in the virtual directory)
— the process of course creation starting with the announcement of a course by a lecturer, automated creation of this course in the Campus Management System with the ability to add several other services to the course, like a course in the LMS (see figure 2), a separate wiki or blog, or code-repositories
   (The process includes automated creation of blog or wiki instances and their connection with existing courses.)
— synchronization of course enrolment (between campus management system, learning management system, e-portfolio-system and personal learning groups, on different abstraction layers)
— e-procurement [11] workflow from procuration over status overview until delivery and payment

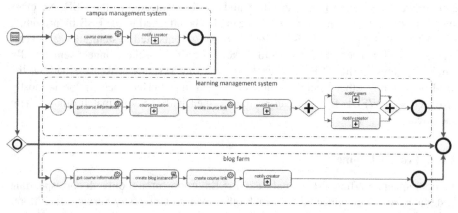

Fig. 2. The BPMN process includes the initial course creation in the CaMS and the optional automated associated course and blog creation in the LMS and the blog farm. The basic tasks of enrolling users and notifying users or the creator are already the result of a previous composition of basic services and are used in this process as basic orchestrated services.

2.3   Identity and Access Management

The Identity & Access Management consists of two main parts. The Identity Management is a virtual directory which holds all institutional digital identities. The access management uses an eXtensible Access Control Markup Language (XACML) database where all access rights and privileges for digital identities are saved. The virtual directory handles the direct flows between the specific *Protected Database Layer*, the databases of the service providers accessed over the Private USB and other legacy systems like existing LDAP's or other databases. The virtual directory has access to sensitive databases (staff data or internal databases), which usually can be accessed by authorized personal only. Specific read and write permissions are stored in the database of the access management to enable data alignment.

The access management consists on the one hand of a role-based access control and on the other hand of a digital rights management. A single role in an institution is not enough to get detailed access right permissions for several systems. For a more generalizable way to define detailed access rights the attribute-based access control is used. Most rules are based on XACML and can be transferred with the use of the security assertion markup language to the requested service provider to grant or prohibit the access to a specific resource or request. In order to keep control, only well-defined generalized roles (like student, faculty member, employee, scientific employee, alumni, guest and admin) are used to specify global user-right-associations.

The IAM provides further services like authentication, authorization and accounting. Moreover, single-sign-on functionality realized with Shibboleth is available when accessing service providers over the USB or managing identities provided by federated identity management systems (e.g. OpenID, OAuth, DFN-AAI).

To provide a personalized view of the content, information on the user accounts has to be saved (e.g. user themes, existing profiles and cross-shared attributes, information like disabilities to provide specific views). The IAM synchronizes this information between the LMS, the PLE profile database and other e-learning systems, if desired by the user, and stores the data in the *Shared Profile Informations Metadirectory* of the PLE databases. In this way, the user is able to use either dedicated profiles for single applications or one common profile for all applications. Furthermore, he is able to edit his profiles in the PLE-GUI or to connect existing external accounts (e.g. google, facebook, dropbox, mircrosoft etc.).

2.4   Portal Server

The implementation of the portal server was realized with the versatile portal software Liferay. The different views are mainly implemented as Java Portlets using the JSR-286 standard to ensure inter-portlet communication. The current solution uses a portlet bridge which allows using either JavaServer Faces or the Google Web Toolkit, depending on the application to be developed, each with its respective frameworks as front-end technologies.

The portal server is the first entrance point or main gateway for everybody in the university to access an application. Widgets or gadgets like from iGoogle can be integrated by the user by means of the OpenSocial API. The reverse away of integrating existing institutional widgets or gadgets into an existing external environment like iGoogle is also possible. Therefore, a valid institutional account including the required privileges to access the widget information is required.

Experience shows that novice users appreciate a pre-defined interface configuration, since otherwise it's too costly for them to arrange things accordingly. The added value must be clearly evident, so we are providing a subset of pre-defined portlets which offer the main information and main functionalities a typical student or teacher needs. Specific user details like the field of study, individual preferences or the like are used to provide a view that is unique for every user. The user is still able to arrange the portlets in a layout of his choice. He is capable of adding and deleting portlets to self-created pages, which in turn can be private or public. Public pages are visible to everybody, where however private pages are only visible to the owner.

Tech-savvy users have the opportunity to develop more complex portlets according to their wishes and to deploy them to the Portal Server. All necessary services are either hosted directly by the USB or connected to it. In addition to the Portal Server view, further pervasive mobile applications are offered which make use of context information on the user and his current situation [10]. They make use of the current location to improve the orientation on campus or to trigger events when somebody is close to the library and has expired books or even suggesting the best train connection to reach the next course in time. All other necessary information can be accessed using the Portal Server which supports device-specific rendering of the content for mobile, tablet or desktop.

3   Experimental Results and Evaluation

After implementation of the PLE framework with its main components and exemplary service providers the following workflow example was evaluated, as depicted in figure 3. A clipping of the portal servers' graphical user interface presenting the workflow is shown in figure 4. The workflow involves only the core components: the portal server, the Private USB, the Identity & Access Management, the process engine including a sample process, the LMS and CaMS as service providers.

The workflow starts with the login process in the portal server, which uses the single-sign-on service of the IAM. All necessary portal information like the system role (e.g. faculty member) is requested and propagated to the portal server (steps 1. to 4.). When accessing the course overview portlet, two simultaneous requests are sent over the Private USB. One goes to the CaMS service provider to get general data of the course (e.g. duration, frequency, room details). Another request goes to the LMS service provider to check whether the course is already created or not. The requests are aggregated by the Private USB and sent back to the portal server (steps 5. to 12.). In this example, the user is a lecturer with only two courses. All information from both systems is aggregated and presented in a single view. Being a lecturer, the user is capable of modifying the course in the CaMS and to create a course in the LMS with triggering the respective process in the workflow engine (steps 13. to 16.). Here, all necessary information (like course description and category) is read from the CaMS, automatically. Afterwards, all enrolled users get enrolled in the newly created course, too, and they will receive a notification about this.

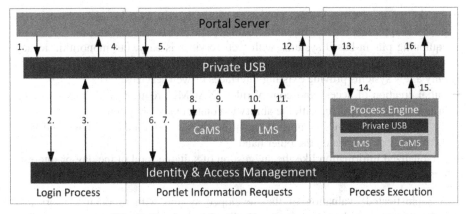

Fig. 3. Simple workflow and involved components

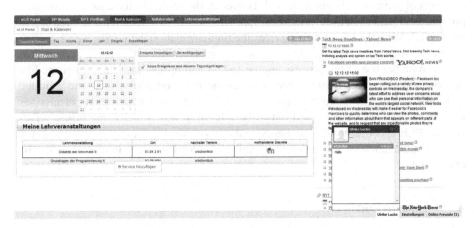

Fig. 4. A page of the portal server including the calendar portlet, the course service portlet with quick navigation to the course service creation and a rss portlet

The evaluation was carried out based on automated tests of the whole process including the respective tests of the involved service providers. Moreover, exemplary user tests focusing on the GUI handling and the desired outcome took place. The crucial goal of the evaluation was to find whether the approach involving several different components works as expected and is comfortable for the users. During the evaluation of our prototype (inter alia with the described process) we obtained the following results:

— it is useful to work with an OpenSource ESB as a fundament; small bugs, a complicated configuration or missing documentation are not necessarily a problem
— the development of web services is easy; to define an generic and easily understandable interface adaptable for other systems is still sophisticated
— with several thousand requests over the Public- and Private USB a scalable architecture and high availability have to be ensured

— the definition of cross-system processes using Activiti as a Java-Framework is a practical approach for development, maintenance and further extensions
— equipping plugin-based systems with web services is easy, but monolithic legacy systems can be hard to handle
— only a few systems provide existing interfaces or web services
— initial creation of access and control rules (XACML) requires a high expense but brings benefit over time, with the ability to connect several systems
— the Portal Server allows to integrate institutional services on the one hand and Web 2.0 widgets or gadgets on the other hand
— personalized information like the suggestion of suitable food of the day or interesting personal contacts are indispensable

A sophisticated evaluation of the developed system with productive users and courses is currently to be scheduled. This will take place as soon as more functionality (in terms of processes) is implemented. However, the results of the existing prototype provide confidence that the presented approach fulfills the requirements defined in section 1.2. With the use of web services the implementation details are well encapsulated and the generic web interfaces ensure the replaceability of existing service providers. With the use of the process engine and an appropriate modeling language like Activiti complex cross-system processes can be modeled, maintained and adjusted with little effort. The summarization of generalizable roles including its permissions in form of XACML rules turned out to be a feasible way. Finally, the portal server and the PLE specific profile databases enable a personalized view on the one hand, and the aggregation of institutional as well as external services in one view on the other hand.

4   Conclusion

The IT infrastructure of universities will continuously grow in the future. However, in order to ensure the operation, development and maintenance of complex software systems the described architecture can help. Especially, the PLE offers for the first time a user-friendly way to combine institutional services and widespread web 2.0 tools in one homogeneous graphical user interface. With the underlying service-oriented architecture, the presented PLE framework offers not only the possibility to extend old services with new generic web service interfaces which can be easily substituted at runtime and so to integrate old services with reasonable expense, but also to adapt itself to changing heterogeneous environments.

It's a hard negotiation process to get read & write access to specific sensible applications or databases. Additionally, it's complicated to examine the leading system, which has rights to override or refresh other service provider databases. Our tasks for the future are to provide more legacy systems with web service interfaces and to integrate them into the existing architecture by connecting them to the USB. All web services that can be used without consideration have to be well documented for a use by external application developers. A token based authentication system has to be introduced when authentication for web services is required. In general, more standards for interoperability of systems and content have to be defined, adopted and implemented. For the field of technology enhanced learning, some research is underway.

With respect to life-long learning we are trying to provide useful import/export opportunities from one system to the other in order to provide possibilities after leaving the institution to continue using data and information collected over several years of institutional belonging.

References

1. Schmeck, H., Müller-Schloer, C., Çakar, E., Mnif, M., Richter, U.: Adaptivity and Self-organisation in Organic Computing Systems. In: Organic Computing A Paradigm Shift for Complex Systems, pp. 5–37. Springer, Basel (2011)
2. Zieliński, K., Szydło, T.: Adaptive Enterprise Service Bus. New Generation Computing 30, 189–214 (2012)
3. Siemens, G.: PLEs – I Acronym, therefore I exist, http://www.elearnspace.org/blog/2007/04/15/ples-i-acronym-therefore-i-exist/ (last visit September 24, 2013)
4. Omar, L.M., Platteaux, H., Gillet, D.: An Institutional Personal Learning Environment Enabler. In: IEEE 12th Int. Conf. on Advanced Learning Technologies (ICALT), Rome, pp. 51–52 (2012)
5. Graf, S., Gergintchev, I., Pätzold, S., Rathmayer, S.: eLearning als Teil einer service-orientierten Hochschulinfrastruktur. DeLFI 2008: Die 6. e-Learning Fachtagung Informatik, pp. 65–76 (2008)
6. Kroop, S., Nussbaumer, A., Albert, D.: Evaluation on Students' and Teachers' Acceptance of Widget- and Cloud-based Personal Learning Environments. Special Issue "Cloud Education Environments". J.UCS. Journal of Universal Computer Science (2013)
7. Casquero, O., Portillo, J., Ovelar, R., Benito, M., Romo, J.: iPLE Network: an integrated eLearning 2.0 architecture from a university's perspective. Interactive Learning Environments 18, 293–308 (2010)
8. Oneto, L., Abel, F., Herder, E., Smits, D.: Making today's Learning Management Systems adaptive. In: Learning in the Synergy of Multiple Disciplines, Proceedings of the EC-TEL. Springer, Heidelberg (2009)
9. Tavangarian, D., Lucke, U.: Pervasive University A Technical Perspective. it – Information Technology 51, 6–13 (2009)
10. Lucke, U., Specht, M.: Mobilität, Adaptivität und Kontextbewusstsein im E-Learning. i-com 11(1), 26–29 (2012)
11. Kaiser, S., Kuhnt, E., Lemcke, S., Lucke, U.: Web-basierte Beschaffung. Erscheint in Proc. Informatik 2013. Köllen Verlag, Bonn (2013)
12. Kieslinger, B., Wild, F., Arsun, O.I.: iCamp – The Educational Web for Higher Education. In: Nejdl, W., Tochtermann, K. (eds.) EC-TEL 2006. LNCS, vol. 4227, pp. 640–645. Springer, Heidelberg (2006)
13. Chatti, M.A., Agustiawan, M.R., Jarke, M., Specht, M.: Toward a Personal Learning Environment Framework. International Journal of Virtual and Personal Learning Environments 1, 66–86 (2010)

Middleware for Dynamically Adaptive Systems

Sihem Loukil, Slim Kallel, and Mohamed Jmaiel

ReDCAD Laboratory, University of Sfax, Tunisia
sihem.loukil@redcad.org,
slim.kallel@fsegs.rnu.tn, mohamed.jmaiel@enis.rnu.tn

Abstract. Dynamically adaptive systems are expected to be able to meet changing user needs and varying environmental conditions they operate in. This motivates current research on developing execution support for such systems. In this context we propose a new middleware that ensures the dynamic reconfiguration of dynamically adaptive systems at runtime. This middleware provides a set of functions enabling the dynamic reconfiguration as well as the monitoring and the consistency of such systems during the reconfiguration.

1 Introduction

Dynamically adaptive systems are be able to detect changes in their execution context and then be adapted at runtime in order to satisfy high reliability and availability requirements. Such systems should be reliable and always available to maintain their usefulness. Two types of adaptations are generally used to ensure the adaptation of these systems : the behavioral adaptations that affect the behavior of the system by changing the behavior of one or several components, and the architectural adaptations (so called architectural reconfigurations) that consist in modifying the structure of the architecture by adding or removing components or connections. These two types of adaptations affect each other since the modification of the structure of the system can cause the change of its behavior and conversely, behavioral changes can cause the addition of new components and connections.

In this context, we proposed, in a previous work [1, 2], an approach for managing of architectural reconfiguration of dynamically adaptive systems. This approach allows the designer to specify the architecture of the system. Then, an automatic code generation process is applied to obtain a system ready to be executed. This code requires a middleware ensuring dynamic reconfiguration as well as monitoring and consistency. This paper focuses on the description of this middleware.

In the literature, several works address the development of middleware supporting dynamically adaptive systems. However, they present several limitations. First, some existing middlewares such as [3, 4] do not support the dynamic reconfiguration in response to execution context changes. Second, other proposed middleware [5, 6] only handles starting, stopping, and connecting components and connectors, but not their addition, removal, and replacement. Third, most

E. Maehle et al. (Eds.): ARCS 2014, LNCS 8350, pp. 72–84, 2014.

of the existing middleware [5–8] consider the system environment context implicitly in the functional code of the system. As such, the system complexity is increased, and the ability to process and manage the context information is limited.

In this paper, we propose a middleware, called DRES4DAS (Dynamic Reconfiguration Execution Support for Dynamically Adaptive Systems), which supports dynamically adaptive systems. This middleware allows performing architectural reconfigurations at runtime that handle starting, stopping, adding and removing components and connectors. It also provides mechanisms to guarantee the monitoring of the execution context in separate modules using the Aspect-Oriented Software Development (AOSD) paradigm. Moreover, our proposed middleware ensures the consistency of the system during reconfigurations.

The remainder of this paper is organized as follows. Section 2 briefly presents our previous work to ensure the architectural reconfiguratioon of dynamically adaptive systems. Section 3 describes the proposed middleware and its implementation. Section 4 illustrates the effectiveness of the proposed approach by considering a case study having dynamic reconfiguration requirements. Section 5 details some related work. Finally, Section 6 concludes this paper and presents future work.

2   Previous Work

We proposed an approach to ensure the architectural reconfiguration of dynamically adaptive systems (figure 1). It supports two types of reconfigurations : planned and unplanned reconfigurations.

For the planned reconfigurations, they are used to monitor the execution context of the running system. These reconfigurations are specified at architectural level using the AOSD paradigm and more specifically the AO4AADL [9, 10] language (Aspect-Oriented extension for AADL). The AO4AADL architectural aspects are associated to a set of AADL (Architecture Analysis & Design Language) component types to form the *Declarative model*. The instantiation of these component types to specify the architecture of the system includes also the instantiation of the AO4AADL aspects. In fact, every aspect has been declared for a type, will be attached to all instances of this type. The resulting model is called *Instance model*. Finally, an automatic code generation process is taken place to generate RTSJ (Real-Time Specification for Java) code from the AADL specification and AspectJ code from the AO4AADL aspects. This code generation is ensured using the Ocarina tool suite [11]. AspectJ aspects are later woven with RTSJ code to form the final application code. We note here that we adopted the RTSJ code because it is the only available java implementation that can be generated from the AADL models.

For the unplanned reconfigurations that can not be anticipated at design time, we used the HOOK methods technique to handle them. These ad-hoc reconfigurations need the manual intervention of the designer and they are triggered in response to new user requirements. The HOOK methods include listeners to capture the evolution of the architecture of application. For example, a Hook method can be used to intercept event messages and then perform customized actions to commit the architectural modifications to the running system.

To ensure a clear representation of the architecture of the modeled system while maintaining its usefulness and reliability, we performed, in a previous work [12], the verification of the reconfiguration actions against a set of imposed architectural OCL invariants. This verification is performed at design level through a verification module. Indeed, the reconfiguration actions are performed first on the instance model to verify the preservation of a set of architectural invariants. If no invariant is violated, the reconfiguration actions are committed to the running system. Otherwise, the new configuration is simply discarded. This allows to save costly executions of roll-back operations on the system. We have opted for selecting eclipse plug-ins to develop a graphical editor allowing the specification of the dynamically adaptive systems. We present in the following, our proposed middleware to support this approach.

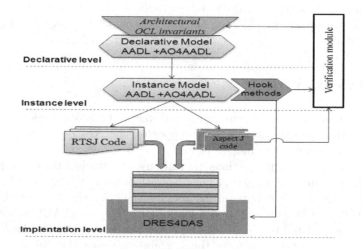

Fig. 1. Architectural reconfiguration of dynamically adaptive systems

3 DRES4DAS Middleware

Our proposed DRES4DAS middleware allows runtime reconfiguration of dynamically adaptive systems and ensures their monitoring and their consistency during the reconfiguration. We assume that our approach is applied on systems with Client/Server architecture and it uses a reliable network and communication protocol that ensures a correct transmission of messages behind distributed systems. The declarative model and the instance model are located at the server machine while the generated code can be distributed on several execution machines. Therefore, our proposed middleware represents a distributed system by a set of interconnected nodes (processes). Each node defines one process of the specified system and includes a set of threads deployed on it. Our proposed middleware (figure 2) ensures various functionalities which consists mainly in :

- Supporting the monitoring of the system by supervising at runtime the execution context of the system (i.e; information of the environment elements relevant for expressing reconfiguration actions) and the topology of the architecture (e.g, getting information about the number of components and connections).
- Ensuring the dynamic reconfiguration of adaptive systems which represents the main function of this middleware.
- Preserving the consistency of the system during and after reconfiguration actions since reconfiguration may lead the system to undesirable states which risks its functioning.

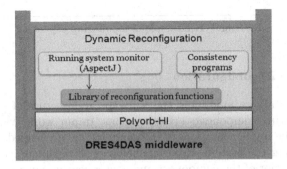

Fig. 2. The proposed middleware

3.1   Aspect-Based Monitoring

The middleware provides a way to detect when it is time to reconfigure the system to build an effective dynamically adaptive system. In this context, we built the *running system monitor* (figure 1) that includes a set of programming aspects that can be easily woven with the functional code of the application. Two types of aspects can be used to monitor the system : generic and specific aspects. Generic aspects can be defined to monitor the whole system in order to get general information such as the number of components running on the system, the number of connections between components, etc. However, specific aspects are used to monitor the execution context variables that are intended to be changed during the execution of the system. These aspects are written in AspectJ language. The specific AspectJ aspects are automatically generated from the AO4AADL aspects using our Aspect generator [9, 10]. Our aspect-based monitor is able to intercept information about the execution context (i.e; messages exchanged through ports and program parameters) of the running system.

Listing 1.1 presents the AspectJ code of an aspect that aims to monitor the battery level of a sensor node. As shown in this code, the pointcut of such aspect (lines 2–3) intercepts the context variable that gives information on the battery level. This information is given through the parameter *battery_level* of the subprogram *Get_Battery_State*. This later is invoked periodically to inform the system on the battery level. The advice code (lines 4–11) enumerates the list of the reconfiguration actions to perform when the battery level drops below a well-determined threshold (lines 6–10). These actions consist in removing the current sensor node and replace it with a new one.

```
1   aspect Battery_State_Aspect{
2     pointcut check_Battery(int battery_level): execution (∗ Subprograms.Get_Battery_State(..))
3                                     && args (battery_level);
4     advice after(int battery_level): check_Battery(battery_level){
5       ...
6       if ( battery_level < threshold){
7         R1:="removeThreadInstance(this)";
8         R2:="addThreadInstance("Sensor_Thread"+","+New_Sensor_Thread+",
9                       "+outport_tab+","+inport_tab+")";
10      ...}
11    ...}}
```

Listing 1.1. Example of monitoring aspect

3.2   Dynamic Reconfiguration

The middleware allows modifying the software architecture of the system by adding or removing components or connections. In our work, we consider that the types and the implementations of the components are defined before deploying and executing the system. However, behavioral reconfigurations returns to modify the behavior of the component and consequently may require the definition of a new type or a new implementation of a component. This needs to stop the system, regenerate the code and re-run it. Thus, the behavioral reconfigurations are not considered in our work.

The architectural reconfigurations supported by our middleware are : (1) *Add connection*: adding a connection between two ports of two threads, (2) *Remove connection*: deleting a connection between two ports of two threads, (3) *Add thread*: creating and deploying a new thread on execution platform and then connecting it with the other components, (4) *Remove thread*: removing its connections with the other components, undeploying it and then deleting it, and (5) *Migrate thread*: moving a thread from a node (process) to another.

A real-time thread is attached to each node of the distributed system. This thread is launched simultaneously with the associated node to detect requests of reconfiguration and perform the necessary reconfigurations affecting this node.

We developed a set of reconfiguration functions in our middleware to ensure the previously presented architectural reconfigurations. For example, Listing 1.2 presents the **addConnection** function used to add a connection between two ports of two threads. This function takes as parameters (line 1) the identifiers of the source port of the connection (*src*) and the destination port of the connection (*dest*), respectively. First, this function looks for the identifiers of the component of the source port (*src_component*) and the destination one (*dest_component*) (lines 2 and 3). Then, it verifies whether these two components are nested in which case both ports that have as identifiers *src* and *dest* must be of the same kind, i.e. input or output ports (lines 4–6). Otherwise, the source port must be an output port and the destination port must be an input port (lines 8 and 9). Moreover, this function verifies that there is no connection between these two ports (line 11). Finally, the connection will be created by adding the *dest* identifier to the set of destinations of the port whose identifier is *src* (line 12).

```
1   addConnection(src,dest:String)
2       String src_component=getComponent(src);
3       String dest_component=getComponent(dest);
4       If ((isNested(src_component,dest_component)
5           and ((isOutputPort(src) and isOutputPort(dest))
6               or (isInputPort(src) and isInputPort(dest))))
7           or
8       (not isNested(src_component,dest_component)
9           and isOutputPort(src) and isInputPort(dest))
10          and
11          not isExistConnection(src,dest)) then
12      addDestinationPort(src,dest);
13      EndIf
```

Listing 1.2. Adding connection

Listing 1.3 presents the **addThreadInstance** function which allows to add a new thread instance to a node and connect it to other components. This function takes as parameters (line 1) : the component type of the new instance (*componentType*), the node where it will be deployed (*node*), the destination list of each output port of this new instance (*outport_dest*) and the list of ports which have in their destinations an input port of this new instance (*source_inport*). After creating a new instance of the specified component type (line 2), this instance is deployed on the node (line 3). The connections of this instance with the other components will be added (as shown in lines 4–9). Adding a new instance of a given type is achieved by calling the constructor of the generated class for this type and providing all necessary parameters.

```
1   addThreadInstance(componentType,node:String; outport_dest[][],source_inport[][]:Hashtable ) {
2       String entity=newInstance (componentType);
3       deploy(entity, node);
4       For i=0 to outport_dest.size() do
5           addConnection (outport_dest[i][1], outport_dest[i][2] );
6       EndFor
7       For i=0 to source_inport.size()do
8           addConnection(source_inport[i][2],source_inport[i][1] );
9       EndFor
```

Listing 1.3. Adding component

3.3 Consistency

In order to avoid reconfigurations that may lead the system to inconsistent states, we propose a set of algorithms to enforce the consistency of the dynamically adaptive system and maintain its correct state. In this context, we distinguish two main problems likely to occur : (1) Problem of conflicting reconfigurations and (2) Problem of removal of architectural elements at runtime.

Problem of Conflicting Reconfigurations : Conflicting reconfigurations may occur when at least two nodes connected to the distributed system launch two contradictory reconfigurations. To avoid such a problem, we propose to lock all the threads affected by the reconfiguration treatments using a common lock. This later allows preventing the connected threads from sending further requests and achieving the treatment of all current requests. These threads are unlocked once the reconfiguration process is achieved.

For each node connected to the communication network, a thread is created to perform the various tasks associated with the reconfiguration process. The role of the used lock is to manage the execution of the various reconfigurations. It guarantees that reconfigurations that are not conflicting with the current reconfiguration (i.e; that do not affect the same architectural elements) can be executed in parallel. For the reconfigurations that affect the same architectural elements, they are executed in mutual exclusion. Hence, these reconfigurations are processed in the order of their arrival. This ensures therefore make reconfiguration decisions consistent in solving conflicts.

Problem of Removal of Architectural Elements at Runtime : Two main cases of dynamic reconfigurations can put the system in an inconsistent state. The first case is related to the removal of a thread that has pending queries. These queries will be unfinished and lost. Thus, the execution of the components interacting with the removed one will be disturbed and even blocked by the non-receipt of the corresponding answers. The second case of this problem is the removal of an active connection that is transmitting messages may have queries that are being evaluated and will not be fully processed.

Avoiding these inconsistencies requires the control on the reconfiguration actions related to the removal of thread instances and connections.

- Control on removing threads : The removal of an instance of a thread is conditioned by the absence of messages in transit destined for this instance. In addition, it should be resting and not currently carrying out any treatments.

  For this purpose, we adopt a verification of the state of the thread instance in case of detection of removing query : if it stills active, the reconfiguration waits until the thread goes into a passive state to proceed the delete action. At the end of each operating cycle of the thread, a program verifies if there is any blocking request of the thread activities (request to delete the thread instance). If so, this thread should be stopped prohibiting the launch of a new cycle. Otherwise, a new cycle is started.

  The removal of the thread is preceded by removing all the connections between this instance and all the other components to ensure a full isolation and avoid the disruption of the rest of the system.

- Control on removing the connections : The middleware verifies if the connection to remove is not transmitting data or messages using the same principle of the removal of threads. At the moment of the reconfiguration request, we verify the state of the connection to remove using its parameters. This allows making the right decision without disturbing the system. If it indicates that the concerned connection is still sending messages then the reconfiguration is blocked until the state of the connection indicates the end of transmission.

3.4 Implementation

We used the PolyORB-HI [13], inspired from the PolyORB middleware architecture [14] to implement our proposed middleware. PolyORB-HI is composed of a minimal middleware core and several automatically generated services. The minimal core presents the common services for all applications while the generated functions are customizable to the needs of the target application. Most of the code of this middleware is generated automatically using the Ocarina tool suite. PolyORB-HI includes three types of middlewares : POLYORB-HI-ADA, POLYORB-HI-C and POLYORB-HI-JAVA that support the execution of the ADA, C and RTSJ code, respectively. However, POLYORB-HI presents some drawbacks. First, examples used to test this middleware are quite simple (two threads communicating where each thread contains at most one input port and one output port). Hence, using POLYORB-HI for a real example (which contains many threads) presents a tedious task. Second, POLYORB-HI carries out a static code generation. In other words, it uses static structures in the generated code. Therefore, once the system is deployed and executed, it can not be reconfigured at runtime. This latter presents a major drawback of the POLYORB-HI middleware.

We developed our middleware in order to deal with these problems. It consists in updating and extending the existing implementation of the PolyORB-HI-JAVA middleware. In this context, we adopted the POLYORB-HI-JAVA middleware since we are interested in the execution of the RTSJ code, as described in [1, 2]. We implemented the functions mentioned in section 3 allowing to perform dynamic reconfigurations. We added then a new class called *Reconfigure* which includes the reconfiguration functions.

In addition to this new class, we updated the existing routines such as the addressing service which manages the components references at runtime. For example we updated the *Context* routine which contains some context parameters used by PolyORB-HI components to allow the deployment and the connections of the components. We replaced the static structures with dynamic ones. In this context, Hash tables are used for ensuring the various dynamic reconfigurations.

Moreover, we implemented the necessary routines for ensuring the consistency of the running system. Indeed, two new programs are included in the new middleware, the first one is responsible of controlling the removal of thread instances and the second one looks for the removal of connections.

4 Case Study

We considered a case study of a FPS (Flood Prediction System) to illustrate the proposed approach allowing the modeling and the reconfiguration of dynamically adaptive systems. This case study presents a set of nodes that communicate and cooperate to carry out flood predictions and notify local authorities to be able to avoid potential hazards. Figure 3 depicts a simplified representation of the general architecture of the FPS using our graphical editor.

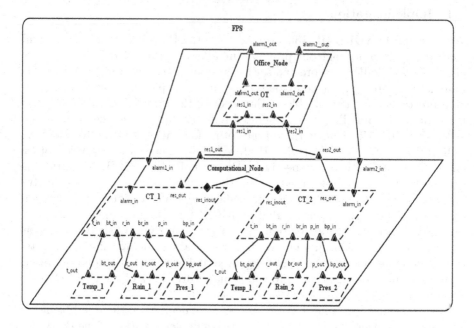

Fig. 3. The graphical representation of the architecture of the FPS system

Three types of components are considered in this case study :

- *Sensors* sense and collect the data relevant for calculations. Several sensors are required such as pressure, rainfall, and temperature sensors.
- *Computational entities* compute flood prediction level according to the values provided by sensor nodes, communicate the predictions to an office node. They also have communication between themselves for detecting malfunctioning of nodes.
- *Office node* verifies the results with the available online information, issues alerts and initiates evacuation procedures.

To illustrate our approach, we define a dynamic reconfiguration that aims at removing a computational thread already deployed in the river when it is no more operational. When such thread is removed, the related sensor threads will be no more connected to a computational thread and the collected information will be lost. The sensor threads should be connected to the nearest operational computational thread in order to tackle this problem.

As mentioned previously, our middleware allows the monitoring of the context information at runtime through AspectJ aspects that are woven with the code of the application.

An AspectJ aspect is intended to intercept a subprogram that indicates whether the thread is still active or no. This subprogram is invoked periodically on each deployed component in the system. We suppose, for example, that the thread *CT_1* is no more operational for a precise period of time. Therefore, our middleware is supposed to follow a dynamic reconfiguration. This reconfiguration consists in removing the computational thread *CT_1* instance of *Computational_Thread* type. For this, the connections of this instance with the computational node (*Computational_Node*), the other computational threads (*CT_2*) and the corresponding sensor threads (*Temp_1*, *Rain_1* and *Pres_1*) should be removed. Moreover, to avoid the loss of information, these sensor threads should be connected to the nearest operational computational thread. In our case, the *CT_2* node is considered as the nearest thread to the *CT_1* thread. The following reconfigurations should be sequentially handled to guarantee the safe reconfiguration of the FPS system:

- Adding connection between *Temp_1* and *CT_2*,
- Adding connection between *Rain_1* and *CT_2*,
- Adding connection between *Pres_1* and *CT_2*,
- Removing connection between *CT_1* and *Temp_1*,
- Removing connection between *CT_1* and *Rain_1*,
- Removing connection between *CT_1* and *Pres_1*,
- Removing connection between *CT_1* and *CT_2*,
- Removing connection between *CT_1* and *Computational_Node*,
- Removing *CT_1* instance of *Computational_thread* component.

Figure 4 shows the execution trace of the reconfiguration actions related to the addition of a connection between *Temp_1* and *CT_2* and the removing of the connection between *CT_1* and *Temp_1*. For example, adding the connection between *Temp_1* and *CT_2* consists in adding connections between the two outports of the *Temp_1* thread to the corresponding inputs of the *CT_2* thread.

After applying efficiently the previously presented reconfiguration actions, we demonstrate also that the consistency is ensured by our middleware using the considered FPS case study. In fact, after this reconfiguration, the system remains consistent. As shown in Figure 5, we note that the temperature sensor thread *Temp_1* continue to collect information and communicate them to the CT_2 thread which in turn continue to compute the flood prediction level and communicate the predictions to the office node through the *Computational_Node* node.

5   Related Work

Several approaches supported the runtime reconfiguration of dynamically adaptive systems. Some of them presented a middleware to ensure such reconfiguration. In the following, we present the most important ones.

RUNES [3] is a component-based middleware that supports the development of software for networked embedded systems. This middleware enables dynamic reconfiguration of components and their interconnections according to changing

```
Computational_Thread_State : CT_1 is no more operational
Dynamic Reconfiguration : Addition of connection between port
29 and port 21
Dynamic Reconfiguration : Addition of connection between port
30 and port 22
Computational_Node : sends 18 bytes to Office_Node node
Computational_Node : sends 15 bytes to Office_Node node
Dynamic Reconfiguration : Removing of connection between port
29 and port 13
Dynamic Reconfiguration : Removing of connection between port
30 and port 14
```

```
Rain_1 : setInvalid : setting invalid for output port 31
Rain_2 : setInvalid : setting invalid for output port 37
Temp_1 : send output from 29 to input port 21 of CT_2 is done
successfully
Temp_2 : send output from 35 to input port 21 of CT_2 is done
successfully
Pres_1 : storeOut : value stored for output port 33
Pres_2 : storeOut : value stored for output port 39
Rain_1 : setInvalid : setting invalid for output port 32
Rain_2 : setInvalid : setting invalid for output port 38
Temp_1 : send output from 30 to input port 22 of CT_2 is done
successfully
Temp_2 : send output from 36 to input port 22 of CT_2 is done
successfully
```

Fig. 4. Part of trace of the dynamic recon- **Fig. 5.** Consistency of the FPS system af-
figuration of the FPS sytem   ter reconfiguration

condition. It encompasses dedicated radio layers, networks, middleware, and specialized simulation and verification tools. Unlike our middleware, RUNES does
not provide monitoring routines of the context changes of the running system.

FRASCATI [4] is a component-based middleware platform for reconfigurable
distributed Service-Oriented Architectures (SOA). It supports runtime adaptation and managing properties of Service Component Architecture (SCA) applications. It allows to introspect an SCA application to discover at runtime its
structure, modify it to add new services, reconfigure the application to take into
account new operating conditions. Unlike our middleware, FRASCATI does not
address the automatic adaptation of components depending on execution context
changes. Moreover, it does not have fully-fledged AOP development technique
for SCA. It uses some notions like *join points* and *advice code* but no grammar
including all the concepts of AOP is provided.

Planit [6] presents a framework for deployment and reconfiguration of
distributed systems. Similarly to our approach, Planit ensures architectural reconfigurations. Ulike our middleware, it only handles starting, stopping, and
connecting components and connectors. The addition, removal and replacement
of components are not taken into account. Similarly to Planit, the approach presented in [5] is not capable of handling the addition, removal and replacement
of components.

The RCES4RTES [8] middleware performs the dynamic reconfiguration of
Distributed Real-time Embedded (DRE) systems. It supports architectural reconfigurations (adding/removing components or connections) as well as behavioral reconfigurations (updating component or updating its implementation). It
provides mechanisms for monitoring DRE systems to observe a system state
during its execution. This monitoring consists in getting the component number
running on the system, getting the connection number between a given component and other components, and getting the last read/write access time to shared
variables. Moreover, this middleware allows to preserve the consistency of the
system during and after reconfigurations. Unlike our middleware, RCES4RTES
provides poor monitoring routines dealing with the structure of the system and
does not allow to monitor the execution context of the running system.

Unlike our proposed middleware, in all the presented middleware above, the code of processing/managing the execution context is implicitly included in the functional code of the system which increases the complexity of the system and limits the ability to manage it. However, in our middleware, the monitoring of the execution context is separated from the functional code of the application. Indeed, it is captured into modular units (aspects) using the AOSD paradigm. Therefore, the complexity of the system is decreased and the management of its execution context becomes easier.

6   Conclusion and Future Work

In this paper, we presented a middleware that supports the architectural reconfiguration of dynamically adaptive systems. This middleware ensures the monitoring and the consistency of the system during reconfigurations. The implementation of our proposed middleware is achieved through updating and extending the existing version of POLYORB-HI-JAVA middleware.

As future work, we plan to provide *reliable* dynamic reconfigurations following two main axes. On one hand, we aim to reduce as much as possible the occurrence of errors (fault prevention). On the other hand, to minimize the damage they cause to the system when errors that could not be prevented actually happen (fault tolerance).

References

1. Loukil, S., Kallel, S., Jmaiel, M.: Runtime adaptation of component based systems. In: Gramoli, V., Guerraoui, R. (eds.) NETYS 2013. LNCS, vol. 7853, pp. 284–288. Springer, Heidelberg (2013)
2. Loukil, S., Kallel, S., Jmaiel, M.: Managing architectural reconfiguration at runtime. International Journal of Web Portals 5, 55–71 (2013)
3. Costa, P., Coulson, G., Mascolo, C., Picco, G.P., Zachariadis, S.: The runes middleware: A reconfigurable component-based approach to networked embedded systems. In: Proceedings of the 16th Annual IEEE International Symposium on Personal Indoor and Mobile Radio Communications, Berlin, Germany (2005)
4. Seinturier, L., Merle, P., Rouvoy, R., Romero, D., Schiavoni, V., Stefani, J.B.: A Component-Based Middleware Platform for Reconfigurable Service-Oriented Architectures. Software: Practice and Experience 42, 559–583 (2012)
5. Sykes, D., Heaven, W., Magee, J., Kramer, J.: From goals to components: a combined approach to self-management. In: Proceedings of the 2008 International Workshop on Software Engineering for Adaptive and Self-managing Systems. ACM (2008)
6. Arshad, N., Heimbigner, D., Wolf, A.L.: Deployment and dynamic reconfiguration planning for distributed software systems. Software Quality Control 15, 265–281 (2007)
7. Morin, B., Barais, O., Jezequel, J.M., Fleurey, F., Solberg, A.: Models@ run.time to support dynamic adaptation. IEEE Computer 42, 44–51 (2009)

8. Krichen, F., Zalila, B., Jmaiel, M., Hamid, B.: A middleware for reconfigurable distributed real-time embedded systems. In: Lee, R. (ed.) Software Engineering Research, Management and Appl. 2012. SCI, vol. 430, pp. 81–96. Springer, Heidelberg (2012)

9. Loukil, S., Kallel, S., Zalila, B., Jmaiel, M.: Toward an Aspect Oriented ADL for Embedded Systems. In: Babar, M.A., Gorton, I. (eds.) ECSA 2010. LNCS, vol. 6285, pp. 489–492. Springer, Heidelberg (2010)

10. Loukil, S., Kallel, S., Zalila, B., Jmaiel, M.: Ao4aadl: Aspect oriented extension for aadl. Central European Journal of Computer Science 3, 43–68 (2013)

11. Vergnaud, T., Zalila, B., Hugues, J.: Ocarina: a Compiler for the AADL. Technical report, Telecom Paristech - France (2006)

12. Loukil, S., Kallel, S., Jmaiel, M.: Verifying runtime reconfiguration of dynamically adaptive systems. In: Proceedings of the 39th Euromicro Conference on Software Engineering and Advanced Applications. IEEE Computer Society (2013)

13. Zalila, B., Pautet, L., Hugues, J.: Towards Automatic Middleware Generation. In: Proceedings of the International Symposium on Object-oriented Real-time distributed Computing, pp. 221–228. IEEE (2008)

14. Vergnaud, T., Hugues, J., Pautet, L., Kordon, F.: PolyORB: A Schizophrenic Middleware to Build Versatile Reliable Distributed Applications. In: Llamosí, A., Strohmeier, A. (eds.) Ada-Europe 2004. LNCS, vol. 3063, pp. 106–119. Springer, Heidelberg (2004)

Mahler: Sketch-Based Model-Driven Virtual Prototyping

Rafael Rosales, Michael Glaß, and Jürgen Teich

University of Erlangen-Nuremberg,
Germany
{rafael.rosales,michael.glass,teich}@cs.fau.de

Abstract. Virtual prototyping and Electronic System Level (ESL) modeling have become valuable resources to cope with the ever-increasing complexity of embedded systems. Their effectiveness, however, is highly dependent on their quick development time and accuracy, both conflicting goals. In this paper, we present a novel tool, *Mahler*, to accelerate the development of ESL models. *Mahler* provides an early design phase playground to manually explore the modeling of functionality at a high level of abstraction and analyze its performance on different architecture implementations very fast. It generates a ready-to-execute source code functional model in an open source SystemC-based language, bridging the gap between a design's very preliminary stage and a more mature design stage that can serve as a starting point for automatic design space exploration on existing ESL design flows. *Mahler* achieves this through the most natural interface: the designer's pen, enabling an intuitive model-driven creation of virtual prototypes following the Y-chart approach; literally sketching actor-oriented functional models at the ESL which are then mapped to the architecture platform for a simulation-based evaluation of power and performance. We demonstrate its advantage in terms of improved design productivity through the implementation of an MPEG-4 encoder virtual prototype.

Keywords: Virtual Prototyping Tool, ESL, Simulation-based Performance and Power Consumption evaluation, Energy Aware Design, Model-Driven Design, Sketch-based User Interface.

1 Introduction and State-of-the-Art

Modern MPSoCs are increasingly complex, as Moore's Law still holds to be true. This has resulted in a productivity gap, where the designers can hardly increase their efficiency at the same pace. Increasing the level of abstraction and modeling at the Electronic System Level (ESL) is an attempt to address this problem, enabling to evaluate the performance of complex systems in a tractable way. Virtual Prototyping, in turn, enables the parallel design of software and hardware and allows to test developed software even before the first hardware prototype has been created, reducing time-to-market considerably.

E. Maehle et al. (Eds.): ARCS 2014, LNCS 8350, pp. 85–97, 2014.
© Springer International Publishing Switzerland 2014

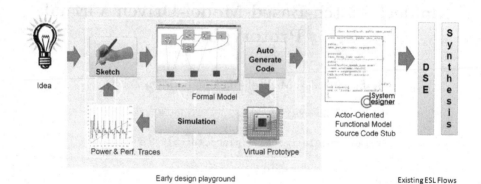

Fig. 1. Mahler sketch-based user interface. A drawn model is auto-generated into a ready-to-execute Virtual Prototype, including XML back-annotations for power and performance evaluation.

Although the creation of a virtual prototype results in an overall time saving, the development effort is significant, and in the case of semi-formal models the designer is involved in writing *code overhead*, such as boiler-plate code, synchronization constructs, or redundant model definitions. For very abstract models, such as those typically used in ESL, the overhead even becomes the major effort factor, hindering design productivity and making maintenance a difficult task.

Several methodologies for the creation of Virtual Prototypes have been developed with the aim to increase the designer's efficiency further. SystemC is the de-facto standard language in industry. It enables the creation of Virtual Prototypes at high levels of abstraction such as transaction-level. Metropolis [1] is a methodology that follows the Y-chart approach [12], separating the modeling of application functionality from the architecture platform. This separation enables to explore different design implementations through a meet-in-the-middle approach, but introduces a non-standard language which system-level designers are required to learn. The SystemCoDesigner methodology [9] [18], also following the Y-chart approach, makes use of SysteMoC [6] [5], an open source SystemC-based language for actor-oriented modeling of functionality. This methodology exploits the formal actor-oriented model for automatic design space exploration (DSE) of hardware/software partitioning [18]. Sesame [4], uses Kahn processes as the formal model to describe functionality and the Pearl discrete event simulation language [2] for the hardware architecture to enable the design space exploration of system architectures. VisualSim [16], is a tool based on PtolemyII [3]. It enables to create actor-oriented functional models through a mouse-based graphical user interface. Its emphasis, however, resides in supporting the functional modeling under different models of computation (MoC) and not automatic DSE of HW-SW partitioning. These established approaches enable the creation of system models, but are limited in their capabilities to rapidly design an executable virtual prototype, hindering the potential of an early manual exploration.

On the user interface side, approaches to improve the productivity of system designers in the modeling process have been developed. In [8], a UML class diagram sketch recognition system is presented. MATLAB/Simulink [19], provides a model-based interface for dynamical systems. In [10], a sketch-based interface for Simulink is described. These sketch-based modeling approaches have shown to improve the efficiency of the designer, but, so far, no complete flow for virtual prototyping exists that enables a sketch-based design to be automatically transformed into an executable virtual prototype, suitable for design space exploration of hardware/software partitioning for power and performance optimization.

This paper introduces *Mahler*, a novel tool to accelerate the development of virtual prototypes, providing an intuitive modeling user interface and aiding to begin design space exploration at a pre-optimized starting point. *Mahler* facilitates the development of an ESL model at its initial stage, where many design choices have to be made before starting established automatic design space exploration iterations. *Mahler* provides an intuitive modeling interface that generates SystemC-based ESL models which can (a) be simulated for power and performance evaluation and (b) serve as a starting point of existing ESL flows, such as automatic design space exploration of hardware/software partitioning.

The main contributions of *Mahler* are:

(I) Fill the gap between the very early model development stage and the starting point of existing automatic design space exploration flows, by providing a very fast sketch-based modeling playground environment.

(II) Reduce the ESL design adoption barrier by enabling a very intuitive manual exploration of actor-oriented modeling and hardware/software codesign choices producing executable SystemC-based virtual prototypes within minutes.

In *Mahler*, the designer is able to literally *sketch* with a pen or touch interface, e.g. a tablet stylus, or a touchless interface, such as Leap Motion controller [14], the functional and architecture model that will be transformed to an executable virtual prototype through *sketch recognition*, see Fig. 1. This intuitive sketch-based approach is shown to be preferred by UML model designers compared to traditional mouse-based user interfaces [8]. This provides not only a direct interface from an idea to an executable implementation, but enables a very fast way to explore actor-oriented functional modeling and hardware/software partitioning. As *Mahler* follows a model-driven approach, the designer is not required to learn the syntax details of a modeling language and, thus, eliminates the overhead and verbosity of plain source code required for trivial tasks, such as plumbing, interconnecting, declarations, instantiation, tagging, etc. This overhead, as we will show, can easily outgrow the size of actual model information, specially in high-level models typical for the ESL, where functionality is abstracted at a coarse level. With *Mahler*, an ESL designer can focus on the actual modeling as in other model-driven approaches, creating a design as on a piece of paper, and almost forget about the coding implementation. This is not only useful in models built from-scratch, but also for porting legacy code to the actor-oriented paradigm, allowing the designer to try different modeling granularities very fast, by drawing simple actors representing very high level functional tasks, or a complex actor network with a more granular task level detail.

Through the use of this actor-oriented paradigm, it is possible to take advantage of techniques for early evaluation of performance such as back-annotation [11] [17], perform a quick simulation of the system, and modify it according to the obtained traces of performance and power consumption. In Fig. 1, it is shown that after the designer has captured the functional model as well as the architecture through sketches, *Mahler* generates the functional model source code in the SystemC-based language SysteMoC [6] as well as the configuration files for simulation. The resulting source code stub is ready for simulation for performance and power estimation, enabling to simulate and visualize power and performance traces immediately after sketching. This provides immediate feedback to the designer on the actual schedule of tasks through time permitting to identify potential optimizations that would lead to reduced power consumption. The sketched model can be modified to explore different architecture hardware mappings, as well as to investigate finer granularities on the functional model and re-run a simulation after some re-sketches. Once a sufficiently good ESL model has been obtained at this high level playground, the actor-oriented source code can be enriched with computational code to specify functionality beyond the formal model. The resulting model can be incorporated into automatic DSE and synthesis toolflows [7], maximizing the reuse of the effort invested.

The rest of the paper is structured as follows: In Section 2, the *Mahler* sketch recognition-based user interface is presented while introducing the functional modeling language and the generation of the source code at the same time. Section 3 describes the modeling of the architecture platform, timing and power consumption annotations, and the simulation of the generated virtual prototype. In Section 4, we present a case study to demonstrate the benefits of modeling with *Mahler*. Finally, we present our conclusions on Section 5.

2   Sketch-Based Functional Modeling

2.1   Functional Model Elements

The actor-oriented formal model SysteMoC [6] used in *Mahler* provides the necessary constructs to model functionality at a high level of abstraction in an implementation-independent manner while providing a well-defined granularity to back-annotate low-level timing-execution values of computational actions. Thereby, it is possible to create an ESL model very fast and obtain estimations of power and performance very early.

We summarize the formal model elements illustrated in Fig.2 in the following:

Definition 1. *An* actor *is a tuple* $a = (I, O, F, R)$ *containing a set of actor ports partitioned into a set of actor input ports* I *and a set of actor output ports* O, *the actor functionality* F, *and a Finite State Machine (FSM)* R.

Definition 2. *The actor FSM is a tuple* $R = (Q, q_0, T)$ *containing a finite set of states* Q, *an initial state* $q_0 \in Q$, *and a finite set of transitions* T.

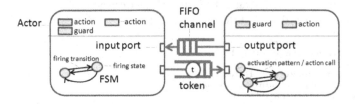

Fig. 2. SysteMoC language elements

Definition 3. *In an FSM $R = (Q, q_0, T)$, a transition is a tuple $t = (q, k, f, q) \in T$ containing the current state $q \in Q$, an activation pattern k, the associated action $f \in a.F$, and the next actor state $q \in Q$. The activation pattern k is a Boolean function that decides if transition t can be taken or not.*

The communication behavior of an actor a (production/consumption of tokens) is coordinated by its FSM R thereby separating clearly the control flow from the processing of data. The latter is modeled by so-called *actions* which are executed if in the current state of the FSM R, an activation pattern associated with a state transition evaluates to true.

Definition 4. *A channel is a tuple $c = (I, O, n, d)$ containing channel ports partitioned into a set of channel input ports I and a set of channel output ports O, its buffer size $n \in N_\infty = \{1, 2, 3, .., \infty\}$, and also a possibly empty sequence $d \in D$ of initial tokens, where D denotes the set of all possible finite sequences of tokens.*

The channels connecting actor ports can be assumed to have FIFO semantics. The complete system functionality is therefore modeled by a *network graph*:

Definition 5. *A network graph is a directed bipartite graph $P_n = (A, C, E)$, containing a set of actors A, a set of channels C, and directed edges $E \subseteq (C.O \times A.I) \cup (A.O \times C.I)$ between actor output ports $A.O$ and channel input ports $C.I$, as well as channel output ports $C.O$ and actor input ports $A.I$, respectively.*

The representation of the formal model in SystemC requires to code each element using the SysteMoC library. As an example, Listing 1.1 shows the source code of a simple actor composed of a single input port and a two state FSM. The transition activation pattern from the first to the second state consists of the existence of a token at the input port. The associated action is the execution of the single actor action.

This source code represents purely the formal model, and can be extended with computational code to operate on the data exchanged. For high level performance estimation however, it is very often unnecessary, and thus the coding of the formal model directly in SystemC becomes a tedious task. With *Mahler*, it is possible to represent the formal model in the most domain-adequate way through sketch recognition from which SystemC code is finally generated automatically.

Listing 1.1. SysteMoC source code

```
1   class ActorClass0 : public smoc_actor {
2   protected :
3   smoc_firing_state state0 ;
4   smoc_firing_state state1 ;
5   public :
6   smoc_port_in <void*> inputport0 ;
7   ActorClass0 (sc_module_name name)
8   : smoc_actor (name, state0 ) {
9   state0 =   inputport0 (1)               >>
10          CALL (ActorClass0 :: action0 )     >>
11          state1 ;
12  }
13  void action0 () {
14  //--Insert your code here if desired--}
15  };
```

In *Mahler*, an *actor* is represented as a rounded-border rectangle. To create an actor, see I of Fig. 3, a rectangle sketch on the drawing canvas is performed. *Mahler* supports any sketch created through mouse, stylus and Leap Motion controller [14] strokes. After finishing the sketch strokes, the sketch-recognition algorithm, based on the shape recognition engine of [15], replaces the sketch with an empty graphical actor instance. This recognition engine is robust enough for the simple sketches required for our formal model, namely rectangles, circles and lines, and it is not a new contribution of *Mahler*.

To begin the specification of the actor FSM, states have to be specified. An FSM *state* is recognized and represented by circles inside the actor area, see II of Fig. 3. FSM Transitions are recognized from a sketched line starting and ending at an actor state. A recognized transition sketch is replaced by an instance of a graphical transition displayed as a directed arrow, see III of Fig. 3.

Ports are created via 'cuts' at the actor borders, i. e., a line starting outside and ending inside of an actor will be recognized as an input port, while a a line starting inside and ending outside of an actor will be recognized as an output port, achieved by testing the coordinates of the first and last strokes. Port instances are displayed by small triangles, see IV of Fig. 3.

Functional *actions* are represented through rectangles inside the actor area,, see V of Fig. 3. A drawn rectangle sketch inside of an actor is replaced with a graphical functional action with a default name. Associated with each FSM transition, a firing rule is specified to define under which conditions the state transition should take place and what functional actions will be executed when taking the transition. To provide the firing rules and actions taken on each FSM transition, the ports and actions are first selected and then associated to a transition through a spring-alike sketch, see VI of Fig. 3. The port conditions are necessary to check for available data tokens at input ports or available slots for output ports. For static data flow models of computation such as SDF, it is not necessary to specify the actual functional action's source code, e. g. the computation of the FFT algorithm, and thus the formal model is complete to specify the functional model for fast evaluation purposes. If a data-dependent algorithm is required to be modeled, the formal model can be used to generate the source code stub and manually insert the code into the functional actions after sketching the actor model.

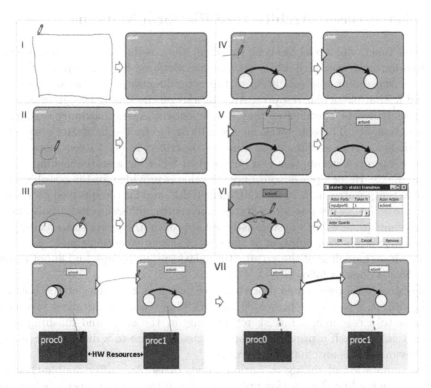

Fig. 3. Sketch-based interface. I) Actor sketch II) FSM State sketch III) FSM Transition sketch IV) Port Sketch V) Action Sketch VI) Action and Firing Rules association VII) Actor interconnection and Hardware Mapping.

Finally, actors are interconnected through FIFO *channels* through their ports. This is done by sketching a line starting and ending on the respective ports.

All graphical modeling elements are not merely drawings, but manipulable object instances, i. e., each element can be moved around, deleted, or modified by switching from 'Sketch mode' to 'Manipulate mode'. Double clicking on elements permits to change their name IDs. In the case of FSM transitions, a dialog displaying the associated firing rules and actions are displayed.

2.2 Functional Model Generation

Once a functional model has been created, *Mahler* generates the source code in the SysteMoC language [6]. This language is based on SystemC, and defines a formal actor model through the members of classes inheriting from the smoc_actor class. Ports and states are value members, while functional actions are represented with the class methods. The construction of the actor FSM is done on the constructor of the class, see Listing. 1.1 for the code generated from the sketched actor at step VI shown in Fig. 3.

3   Sketch-Based Architecture Platform Mapping

Once the functional model has been specified, it is possible to map each single actor to a hardware resource in the *architecture platform*. Such a mapping defines that the scheduling and execution of the actor functional actions will be performed in that particular resource. Annotations on the timing execution of each action can then be specified as they are dependent on the hardware executing the functionality. These annotations are interpreted by the hardware resource's performance model at simulation time as described in [17]. Even more, each resource's power consumption can be specified following a state-machine based approach [20]. Here, a power consumption value is provided for the possible processor activity states, namely RUNNING or IDLE, and for the specified processor power state, i. e., a discrete set of states representing different clock frequencies. During simulation, using a hysteresis-based approach, the power state is changed to minimize power consumption at the cost of slower execution time.

The above modeling of the architecture platform, mappings, and annotations in *Mahler* is done as follows:

Hardware resource such as processors are drawn as rectangles at the bottom of the canvas. They are represented as dark blue rectangle instances. To map an actor to a resource, a line sketch starting at the actor and finishing at a resource is drawn. If a previous mapping existed before to a different resource, the previous one is automatically removed.

The annotation of timing execution values takes place after double-clicking on the mapping line. This action opens a dialog, listing all the actions belonging to the mapped actor and providing a space to fill the estimated timing values, in nanoseconds for example, for each action when run on this particular resource. Power consumption annotations are included on the dialog box opened after double-clicking the respective resource. A list of power states can be specified to establish the amount of power consumed, and the associated clock frequency for each particular power state.

3.1   Generated XMLs

The mapping of actors to the architecture platform, the execution timing annotations as well as the power consumption parameters are then generated by *Mahler* as XML configuration files. These configuration files are used for the simulation-based power and performance evaluation, see Listing 1.2 for the generated XMLs for the functional model of Fig. 3 mapped to an architecture platform consisting of two processors: proc0 and proc1, as shown in VII of Fig. 3.

Listing 1.2. Snippet of generated XML

```
1   <FunctionalityMapping>
2     <Map FuncUID="actor1" ArchUID="proc0"/>
3   </FunctionalityMapping>
4   <TimingAnnotations>
5     <Resource id="proc0" frequency="130" units="MHz">
6       <Timing action="actor1::action0" value="22146" units="us"/>
7     </Resource>
8   </TimingAnnotations>
9   <PowerAnnotations>
10    <Resource id="proc0">
11    <ComponentState id="RUNNING">
12    <PowerState id="fast" powerConsumption="94 mW" frequency="200 MHz"/>
13    <PowerState id="slow" powerConsumption="35 mW" frequency="130 MHz"/>
14    </ComponentState>
15    <ComponentState id="IDLE">
16    <PowerState id="fast" powerConsumption="90 mW" frequency="200 MHz"/>
17    <PowerState id="slow" powerConsumption="33 mW" frequency="130 MHz"/>
18    </ComponentState>
19    </Resource>
20  </PowerAnnotations>
```

3.2 Simulation

The generated source code and configuration files contain the necessary information to start a simulation-based evaluation of performance. By following a similar virtual processing approach as provided in [17] [11], the functional model is simulated along with a performance model for each hardware resource to obtain the respective scheduling and power consumption traces. In this approach, each hardware resource defines a single SystemC process, and schedules the execution of the actors mapped to it. The execution time of each functional action is simulated according to the parameters provided in the configuration file. An embedded power management service on each processing element drives the power state machine to manage power consumption. Integrating as well a GUI for trace visualization makes it possible to visualize the performance of the sketched model after a single click. After obtaining the traces, it is possible to modify the functional model to regenerate the source code for compilation, simulation and visualization. If the changes involve only a change in the mapping of actors, or the annotation of their timing or power consumption values, no recompilation is necessary as only new configuration files will be created.

4 Use Case

To demonstrate the design productivity improvement using *Mahler*, we have chosen to model an MPEG-4 Encoder Use Case. We would like to show what little effort is needed to model such an encoder at the ESL and to estimate if the performance constraints are met while taking into account the respective power consumption for two different scenarios: one implementing the encoder in software running on a single processor, and another one splitting the workload into three application-specific processors.

The MPEG-4 Encoder system-level model is taken from [13]. We model each MPEG-4 Encoder algorithm block as a separate actor, namely: discrete cosine

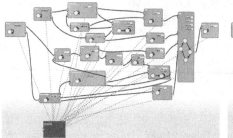

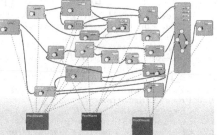

Fig. 4. MPEG-4 Use case - All actors running on a single processor

Fig. 5. MPEG-4 Use case - Actors mapped to multiple hardware resources

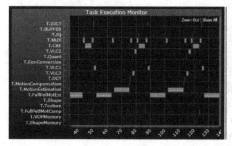

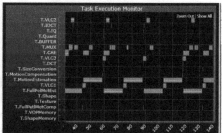

Fig. 6. Scheduling simulation results - Shown is the sequential scheduling and execution of the actions of (a) all actors mapped to a single processor and (b) the parallel execution of actors mapped on three different processors

transform (DCT), quantization, inverse quantization (IQ), motion compensation, motion estimation, Content Based Arithmetic Encoding (CAE), variable length coding (VLC). The encoder follows a dataflow paradigm, thus we proceed to define simple FSMs for most of the actors, where the periodic execution of its functional action is conditioned to the existence of tokens at the input ports before trying to compute an action as well as enough FIFO space available before producing one token of data at the output ports, see Figure 4. As at this level of abstraction we are not interested in the functional (algorithmic) execution of the specified actor actions but rather in a loosely timed execution according to the annotated timing values. For this case study, the majority of the FSMs simply contain one state and one transition to account for the dataflow dependencies with the other actors. The multiplexor actor, in contrast, defines the multiplexing order through a four-state FSM.

Now that the functional model has been sketched including 20 actors, we proceed to set-up the architecture platform to then map the functional actors to hardware resources and thus be able to provide timing annotations for execution as well as power consumption parameters on each resource.

The annotated execution time values can be obtained from data sheets of previous designs, or be expert's estimations. In this use case, we obtained these numbers from the relative load profile of a single RISC processor [13].

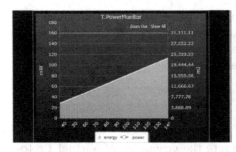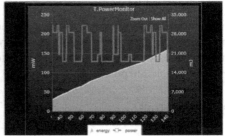

Fig. 7. Power consumption simulation results - Constant power consumption of fully active single processor vs. variable power consumption values due to idle periods of time of inactive processors

On the LHS of Figures 6 and 7, we can see the simulation results of the one RISC processor mapping. The actors, shown at different Y-axis levels, are executed sequentially, and their periodic execution can be observed as well. The power consumption is constant due to the 100% usage of the processor.

We proceed now to evaluate this encoder for a three processor solution proposed in [13], in which algorithms with similar properties are assigned to the most appropriate processor or accelerator. Blocks with high data parallelism, such as DCT, IDCT, and motion estimation, have been mapped to hardware accelerator, whereas stream oriented blocks, such as VLC have been mapped to a different processor, see Figure 5. As processors will not be completely utilized all of the time, we make use of low power modes to save power while idle as well as reduce the processor frequency. The respective timing annotations were scaled to the expected operating frequency of the dedicated processors. The RHS of Figures 6 and 7 shows the resulting task schedule and power consumption. It is now possible to observe the parallel execution of tasks and their duration, and the different system power consumption values according to the number of active processors and their power mode. The corresponding number of Lines of Code for the generated functional model and XML annotation files for the MPEG-4 use case and the first introduced source-sink model of step VII of Fig. 3 are summarized in Table 1. It is easy to appreciate that even though the use case functional model actors were only a bit more complex than the simple functional model of Fig. 3 VII, this results in a significant increase of a factor of 40x or more of LoC. The time taken to model the complete use case was less than an hour, and the investigation of the alternative scenario took less than 10 minutes

Table 1. LoC generated for the simple Source-Sink and MPEG-4 Encoder Use Case

	Complexity	LoC
Simple Functional Model	2 actors	20
MPEG-4 Functional Model	20 actors	850
MPEG-4 XMLs	Single Processor	74
MPEG-4 XMLs	Three Processors	104

to set-up. With *Mahler*, we have reduced the modeling effort significantly, saving us to write so many LoC, and furthermore, we can reuse our generated model on automatic DSE tools to obtain a more optimal mapping of functionality into hardware, as well as instrument the model with real algorithm computations for HW synthesis purposes.

5 Conclusions

We have presented a novel tool to accelerate the generation of Virtual Prototypes and ESL specifications from graphically sketched actor models through a model-driven natural interface. To the best of our knowledge, this is the first ESL modeling tool to provide a consolidated sketch-based interface for actor-oriented-based model development that generates ready to execute virtual prototypes for simulation-based power and performance evaluation reducing the initial modeling stage of actor-oriented and hardware/software codesign choices thanks to its model-driven and natural interface approach. Its benefits may be summarized as follows: i) It allows to very quickly pre-optimize an initial design through very short design iterations before beginning automatic design space exploration thanks through its intuitive playground environment, increasing the efficiency of a virtual prototype designer, by enabling the creation of a fully executable ESL virtual prototype within minutes with the same accuracy as state-of-the-art approaches ii) The generated functional code can be integrated into existing ESL design flows for further design phases. Furthermore, being a model-driven approach it also features: iii) No necessity to master a new language or dialect to create a system model, reducing the learning curve and facilitating the adoption of system-level design techniques. iv) Enabling the designer to focus on model development, and not on boiler-plate code such as declarations, instantiations, interconnections, associations, etc. which usually introduce more complexity into the model than the model information itself.

Acknowledgment. We would like to thank the support of the team of Dr. Ralph Hasholzner at Intel Mobile Communications, Munich, Germany, for their valuable feedback. This work was supported in part by the Project PowerEval funded by Bayerisches Wirtschaftsministerium, support code IUK314/001.

References

1. Balarin, F., Watanabe, Y., Hsieh, H., Lavagno, L., Passerone, C., Sangiovanni-Vincentelli, A.: Metropolis: an integrated electronic system design environment. Computer 36(4), 45–52 (2003)
2. Coffland, J.E., Pimentel, A.D.: A software framework for efficient system-level performance evaluation of embedded systems. In: Proceedings of the 2003 ACM Symposium on Applied Computing, pp. 666–671. ACM (2003)
3. Eker, J., Janneck, J.W., Lee, E.A., Liu, J., Liu, X., Ludvig, J., Neuendorffer, S., Sachs, S., Xiong, Y.: Taming heterogeneity-the Ptolemy approach. Proceedings of the IEEE 91(1), 127–144 (2003)

4. Erbas, C., Pimentel, A.D., Thompson, M., Polstra, S.: A framework for system-level modeling and simulation of embedded systems architectures. EURASIP J. Embedded Syst. 2007(1), 2 (2007)
5. Falk, J.: SysteMoC (2008), http://forge.greensocs.com/en/projects/SysteMoC
6. Falk, J., Haubelt, C., Teich, J.: Efficient representation and simulation of model-based designs in SystemC. In: Proc. FDL 2006, Forum on Design Languages 2006, Darmstadt, Germany, pp. 129–134 (September 2006)
7. Gerstlauer, A., Haubelt, C., Pimentel, A., Stefanov, T., Gajski, D., Teich, J.: Electronic system-level synthesis methodologies. IEEE Transactions on Computer-Aided Design of Integrated Circuits and Systems 28(10), 1517–1530 (2009)
8. Hammond, T., Davis, R.: Tahuti: A geometrical sketch recognition system for UML class diagrams. In: ACM SIGGRAPH 2006 Courses, p. 25. ACM (2006)
9. Haubelt, C., Falk, J., Keinert, J., Schlichter, T., Streubühr, M., Deyhle, A., Hadert, A., Teich, J.: A SystemC-based design methodology for digital signal processing systems. EURASIP J. Embedded Syst. 2007(1), 15 (2007)
10. Kara, L.B., Stahovich, T.F.: Hierarchical parsing and recognition of hand-sketched diagrams. In: ACM SIGGRAPH 2007 Courses. ACM, New York (2007)
11. Kempf, T., Doerper, M., Leupers, R., Ascheid, G., Meyr, H., Kogel, T., Vanthournout, B.: A modular simulation framework for spatial and temporal task mapping onto multi-processor SoC platforms. In: DATE, vol. 2, pp. 876–881. IEEE Computer Society, Washington, DC (2005)
12. Kienhuis, B., Deprettere, E.F., van der Wolf, P., Vissers, K.A.: A methodology to design programmable embedded systems - The Y-Chart approach. In: Embedded Processor Design Challenges: Systems, Architectures, Modeling, and Simulation - SAMOS, pp. 18–37. Springer, London (2002)
13. Kneip, J., Bauer, S., Vollmer, J., Schmale, B., Kuhn, P., Reissmann, M.: The MPEG-4 video coding standard-A VLSI point of view. In: 1998 IEEE Workshop on Signal Processing Systems, SIPS 1998, pp. 43–52. IEEE (1998)
14. Leap Motion Inc.: Leap Motion (2013), https://www.leapmotion.com/
15. Microsoft: Ink analysis framework. http://msdn.microsoft.com/en-us/library/windows/desktop/ms704040%28v=vs.85%29.aspx
16. Mirabilis Design Inc.: Visual Sim (2008), http://www.mirabilisdesign.com/Pages/Product/mdi_products.htm
17. Streubühr, M., Gladigau, J., Haubelt, C., Teich, J.: Efficient approximately-timed performance modeling for architectural exploration of MPSoCs. In: Forum on Specification Design Languages, FDL 2009, pp. 1–6 (September 2009)
18. Teich, J.: Hardware/software codesign: The past, the present, and predicting the future. Proceedings of the IEEE 100, 1411–1430 (2012) (Centennial-Issue)
19. The Mathworks Inc.: Simulink (2013), http://www.mathworks.com
20. Xu, Y., Rosales, R., Wang, B., Streubühr, M., Hasholzner, R., Haubelt, C., Teich, J.: A very fast and quasi-accurate power-state-based system-level power modeling methodology. In: Herkersdorf, A., Römer, K., Brinkschulte, U. (eds.) ARCS 2012. LNCS, vol. 7179, pp. 37–49. Springer, Heidelberg (2012)

Formal Architecture Specification for Time Analysis

Hajer Herbegue, Mamoun Filali, and Hugues Cassé

CNRS-IRIT, Université de Toulouse
Toulouse, France
firstname.lastname@irit.fr

Abstract. WCET calculus is nowadays a must for safety critical systems. As a matter of fact, basic real-time properties rely on accurate timings. Although over the last years, substantial progress has been made in order to get a more precise WCET, we believe that the design of the underlying frameworks deserve more attention. In this paper, we are concerned mainly with two aspects which deal with the modularity of these frameworks. First, we enhance the existing language Sim-nML for describing processors at the instruction level in order to capture modern architecture aspects. Second, we propose a light DSL in order to describe, in a formal prose, architectural aspects related to both the structural aspects as well as to the behavioral aspects.

Keywords: Hardware, microarchitecture, pipeline, WCET, architecture language, formalization, constraints.

1 Introduction

System-on-chip and processor modeling methodologies are continuously improved to overcome the increasing complexities of critical embedded systems. Designers have to deal with complex features of new architectures and develop application/domain specific processors. It is highly desirable, as intending to reduce the costs and time-to-market, that the software design tool can be synthesized automatically from high level processor specifications. In this scope, there is a surge in architecture description languages. ADLs have been used in retargetable tools generation, design space exploration, hardware synthesis, verification and time analysis [14,16]. In order to have reliable and powerful design and analysis flows, ADLs have to convey the informal processor specification provided by vendors to the development tools, as closely as possible. Furthermore, the validation (and verification) is an important task in the system-on-ship design process, that ensures the correction of the system with respect to the correctness requirements and real-time constraints. Such a task is arduous because of the architecture complexity and lack of clear and explicit syntax and semantics in currently used architecture languages. Indeed, to ensure the completeness of the architecture requirements at the design stage, it is essential to have a precise and formal processor specification. ADL-driven flows for worst case execution time (WCET)

E. Maehle et al. (Eds.): ARCS 2014, LNCS 8350, pp. 98–110, 2014.

analysis, like the OTAWA framework [4], need a clear and explicit syntax and semantics for the architecture description to provide the required accuracy.

At the present time, OTAWA allows the time analysis using a constraint-based approach, in addition to the validation and the animation of time results [12] and the generation of fine-grained simulators at pipeline level. In this paper, we enhance the OTAWA work flow with a logic-based description that formalize the architecture properties. This description is used, with the architecture model described in the Sim-nML language, to generate a constraint-based description for the WCET computation. We first present how advanced architecture features, specially instruction with complex behaviors, can be handled by the OTAWA ADL description. Second, we give, in a formal prose, the operational properties of the hardware components and the instruction set. These properties describe the instructions behavior regarding to resources allocation, dependencies, parallel execution, etc. This description also provides a good basis for formal verification of time analysis methods.

The paper is organized as follows. Section 2 gives an overview of the ADL-based approach and our contribution. In Section 3, we present the Sim-nML language and its extension to describe advanced features of real-life architectures. In Section 4, we present the logic-based description, illustrated through a processor use case. In Section 5, we present an overview of related works and draw a comparison between their respective description languages. Section 6 concludes the paper.

2   ADL-Based Approach for Time Computation

OTAWA [4] is a framework dedicated to WCET computation of a program executed on a given processor. The time analysis is based on an abstraction of the target architecture and the binary. The WCET of a program corresponds to the execution time of the longest execution path, which is identified on the control flow graph (CFG) of the program. An execution path is a sequence of code snippets, called *basic blocks*. The WCET is a function of the time cost of the basic blocks and their execution counts [18]. In this paper, we focus on the computation of the basic block execution time. The pipeline analysis consists of modeling the instruction behavior of the pipeline and evaluating the impact of the hardware features on the instruction execution times [17]. The framework OTAWA was enhanced with an ADL-based approach [11] that aims at computing the time cost of a basic block considering the pipeline features. The carried analysis considers as input (1) the program binary, (2) the basic block as an instruction sequence and (3) the architecture description in the Sim-nML language [10] (see figure 1). Sim-nML was extended to support, in addition to the ISA description, the micro-architecture description of the target processor. The architecture description includes the resources accessed by the instructions such as pipeline stages, buffers, etc. and the execution model of instructions. The execution model describes the instruction behavior in terms of resource allocation. From the Sim-nML language and the binary, we generate an internal

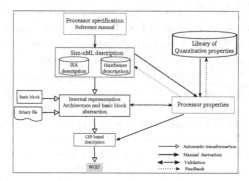

Fig. 1. ADL-based flow for time analysis

representation of the architecture and of the basic block. Then, a constraint-based description is automatically generated from the execution models of the instructions and the pipeline description. These constraints are combined to formulate a constraint satisfaction problem (CSP) [8], whose resolution provides the time cost of the basic block.

In this paper, we intend to provide a formal description of the architecture constraints, in which we can express the architecture elements and properties, regardless of the resolution method and the language used later for time computation. We propose a domain specific language that allows a logic description of the architecture properties. The idea is to provide a library in which the architect-user can find a set of reusable quantitative properties that assist him in (1) the definition of architecture high-level constraints that would be used for time analysis and (2) the validation of the correctness and the consistency of the architecture model with respect to the initial specification. Indeed, according to the initial Sim-nML description and what is provided in the properties library, the user defines a set of properties that will be used further to compute WCETs.

3   The Sim-nML Description Language Extension

Sim-nML [10] is a hierarchical and a highly structured language that describes the processor at instruction level, using an attributed grammar. The instructions and the addressing modes are described using pre-defined attributes. The *syntax* attribute defines the assembly representation of the instruction. The attribute *image* gives the binary representation and *action* defines the semantics of the instruction (register transfer). Our extension to the Sim-nML language [11] allows the definition of the processor resources and the execution model of the instruction set, giving how and when the resources are accessed by each instruction. The properties of the hardware components are specified as attributes. So, we can declare stages, buffers, registers and memories. Concerning stages, we can specify out-of-order execution, superscalarity, cache characteristics, if relevant for time analysis, etc. The instructions definition is extended with an attribute

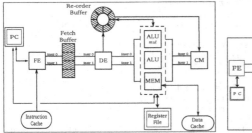
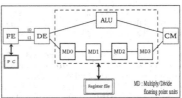

Fig. 2. An out-of-order superscalar processor

Fig. 3. Floating point pipeline

uses that describes the execution model. In fact, to start execution on a stage, an instruction has to wait for its resources to be available, including the operands, the executing stage, the memory, etc. Therefore, the execution time of an instruction is impacted by the resources state. The *uses* attribute defines, in a timed sequence called *clause*, the resources required by an instruction in each step of its execution. A sequence is defined using commas. Every clause in a sequence represents a step of the instruction execution. In every step, one or more resources are required, and access can be in read or write mode. Parallel access is expressed by the operator &. Access to some resources takes a fixed duration t, that is specified as #{t}. An example of a 2-scalar out-of-order processor is illustrated in figure 2 and described in Sim-nML in lines 1-12 of listing 1.1. The language extension was amenable to describe some complications of instruction set architectures. In next paragraphs, we show how we extend the Sim-nML in order to handle pipelines with complex and long-running instructions.

Not-fully symmetric ALU. Specialized functional units are designed for specific operation patterns to achieve shorter delays. In the processor of figure 2, we assume that the first *ALU* occurrence implements a multiplier component executing multiply operations and ordinary data processing operations. Usually, processors include only one specialized ALU because it is expensive and there are more additions than multiply operations. Thus, arithmetic instructions are executed by any of the *ALU*. So no occurrence is specified in the *ADD* execution model (lines 18-19 of listing 1.1). While, in the execution model of *MUL*, we specify *ALU*[0] as the required stage occurrence (lines 23-24 of listing 1.1). This will be used when scheduling instructions to be issued to the *ALU* units. Different latencies has been associated to the execution of the *ADD* and *MUL* instructions on the *ALU* unit.

Listing 1.1. Sim-nML processor description

```
1   stage FE , DE , ALU[2]  , MEM , CM
2   extend FE , DE , CM
3       capacity = 2          // super-scalarity degree
4       inorder = true        // in-order stages
5   extend ALU , MEM
```

```
6        inorder = false // out-of-order stages
7
8     buffer FBuf [4]  , RoB [8] // Fetch Buffer and Re-order Buffer
9
10    reg PC [1,card(32)] // 32-bit PC register
11    reg R [16,card(32)] // 16 registers of 32 bits
12    mem M [32,card(8)]// a memory of 2^32 8-bit words
13
14    op ADD (rd:card (4),rs:card (4),rn:card (4))
15      syntax = format ("add r%d r%d r%d",rd,rs,rn)
16      image = format ("00%2b%2b%2b",rd,rs,rn)
17      action = {R[rd] = R[rs] + R[rn] ;}
18      uses= FE & FBuf & PC.read, DE, ALU & RoB & R[rs].read &R[rn].read
19           & R[rd].write#{1}, CM
20
21    // Multiply instruction executed on the specilized ALU
22    op MUL
23      uses= FE & FBuf & PC.read, DE, ALU[0] & R[rd].write & R[rm].read
24           & R[rs].read & RoB#{5},CM
25
26    // load multiple instruction
27    op load_multiple (rlist: card(16) , rn: card(4) )
28      uses = FE & PC.read & FBuf, DE ,
29    if rl<0..0>==1 then MEM & M.read & R[rn].read & R[0].write & RoB
           endif ,
30    if rl<1..1>==1 then MEM & M.read & R[rn].read & R[1].write & RoB
           endif , ..,CM
31
32    // branch instruction dumped after decode
33      var taken[1,u1]
34    extend B_Cond
35      uses = FE & PC.read & FBuf,DE & (if (taken==1) then PC.write endif)
```

Multi-cycle instructions. Some complicated arithmetic operations, such as multiply, divide and floating point operations, can require complex hardware with significantly longer delays than a single *ALU*. One solution is to have parallel pipelines for different multi-stage instructions. For example, division is frequently implemented using this scheme even in high performance superscalar processors. In addition, such an instruction stays many cycles on the same stage, mostly the first. In the pipeline of figure 3, we have a pipelined multiply/divide functional unit *MD*. The *ALU* unit executes simple operations. Instructions are issued in the *MD* floating point pipeline out-of-order. The listing 1.2 presents the execution model of the divide and multiply instructions. The *DIV* and *MUL* instructions have different latencies on the first stage of the pipelined *MD* unit. In fact, stages with different latencies is also a relevant pipeline property for hazards detection and the instructions scheduling, which is critical in an out-of-order issue processor. These latencies will be considered when generating the timing constraints to compute the execution time of instructions.

Listing 1.2. Floating point pipeline

```
1    stage FE, DE, ALU, MD0 , MD1 , MD2 , MD3, CM
2    extend FE , DE , CM
3            capacity = 2       // 2-superscalar stages
4    extend ALU , MD0
5            inorder = false // out-of-order stages
6    extend MUL
7      uses= FE#{1}, DE#{1}, MD0 & R[rd].write & R[rm].read & R[rs].read
           #{1},
```

```
 8           MD1#{1}, MD2#{1}, MD3#{1}, CM#{1}
 9   extend DIV
10     uses= FE#{1}, DE#{1}, MD0 & R[rd].write & R[rn].read & R[rm].read
           #{21},
11           MD1#{1}, MD2#{1}, MD3#{1}, CM#{1}
```

Micro-coded Instructions. Multiple register transfer instructions provide an efficient way of moving the contents of several registers to and from memory. These instructions take one cycle to issue but then use multiple memory cycles to load/store all the registers. We consider the pipeline of the figure 2. The load multiple instruction is given in lines 27-30 of listing 1.1. The list of registers to load is given by the operand rl coded on 16 bits. Every bit refers to a register and is set to one if the register is to load. So, if the register is loaded, then we have a clause in which the MEM unit, the memory and the register with the appropriate access mode are required. Otherwise, we have an empty clause. In order to have a wellformed final clause, with a valid pipeline path, we defined a semantic rule that states that: *in a clause sequence, if a clause is empty, then it is removed from the sequence: cl , $\emptyset$, cl' $\Rightarrow$ cl , cl'.* For example, we have the following instantiated clause for the instruction ldmia r13, {, r11, r13, r15}:

FE & PC.read&FBuf, DE , MEM&M.read&R[13].read&R[11].write&RoB , MEM&M.read&
R[13].read&R[13].write&RoB ,MEM&M.read&R[13].read&PC.write&RoB , CM.

Branch Instruction. Some processors resolve branch target at the decode stage. The branch instruction is no longer used on next stages. So a branch instruction is dropped after the decode stage (lines 33-35 of listing 1.1). This is useful in out-of-order pipelines, since it reduces the structural hazards on functional units.

4   Formal Architecture Description

We formalize an architecture description through the architecture denoted by $\mathcal{A}$ and the instruction clauses of the basic block $\mathcal{BB}$. We generate an equation system $\mathcal{E}q(\mathcal{BB}, \mathcal{A})$ representing the analyzed $\mathcal{BB}$, with respect to $\mathcal{A}$. In $\mathcal{E}q(\mathcal{BB}, \mathcal{A})$, the execution times are not computed. In order to do that, we formulate a set of structural and temporal high-level constraints $Constraints\_\mathcal{A}$. The resolution of $\mathcal{E}q(\mathcal{BB}, \mathcal{A})$ and $Constraints\_\mathcal{A}$ provides an equation system where the instructions execution times have been computed (figure 4).

Fig. 4. Formal approach for time analysis

4.1   A Light DSL for Architecture Constraints

We introduce a light DSL (Domain Specific Language) for expressing the architecture and basic block properties. We derive from every instruction of the basic block a set of tasks that are divided into levels:

- *ISA level.* The task represents the lifetime of the instruction on the pipeline. It starts when the instruction enters the pipeline and finishes when it leaves. The task is given by the instruction index in the basic block.
- *Step level.* The task models the execution of an instruction on a stage or a functional unit, what we call a *step*. Hereinafter, we use processing units to refer to stages or functional units.
- *Resource level.* Basic tasks or leaves represent the resource allocation within an instruction step. This includes stages, functional units, buffers, registers and memory allocation.

The lifetime of every task is modeled using an interval. Table 1 summarizes the architecture DSL. We also consider the predefined functions $scal(st)$ and $nb(r)$ returning respectively a stage scalarity and a resource occurrences number. We consider the instruction sequence of figure 5 executed on the processor of figure 2 as a use case. From the Sim-nML description, the non terminal $\langle Stage \rangle$, $\langle Register \rangle$ and $\langle Memory \rangle$ are instantiated as in (1).

Table 1. Architecture DSL

Architecture domain
$\langle Stage \rangle$, $\langle Register \rangle$, $\langle Memory \rangle$, $\langle Buffer \rangle$, $\langle Resource \rangle ::= \langle Register \mid Buffer \mid Memory \rangle$

Basic block domain (of length n)
$\langle instruction \rangle ::= nat$, $\langle step \rangle ::= nat$, $\langle interval \rangle ::= string$

ISA level tasks:	Step level tasks:
$\langle ISA \rangle_{\langle instruction \rangle}^{\langle interval \rangle}$	$\langle Step \rangle_{\langle instruction \rangle, \langle step \rangle}^{\langle interval \rangle}$

Resource level tasks (leaves):
$_{\langle occurrence \mid ? \rangle}\langle Stage \rangle_{\langle instruction \rangle, \langle step \rangle}^{\langle interval \rangle}$ $\mid$ $_{\langle occurrence \mid ? \rangle}^{[r \mid w]}\langle Resource \rangle_{\langle instruction \rangle, \langle step \rangle}^{\langle interval \rangle}$

$$\langle Stage \rangle ::= \{FE, DE, ALU, MEM, CM\} \ , \ \langle Register \rangle ::= \{R, PC\}, \qquad (1)$$
$$\langle Memory \rangle ::= \{M\}, \langle Buffer \rangle ::= \{FBuf, RoB\}$$

We assume the following semantic sets that we automatically generate from the architecture and the basic block:

- $\mathcal{I}$ denotes the set of tasks of the ISA level.
- $\mathcal{S}$ denotes the set of steps of all the instructions in the basic block,
- $\mathcal{L}$ denotes the set of synthesized leaves,
- $\mathcal{U}$ denotes the subset of leaves concerning stages or functional units,
- $\mathcal{B}, \mathcal{R}$ and $\mathcal{M}$ denote respectively the subset of leaves concerning buffers, registers and memories.

We consider the following dedicated quantifiers where $\forall_\mathcal{I}, \forall_\mathcal{S}, \forall_\mathcal{L}, \forall_\mathcal{U}, \forall_\mathcal{B}$ quantifies respectively over the basic block instructions, the steps, the leaves, the processing units and the buffers. We also use the predefined functions $Last_\mathcal{S}(i)$, $Buffer(i, s)$ and $Unit(i, s)$ that return respectively the last step task of i, the set of buffers and processing units of i at the step s.

$$\mathcal{I} = \{o_0^{t\_0} \, , \, o_1^{t\_1} \, , \, o_2^{t\_2}\} \quad , \quad \mathcal{S} = \mathcal{S}_0 \cup \mathcal{S}_1 \cup \mathcal{S}_2 \quad , \quad \mathcal{L} = \mathcal{L}_0 \cup \mathcal{L}_1 \cup \mathcal{L}_2$$

In the following, we detail the sets $\mathcal{S}_2, \mathcal{U}_2, \mathcal{R}_2, \mathcal{B}_2$ and $\mathcal{M}_2$ which are respectively the set of steps, stages, registers, buffers and memories of o_2. The instruction o_2 is a load multiple and loads **3 registers** from memory. So, we can observe that, based on the execution model in listing 1.1, **6** steps are generated, including **3** relative to the execution on the MEM unit. The instruction decomposition is illustrated in figure 6.

$$\mathcal{S}_2 = \{s_{2,0}^{t\_2\_0} \, , \, s_{2,1}^{t\_2\_1} \, , \, s_{2,2}^{t\_2\_2} \, , \, s_{2,3}^{t\_2\_3} \, , \, s_{2,4}^{t\_2\_4} \, , \, s_{2,5}^{t\_2\_5}\}$$

$$\mathcal{L}_2 = \mathcal{U}_{i2} \cup \mathcal{R}_{i2} \cup \mathcal{B}_{i2} \cup \mathcal{M}_{i2}$$

$$\mathcal{U}_2 = \{_0FE_{2,0}^{tu\_2\_0} \, , \, _0DE_{2,1}^{tu\_2\_1} \, , \, _0MEM_{2,2}^{tu\_2\_2} \, , \, _0MEM_{2,3}^{tu\_2\_3} \, , \, _0MEM_{2,4}^{tu\_2\_4} \, , \, _0CM_{2,5}^{tu\_2\_5}\}$$

$$\mathcal{R}_2 = \{_0^rPC_{2,0}^{tr\_2\_0} \, , \, _{13}R_{2,2}^{r\_2\_2} \, , \, _{11}R_{2,2}^{w\_2\_2} \, , \, _{13}R_{2,3}^{r\_2\_3} \, , \, _{13}R_{2,3}^{w\_2\_3} \, , \, _{13}R_{2,4}^{r\_2\_4} \, , \, {}^wPC_{2,4}^{tr\_2\_4}\}$$

$$\mathcal{B}_2 = \{_?FBuf_{2,0}^{tb\_2\_0} \, , \, _?RoB_{2,2}^{tb\_2\_2} \, , \, _?RoB_{2,3}^{tb\_2\_3} \, , \, _?RoB_{2,4}^{tb\_2\_4}\}$$

$$\mathcal{M}_2 = \{_0^rM_{2,2}^{tm\_2\_2} \, , \, _0^rM_{2,3}^{tm\_2\_3} \, , \, _0^rM_{2,4}^{tm\_2\_4}\}$$

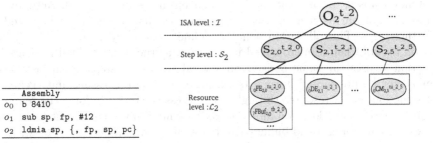

Assembly	
o_0	b 8410
o_1	sub sp, fp, #12
o_2	ldmia sp, {, fp, sp, pc}

Fig. 5. Basic block

Fig. 6. Decomposition of instruction o_2

4.2 Architecture Properties

In this section we give a set of structural and dynamic properties that describes the architecture and instruction behavior. We use Allen intervals to express temporal relations between intervals. The properties are parametrized by the architecture and the basic block equations presented in the previous section.

Instruction Continuity. An instruction starts when its first step ($s = 0$) starts and terminates when its last step terminates. Considering two successive steps of an instruction, a current step finishes when the next step starts (2).

$$\forall_{\mathcal{I}} \, o_i^t. \, \forall_{\mathcal{S}} \, s_{i,0}^{t'}. \, t \text{ \textbf{Starts} } t'$$
$$\forall_{\mathcal{S}} \, s_{i,s}^{t}. \, \forall_{\mathcal{S}} \, s' \, {}_{i,s+1}^{t'}. \, t \text{ \textbf{Meets} } t' \qquad (2)$$
$$\forall_{\mathcal{I}} \, o_i^t. \, \forall_{\mathcal{S}} \, s_{i,Last_S(i)}^{t'}. \, t \text{ \textbf{Finishes} } t'$$

Instruction Support. We assume that, within a step, an instruction requires one and only one stage and at the most one buffer resource (3a). This is a structural property used for architecture correctness validation. Two cases arise. First, if a buffer is required within a step, then this buffer is unique and is the support of the instruction during that step. Indeed, the instruction is contained in the buffer slot throughout the step. The buffer is allocated since the instruction starts execution within the step, and remains so until the resources on the next step become available. The buffer is released when the instruction starts the next step (3b). Second, if no buffer is used, thus, the stage is the instruction support. It is blocked until the instruction starts the next step, i.e. next step resources are available (3c).

$$\forall i. \; \forall s. \; \mathbf{card} \; (Buffer(i,s)) \; \leq \; 1 \wedge \mathbf{card} \; (Unit(i,s)) \; = \; 1 \tag{3a}$$

$$\forall_S \; s_{i,s}^t. \; \mathbf{card} \; (Buffer(i,s)) \; = \; 1 \; \Rightarrow \; \exists!_? b_{i,s}^{t'} \in Buffer(i,s). \; t = t' \tag{3b}$$

$$\forall_S \; s_{i,s}^t. \; \mathbf{card} \; (Buffer(i,s)) \; = \; 0 \; \Rightarrow \; \exists!_o st_{i,s}^{t'} \in Unit(i,s). \; t = t' \tag{3c}$$

Resources Allocation Policy. An instruction executes on a given stage, once it gets all its required resources, including the stage. Thus, all required resources are allocated at the beginning of the step (4a). After the execution latency elapses, all or some of the owned resources are released. Actually, we assume that an instruction keeps the resources that are going to be asked on further steps. This allocation policy is defined to avoid deadlocks. Such a situation occurs when a micro-coded instruction, as the multiple load presented in section 3, uses the same register on several successive steps. Such instruction must not be preempted during its execution on the processing unit. When an instruction uses a resource through two successive steps, we force the temporal continuity on the allocation intervals, as presented in the constraint (4b). Some resources, like stages and buffers, can be required in *non-deterministic* way: the instruction requests for any of the available occurrences, or in a *deterministic* way: the instruction requests for a specific occurrence. For a resource r, we have to insure that no more then $nb(r)$ occurrences are allocated at the same time. This contention problem occurs in case of non-deterministic resources with dynamic scheduling. Currently, the property (4c) concerns stages and buffers.

$$\forall_S \; s_{i,s}^t. \; \forall_{\mathcal{L}} \; {}_o^a res_{i,s}^{t'}. \; t \; \mathbf{Starts} \; t' \wedge t' \; \mathbf{During} \; t \tag{4a}$$

$$\forall_{\mathcal{L}} \; {}_o^a r_{i,s}^t. \; \forall_{\mathcal{L}} \; {}_o^a r_{i,s+1}^{t'}. \; t \; \mathbf{Meets} \; t' \tag{4b}$$

$$\forall_{\mathcal{U} \cup \mathcal{B}} \; {}_o x_{i,s}^t. \; \mathbf{card} \; (\{ {}_o x_{i',s'}^{t'} \in \mathcal{U} \cup \mathcal{B} \mid t \; \mathbf{Overlaps} \; t' \}) \; \leq \; nb(x) \tag{4c}$$

Stage Specific Constraints. These constraints depend on the stages execution features. For a simple-scalar stage with in-order execution, only one instruction is issued to the stage per cycle and is issued before its successor in the program (5a).

$$\forall_{\mathcal{U}} \; {}_o st_{i,s}^t. \; \forall_{\mathcal{U}} \; {}_o st_{i',s'}^{t'}. \; i < i' \Rightarrow t \; \mathbf{Before} \; t' \tag{5a}$$

$$\forall_{\mathcal{U}} \; {}_o st_{i,s}^t. \; \mathbf{card} \; (\{ {}_o st_{i',s'}^{t'} \in \mathcal{U} \mid t \; \mathbf{Overlaps} \; t' \}) \; \leq \; scal(st) \tag{5b}$$

$$\forall_{\mathcal{U}} \; {}_o st_{i,s}^t. \; \forall_{\mathcal{U}} \; {}_o st_{i',s'}^{t'}. \; i' < i + scal(st) \Rightarrow t \; \mathbf{StartsBeforeBegin} \; t' \tag{5c}$$

$$\forall_{\mathcal{U}} \; {}_o st_{i,s}^t. \; \forall_{\mathcal{U}} \; {}_o st_{i+scal(st),s'}^{t'}. \; t \; \mathbf{Before} \; t' \tag{5d}$$

In case we have a super-scalar stage st, at most $scal(st)$ successive instructions can be issued in parallel (5b). However the overall program order must be maintained. Thus, an instruction of index i can be executed in parallel with an instruction of index j such that $j < i + scal\,st$. We introduce a new time relation $StartsBeforeBegin$ that define a priority relation between two intervals (5c). The scalarity limit of the stage is expressed by a forced precedence between instruction i and instruction $i + scal(st)$ (5d). For out-of-order stages, no precedence is defined except those implied by the data dependencies.

Data Dependencies. Memories and registers can be owned in a read or a write mode. For example, when a register is accessed by two successive instructions such that the first request is a read access and the second is a write access, then, the read access must occur before the write access. Read After Write (RAW) hazards are explicited when instructions access registers and memories. Write After Write (WAW) hazards must be explicited for memory accesses.

$$\forall_{\mathcal{R}} \ {}^r_o reg^{el}_{i,s}. \ \forall_{\mathcal{R}} \ {}^w_o reg^{el'}_{i',s'}. \ i \leq i' \Rightarrow el \ \textbf{Before} \ el'$$
$$\forall_{\mathcal{R}} \ {}^a_o m^{el}_{i,s}. \ \forall_{\mathcal{R}} \ {}^w_o m^{el'}_{i',s'}. \ i \leq i' \Rightarrow el \ \textbf{Before} \ el' \tag{6}$$

To elaborate the constraints $Constraints\_\mathcal{A}$, we instantiate all (or some of) the constraints presented in equations from 2 to 6, with respect to the architecture $\mathcal{A}$ and the basic block sets. We detail here the constraints of the instruction o_0 which is a branch (the corresponding execution model is in listing 1.1):

(2) $\rightarrow$ t_2 **Starts** t_2_0 $\wedge$ t_2_0 **Meets** t_2_1 $\wedge$ ... t_2_1 **Finishes** t_2
(3) $\rightarrow$ $tb\_2\_0 = t\_2\_0$ $\wedge$ $tu\_2\_1 = t\_2\_1$ $\wedge$ $tb\_2\_2 = t\_2\_2$ $\wedge$ $tb\_2\_3 = t\_2\_3$ $\wedge$ ...
(4) $\rightarrow$ tu_2_2 **Meets** tu_2_3 $\wedge$ tu_2_3 **Meets** tu_2_4 $\wedge$ tb_2_2 **Meets** tb_2_3 $\wedge$ ...
(6) $\rightarrow$ t_0_1 **Before** t_2_0 $\wedge$ t_1_2 **Before** t_2_2 $\wedge$ ...

These high-level constraints are used to generate a constraint description to be processed by a given solver. In [11], we show how to solve these constraints with the CSP/CHOCO [1]. The resolution of the constraints for the basic block of the figure 5 executed on the processor of figure 2 gives the following values, among others $:t\_0 = [0, 2]$; $t\_1 = [2, 6]$ *and* $t\_2 = [2, 9]$. In [12], we also show how to animate such properties through the timed automata provided by the UPPAAL tool [7].

5   Related Work

There have been a lot of research efforts in architecture description languages that aim to formalize the processor specification provided in user manuals. Most of these efforts was based on ADLs like ArchC [15], LISA [13], HARMLESS [5] and Sim-nML [11], that was used to generate retargetable tools. Since these ADLs are actually mature regarding the ISA level description, modern ISAs are currently supported and accurate simulators can be generated. Nevertheless, these approaches assume simple pipelines like DLX, since the micro-architecture is not handled or limited to its structure. Our general approach based on Sim-nML supports the retargetable tool generation, in addition to complex instruction execution models. Retargetable WCET analysis tools based on processor description are presented, among others, in [14] [19] [6] [9]. Timed automata was observed in [6] [9] as a formal processor description. This model is difficult to elaborate and is hand-made, which limits experimentations to simple five stage pipelines with in-order execution. Our approach offers a high-level processor description that can be used to generate timed automata. The work of [19] is close to ours. The authors use the EXPRESSION language to describe the ISA and the micro-architecture and generates execution graphs for the analysis. However, the ADL description only includes the pipeline structure. The hardware components behavior, such as out-of-order execution and superscalarity, are specified in C++ external libraries. The use of many formalisms to processor description makes it not suitable for validation. Other methods verify program behavior and the memory design [3] on PowerPC and ARM architecture using a formalization. This approach uses the L3 language [2] for the ISA description and the generation of a HOL specification used for verification. The formal description is limited to the ISA level and cannot be used for time analysis. The table 2 summarizes the architecture languages capabilities.

Table 2. Architecture languages summary table

	ArchC	Chronos	LISA	Harmless	Expression	L3	Otawa
Code optimization							
Simulation	•	•	•	•			•
Retargetable tool generation	•		•	•			•
Design space exploration	•		•		•		
Time analysis		•			•		•
Formalization	•			•	•	•	•
Verification/Validation					•	•	•
Out-of-order pipeline		•				•	•
Superscalar pipeline	•	•	•			•	•
Complex instruction set	•		•			•	•

6   Conclusion

In this paper, we have showed how advanced architecture features can be described through an extension of the Sim-nML architecture description language. We have presented the syntax for describing advanced pipelines structure and instructions with complex execution models. We have also presented a specification language that aims to formalize the architecture features. We have elaborated a set of generic properties that can be used for the generation of architecture constraints for time analysis and the validation. This formalization can be a basis for formal verification, required to obtain certified WCET computation methods. The proposed approach for time analysis is modular since it is based on the hardware description and the basic block, each one independent from the other. Modularity also comes from the fact that the Sim-nML description of the ISA and the micro-architecture are separated in implementation terms, so that the same ISA description can be reused for different pipelines. High-level constraint description present a significant advantage since the user is free to choose the resolution method for WCET computation. We have drawn a comparison between currently used description languages and formalism. In this paper we have used a processor model that possess real word processor features to test our approach. We are currently validating our formalization on real-life processors that are rolling out on the market, among which the Cortex-A8.

References

1. CHOCO: An Open Source Java Constraint Programming Library, http://choco.mines-nantes.fr
2. L3: An ISA Specification Languag, http://www.cl.cam.ac.uk/~acjf3/l3/
3. Alglave, J., Fox, A., Ishtiaq, S., Myreen, M., Sarkar, S., Sewell, P., Nardelli, F.Z.: The semantics of power and arm multiprocessor machine code. In: Workshop on Declarative Aspects of Multicore Programming (DAMP), pp. 13–24 (2008)
4. Ballabriga, C., Cassé, H., Rochange, C., Sainrat, P.: OTAWA: An Open Toolbox for Adaptive WCET Analysis. In: Min, S.L., Pettit, R., Puschner, P., Ungerer, T. (eds.) SEUS 2010. LNCS, vol. 6399, pp. 35–46. Springer, Heidelberg (2010)
5. Béchennec, J.L., Briday, M., Alibert, V.: Extending harmless architecture description language for embedded real-time systems validation. In: International Symposium on Industrial Embedded Systems, pp. 223–231 (2011)
6. Béchennec, J.L., Cassez, F.: Computation of wcet using program slicing and real-time model-checking. CoRR (2011)
7. Behrmann, G., David, A., Larsen, K.G., Håkansson, J., Pettersson, P., Yi, W., Hendriks, M.: Uppaal 4.0. In: QEST, pp. 125–126 (2006)
8. Beldiceanu, N., Carlsson, M., Demassey, S., Petit, T.: Global constraint catalogue: Past, present and future. Constraints 12, 21–62 (2007)
9. Dalsgaard, A., Olesen, M., Toft, M., Hansen, R., Larsen, K.: METAMOC: Modular execution time analysis using model checking. In: Workshop on Worst-Case Execution Time Analysis (WCET), vol. 15, pp. 113–123 (2010)
10. Fauth, A., Van Praet, J., Freericks, M.: Describing instruction set processors using nML. In: European Design and Test Conference (EDTC), pp. 503–507 (1995)
11. Herbegue, H., Cassé, H., Filali, M., Rochange, C.: Hardware architecture specification and constraint based wcet computation. In: International Symposium on Industrial Embedded Systems (SIES), pp. 259–268 (2013)
12. Herbegue, H., Filali, M., Cassé, H.: A constraint-based wcet computation framework. In: Junior Researcher Workshop on Real-Time Computing (JRWRTC), pp. 33–36 (2013)
13. Hohenauer, M., Scharwaechter, H., Karuri, K., Wahlen, O., Kogel, T., Leupers, R., Ascheid, G., Meyr, H., Braun, G., Someren, H.V.: A methodology and tool suite for c compiler generation from adl processor models. In: Design, Automation and Test in Europe Conference and Exhibition, vol. 2, pp. 276–1281 (2004)
14. Li, X., Roychoudhury, A., Mitra, T.: Modeling out-of-order processors for WCET analysis. Real-Time Systems 34, 195–227 (2006)

15. Miele, A., Pilato, C., Sciuto, D.: An automated framework for the simulation of mapping solutions on heterogeneous mpsocs. In: International Symposium on System on Chip (SoC), pp. 1–6 (2012)
16. Mishra, P., Dutt, N.: Modeling and validation of pipeline specifications. ACM Trans. Embed. Comput. Syst., 114–139 (2004)
17. Rochange, C., Sainrat, P.: A context-parameterized model for static analysis of execution times. High-Performance Embedded Architectures and Compilers II (2009)
18. Wilhelm, R., Engblom, J., Ermedahl, A., Holsti, N., Thesing, S., Whalley, D., Bernat, G., Ferdinand, C., Heckmann, R., Mitra, T., Mueller, F., Puaut, I., Puschner, P., Staschulat, J., Stenström, P.: The Worst-Case Execution-Time problem–overview of methods and survey of tools. ACM Transactions on Embedded Computing Systems (TECS), 36:1–36:53 (2008)
19. Xianfeng, L., Abhik, R., Tulika, M., Prabhat, M., Xu, C.: A retargetable software timing analyzer using architecture description language (2007)

Hardware APIs: A Software-Centric Approach for Automated Derivation of MPSoC Hardware Structures Based on Static Code Analysis

Matthias Meier, Mark Breddemann, and Olaf Spinczyk

Technische Universität Dortmund, Department of Computer Science 12

Abstract. Multiprocessor systems on a chip (MPSoCs) are a popular class of course-grained parallel computer architectures, which are very useful, because they support re-use of legacy software components and application-specific tailoring of hardware structures at the same time. Furthermore, model-driven design frameworks for MPSoCs such as Xilinx' EDK or our own LavA-framework facilitate very fast system development. However, in this paper we argue that these design frameworks are not ideal from the development process perspective. Instead, we propose a software-centric approach that is based on the hardware API concept. The API is a representation of hardware components on the software level, which is generated from a hardware meta-model. It allows us to automatically derive a hardware structure based on access patterns in software, revealed by a static code analysis. This trick reduces the number of hardware details the developer needs to deal with and avoids configuration inconsistencies between the hardware and software levels by design.

1 Introduction

Configurable hardware is becoming increasingly powerful and less expensive. This allows embedded system developers to exploit hardware parallelism in order to improve real-time properties and energy efficiency. Multiprocessor systems on a chip (MPSoCs) are a popular class of course-grained parallel computer architectures, which are very useful, because they support re-use of legacy software components and application-specific tailoring of hardware structures at the same time. Hardware accelerators for timing-critical operations can be easily integrated due to standardized on-chip busses, leading to acceptable system performance.

In a previous paper we have presented our LavA-framework [10], which follows a model-driven approach to synthesize MPSoC hardware structures based on high-level descriptions. From a user's perspective it resembles Xilinx' well-known Embedded Development Kit (EDK), but is completely based on configurable open source components and easily extensible. Frameworks such as EDK and LavA free application developers from the burden to cope with the underlying hardware description language, such as VHDL or Verilog, hide implementation details, and are thus very popular.

E. Maehle et al. (Eds.): ARCS 2014, LNCS 8350, pp. 111–122, 2014.

However, in systems with complex infrastructure software, such as operating systems, communication libraries, or language runtimes, the semantic gap between the application-code level and the hardware model, on which hardware design frameworks rely, is still very big. Besides this difficulty, the developer is left alone with the problem to fit the infrastructure software layers, which are typically highly configurable, between the application and the hardware.

In contrast, our approach aims at a seamless co-configuration of hardware structures and infrastructure software based on the application software's requirements. This avoids misconfiguration, which would lead to waste of resources, and improves separation of responsibilities between application and platform developers. The approach is "software centric" in the sense that the configuration process starts with a static code analysis of the application software and configures all infrastructure software layers as well as the MPSoC hardware structure in a top-down manner. A key question in the design of this process, which we have implemented as an extension of our LavA framework, is how to derive the hardware structure from usage patterns on the lowest level of the software stack. This question will be the focus of this paper and the "hardware API", which represents the hardware components in software, is the answer.

The outline of this paper is as follows: In Section 2 we will discuss existing approaches from related literature and we will present the differences and advantages of our software-centric approach compared to other MPSoC design processes. The details of our own approach including the notion of a hardware API will be presented in sections 3 and 4. The sections 5 and 6 provide additional insights into the implementation. An example project will be presented in Section 7. The paper ends with a discussion in Section 8 and a short conclusion in Section 9.

2   State of the Art

Many research groups work on the automated configuration of MPSoC structures based on application knowledge. Typically, these works based on a similar workflow as presented on the left-hand side of Figure 1. The input for the workflow is usually represented by an abstract application model. This model combined with a design space exploration (DSE) is used to automatically generate the application code and the hardware structure. For instance, Arpinen et al. present a configurable multiprocessor platform that supports distributed execution of applications described in UML 2.0 [1]. Several others use Kahn Process Networks [4] or similar process networks as a model to describe the application and map the processes to hardware resources based on different optimization criteria, such as performance, energy consumption, or chip space demands [6,15,16]. However, the process networks are suitable for the purpose of mapping optimizations rather than the configuration of an entire multiprocessor system, including peripheral devices. Further, some approaches introduce their own specifications to describe multiprocessor or manycore systems. These systems are specified by high-level system specifications [9], textual [8] or XML-based descriptions [18].

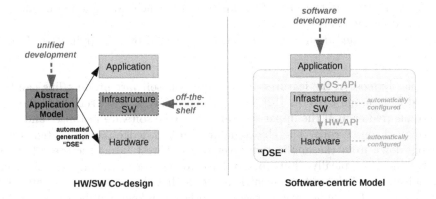

Fig. 1. HW/SW Design Methodologies

Besides the fact that the information is not extracted from the software, we think that these specifications are too far away from the application and thus not amenable to application developers.

Only very few publications address the role of infrastructure software in this domain. This is surprising, because computer scientists tend to regard computer systems as a stack of hardware and software layers with several infrastructure software layers between the hardware and the application code [14]. Ignoring these layers comes at the risk of designing solutions that cannot cope with the demands of complex real-world applications. Furthermore, the subsequent integration of off-the-shelf infrastructure software between the application and the hardware layer is difficult and can lead to inconsistencies between the layers, because both adjacent layers have to be considered and the designer has to adapt the operating system by hand. HeMPS [2] is a framework that integrates a microkernel for scheduling and task communication into the workflow for NoC-based MPSoCs. The configuration of HeMPS is done by a graphical user interface and not automated derived from the application. In [1] they use the RTOS eCos in a configurable multiprocessor platform, but the operating system is not directly integrated in the architecture exploration of the application and the hardware. There is also some work [3, 19] that deals with the co-simulation of operating system and hardware. These simulations are rather intended for the fast validation or partitioning of embedded systems than a refinement of the DSE results by the consideration of the operating system.

Based on experience with the configuration of vertically composed software product lines [13], we favor a straight *top-down* configuration process for complex embedded hardware/software stacks (right-hand side of Figure 1). This software-centric model provides a streamlined design flow from the application over the infrastructure software to the hardware layer. At the boundary between each pair of adjacent layers, there are two sources of configuration information for the lower layer:

1. *Usage patterns* in the code of the upper layer, which can be found by means of static code analysis.
2. *Explicit configuration decisions* that are provided by the application developer.

Typically most of the features of a configurable software product line can be derived from usage patterns [12]. For the code analysis it is crucial to analyze the configured code of the upper software layer (the software instance) and not the original source code. Thereby configuration knowledge is transported step-by-step down from the application layer to the lowest infrastructure software layer, which is typically—but doesn't have to be—an operating system. The first advantage of the software-centric model is that the infrastructure software is included in the configuration process, and layer-by-layer will be generated in the top-down configuration process in order to prevent inconsistencies between them. The second advantage is that no abstract application model is needed and the configuration information can directly be obtained from the highest software layer, simply by using the API. The lower layers can be configured automatically afterwards. In this paper we focus on the step from the hardware API to the hardware structure. Therefore, we need a representation of MPSoC hardware components on the software level that can be analyzed statically at compile time to derive a hardware design. There are several approaches that are dealing with the representation of hardware in software. Kumar et al. present an object-oriented technique to model hardware in C++ in their work [7]. They focus on the states of the hardware and the operations that modify these states. In order to create hardware components they instantiate C++ classes at runtime. However, since we need to analyze the software statically at compile time to obtain the MPSoC configuration, we need another mechanism to represent the MPSoC hardware. In [11] a high-level design methodology to describe hardware in C++ is presented. For this purpose, they extend C++ with new class libraries to provide concurrency and reactivity in order to describe hardware in software. This approach is quite similar to the common C++ extension SystemC and is rather intended to describe the behavior of hardware than application-specific requirements on the hardware component configurations.

3   LavA Configuration Process

The main idea behind the LavA configuration process is to extend the straight top-down configuration process from the software layers down into the layer of configurable MPSoC hardware. An overview of the process is given in Figure 2. In order to detect usage patterns for the hardware layer within the application/infrastructure software layer statically, a representation of hardware components on the software level is needed. We call this representation the *hardware API*. In the case of the LavA-framework this API could be generated automatically from the meta-model, which describes the set of all hardware components available in the LavA platform. By means of the hardware API the software can instantiate

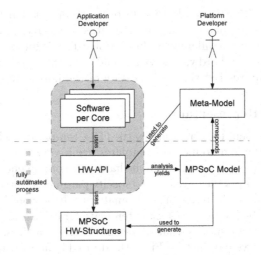

Fig. 2. LavA Configuration Process

and use hardware components as if they were ordinary software. The static code analysis detects these instantiations and uses this information to generate an MPSoC model, which will finally be used for the hardware synthesis.

This approach is beneficial for both, the application developer and the hardware platform developer. The application developer only needs to write the application software and does not have to deal with low-level hardware structures, hardware description languages or other unamenable representations of the hardware for an application developer at all. The platform developer only has to provide a meta-model for his platform. In case of an extension, for example the integration of a new kind of I/O device, an extended version of the hardware API will be generated automatically and is ready to be used as soon as the meta-model got extended. All steps of the LavA approach below the dashed line are fully automated. In the following sections the LavA approach is described in greater detail.

4   Representation of Hardware in Software

The essential question which had to be answered, was: How to represent the several hardware components of an MPSoC in software in order to obtain the MPSoCs configuration at compile time? As the software for embedded systems is frequently written in C or C++, we looked for a suitable language element in these languages to represent the hardware components. The required software language element to represent the hardware has to be flexible enough to deal with the vast amount of possible hardware configurations. Especially, when considering hardware structures like MPSoCs, which are typically composed out of processing elements, communication infrastructure, peripheral devices and memories. At the same time it has facilitate the analysis of the hardware representing

source code statically at compile time in order to detect and to configure the
MPSoC hardware components. Furthermore, it is necessary to represent devices
of the same kind but with different configurations. This is important, since otherwise every instance of a hardware device would have the same properties, which
would unnecessarily restrict the configuration of the hardware structure.

4.1   Hardware Representation

We decided to represent the hardware by the C++ template mechanism, because
it matches all of our requirements. Templates are a very powerful and generic
mechanism. They allow us to configure the hardware components at compile time
since the language forces the developer to specify parameters as constants. This is
absolutely essential for the usage of static analysis. The various hardware devices
are basically described with a C++ class template for each kind of device. Figure
3 exemplarily shows a template that represents UART[1] devices. The UART can
be configured with two parameters: First, the desired baud rate has to be defined,
and then the interrupt configuration for this device follows. The required I/O
address range is indicated in bytes by the symbolic constant Size.

```
template < int Baud = 57600, int IRQLines = 1 >
struct UART : public AbstractDevice<IRQLines> {
    enum { Size = 8 };
};
```

Fig. 3. The UART template – Part of the Hardware API

4.2   Hardware Instantiation

In order to create a hardware instance for a specific device in software, the
corresponding class template has to be instantiated as global object. By the
use of inheritance or composition, the developer has manifold possibilities to
instantiate the hardware. Thus, for example, a device driver may use a hardware
object as attribute, or the device driver class inherits from the hardware class
template in order to instantiate the hardware by itself. Several examples of the
hardware instantiation with different parameters are presented in Figure 4.

4.3   Interrupts and Device Addresses

The interrupt numbers and addresses for the memory-mapped I/O devices are
assigned automatically during the LavA HW/SW synthesis process. Therefore,
the application developer does not have to care about their correct and consistent
assignment. However, he can use the provided member functions of the hardware
class templates to query the assigned interrupt numbers and I/O addresses.

---

[1] Universal Asynchronous Receiver/Transmitter.

```
// Object in global namespace
UART<9600, 0> globalUART;

// Multiple instantiation with array
UART<57600, 1> threeUARTs[3];

// Instantiation after inheritance
class DerivedUART : public UART<> {} DerivedUART derivedUART;

// Instantiation after composition
class CompUART {
    public:
        UART<19200, 1> uart1, uart2;
} CompUART compUART;
```

Fig. 4. Instantiation of UART Template

5 Model-Driven Development of Hardware API

The presented hardware class templates constitute the hardware API, the lowest layer of the software stack. It fulfills two purposes: first, the instantiation of the API is detected to configure the MPSoC and second, the resulting code will be used at runtime to access the synthesized hardware component. The hardware API interacts directly with the hardware structure, and is thus closely linked to it. Extensions to the hardware may also have an impact on the hardware API. Therefore, LavA uses a model-driven approach to keep the hardware as well as the hardware API consistent.

The meta-model plays the central role of the model-driven approach. It defines the formal structure and the construction rules for LavA's MPSoC hardware structure (Figure 5). In addition, it specifies the relationships and operations for the arrangement of the hardware components. On the top level, the MPSoC is composed of nodes, connections and shared memories. In this context a node signifies one processor of the MPSoC with its local peripherals and communication interfaces. The nodes, or rather the processors, can be associated with connections in order to communicate by a message-based mechanism with any number of other processors. Additionally, all hardware components provide a minimal required set of attributes, for instance the size of the message queue for a connection, or the width of a timer register. Attributes that are declared constant, are fixed for all instances of the same kind, whereas the other attributes are used as parameter for the hardware class templates. These attributes express the variations for hardware instances of the same kind.

We developed the meta-model with EMF[2] (Eclipse Modeling Framework), an open-source framework for model-driven software engineering and code

---

[2] http://www.eclipse.org/modeling/emf/

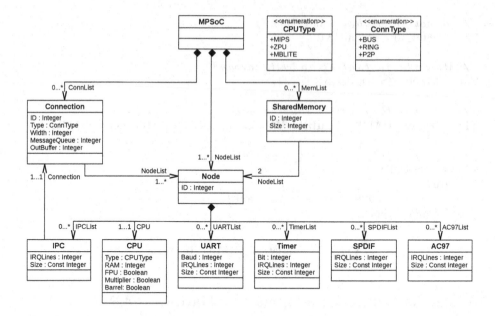

Fig. 5. Excerpt of the LavA Meta-Model

generation, which allows us to generate the hardware API class templates directly from the meta-model.

6   Static Code Analysis

To generate an instance of the meta-model, that is, a hardware model for a concrete MPSoC, we have to analyze the software stack (in our case: application and operating system) by searching for global instances of hardware API class templates. We use an extended version of the C++ parser library PUMA [17] for this purpose. By means of these detected hardware instances and the initialization parameters the hardware model is being created and filled. The only exceptions are the interrupt numbers and the device addresses. Due to the cyclic dependencies between the software and hardware layer it is not possible to assign these numbers and addresses before the hardware structure is determined. After PUMA finds each hardware instantiation in the software, the devices get assigned their interrupt numbers, one by one, and the address space will be continuously partitioned according to the symbolic constant Size. Finally, PUMA generates a hw_init function that is executed during the boot-up time of the operating system. Within this function the interrupt numbers and the device addresses are set to the attributes of any peripheral device representing object. The result of this step is extended C++ source code and an EMF model representing the hardware.

Based on the model and LavA's extensible library of VHDL-based opensource IP components, which are extended with component-specific configuration options, we finally create the hardware instance. More details on how to configure LavA's hardware platform from the EMF model can be found in [10].

7   Example: Audio Decoder

To exemplify our approach we here present the implementation of a Dolby Digital[3] audio decoder. The application reads the encoded audio bit stream from a DVD Player using an S/PDIF interface, decodes the audio signal and outputs this to an AC'97 module. The workload is divided accordingly using a pipelined design with three stages:

1. *extraction* of *synchronization frames* from the bit stream, which contain the encoded audio signals for 6 audio channels
2. *decoding* the extracted frames and mixing the 6 channels down to a stereo signal
3. *output* of audio samples to AC'97

In this scenario, the extraction and output stages are performed on an own processor each. Since synchronization frames can be decoded independently, we further parallelized the decoding stage, using three processors. In the future we plan to gain the task mapping automatically from a design space exploration. For the audio decoder we could even re-use a standard decoding library initially developed for x86 (liba52[4]). Within each application software task we instantiated the required hardware components, namely processors, communication infrastructure and devices, and configured them by the template parameters. For example, the hardware instantiations for one of the decoding processors look as follows: Node<2>, CPU<MBLITE, 96, true, true, true>, SharedMemory<1, 4>, SharedMemory<4, 4>, Connection<1, BUS, 32, 5, 5>, IPC<1>, and Outport<2>. The used template parameters correspond to the attributes of the meta-model for each hardware component. For instance, the type of the processor is *MBLITE*, its local memory allocates 96 kB and the three optional hardware accelerators are enabled in the processor. Modifications to the hardware, for example due to performance issues, can easily be done by the replacement of the CPU type with a more powerful processor. After the software for each processor is programmed the PUMA parser analyzes the five software stacks, generates the hw_init functions for each processor and creates the hardware model. Finally, the VHDL source code is generated from the hardware model by the EMF. All steps after the application development are fully automated. Only the User Constraints File for the hardware synthesis has to be prepared manually. Due to LavA's automated design flow the application-specific MPSoC in the form of VHDL source code can be generated in seconds after the developer has finalized the application.

---

[3] Dolby Digital (ATSC A/52) is a standard for 6 channel audio compression. It uses AC-3 as audio bit stream, which contains a sequence of synchronization frames. Each frame contains 6 audio blocks. A synchronization frame is the smallest independently decodable unit of the audio bit stream.

[4] http://liba52.sourceforge.net/

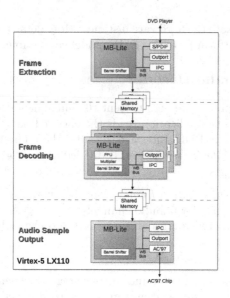

Fig. 6. Hardware Platform: Dolby Digital Audio Decoder

The final hardware platform generated for the case study is shown in Figure 6. The MPSoC is composed out of five MB-Lite[5] processors arranged in three stages. The MB-Lite is an instruction set and cycle compatible open-source version of the Xilinx's MicroBlaze processor. We tested this MPSoC on a Xilinx Virtex-5 LX110 FPGA (speed grade -1) at a frequency of 33 MHz. On this FPGA the MPSoC occupies 35,711 6-input LUTs[6] (51 %).

8   Discussion

8.1   Top-Down vs. Bottom-Up Configuration

In the embedded systems domain all re-usable hardware and software components tend to be configurable according to application-specific requirements. In a complex hardware/software stack the configurations of all layers have to be consistent, thus top-down or bottom-up configuration processes are possible. The hardware manufacturer Xilinx provides tool support for bottom-up configuration while the software engineering community seems to favor top-down configuration starting with highly abstract configurable *features* [5]. The approach presented here is top-down. This allows application developers to abstract from hardware structures. It is more "programmer compatible". On the other hand, we are aware that the lack of control over the synthesized hardware might induce a

---

[5] http://www.opencores.org/project, mblite.

[6] The area-wise most expensive component is the floating-point unit (FPU) with 6,432 6-input LUTs per instance. However, due to real-time constraints, the FPU cannot efficiently be replaced by a software algorithm.

certain overhead. We haven't experienced this problem in our example, but will investigate it in the future.

8.2 General Applicability of the Approach

The presented approach is neither limited to be used in conjunction with the LavA-framework nor is it required to have an operating system on top of the hardware. The hardware API can be used by a complex software stack as well as by simple applications. In any case it hides the hardware details from the application developer. It is also conceivable to replace LavA's hardware platform, for instance, by Xilinx's EDK or by a software-based emulation of the hardware components. It would merely be necessary to provide a meta-model that reflects the respective configuration options and a transformation of the resulting hardware model into the model that is needed by the respective framework for hardware synthesis. It is furthermore interesting to note that two frameworks with a compatible meta-model would also have a compatible hardware API. As a consequence, software written for one framework would also work with the other, e.g. switching between LavA and EDK would only be a matter of configuration.

9 Conclusion

In this paper we have introduced a methodology and a tool chain for tailoring MPSoC hardware structures solely based on static code analysis. By automating the configuration process we simplify application development, because no knowledge about computer architecture or hardware description languages is required, and configuration inconsistencies are avoided by design. We regard the *hardware API*, i.e. the generated representation of configurable hardware components on the software level, as the key innovation of this work. Our experiences with an audio decoder example are positive and encourage us to validate the approach with bigger case studies.

Acknowledgments. This work is supported by the German Research Foundation (DFG) under grant no. SP 968/4-2.

References

1. Arpinen, T., Kukkala, P., Salminen, E., Hännikäinen, M., Hämäläinen, T.D.: Configurable multiprocessor platform with RTOS for distributed execution of UML 2.0 designed applications. In: Proceedings of the Conference on Design, Automation and Test in Europe (DATE 2006), Washington, D.C., USA (2006)
2. Carara, E., de Oliveira, R., Calazans, N.L.V., Moraes, F.: Hemps - a framework for noc-based mpsoc generation. In: IEEE International Symposium on Circuits and Systems (ISCAS 2009), pp. 1345–1348 (2009)
3. Honda, S., Wakabayashi, T., Tomiyama, H., Takada, H.: Rtos-centric hardware/software cosimulator for embedded system design. In: Int. Conf. on Hardware/Software Codesign and System Synthesis (CODES+ISSS 2004), pp. 158–163 (2004)

4. Kahn, G.: The semantics of a simple language for parallel programming. In: Rosenfeld, J.L. (ed.) Information Processing, Stockholm, Sweden, pp. 471–475. North Holland, Amsterdam (1974)
5. Kang, K., Cohen, S., Hess, J., Novak, W., Peterson, S.: Feature-oriented domain analysis (FODA) feasibility study. Technical report, Carnegie Mellon University, Software Engineering Institute, Pittsburgh, PA (November 1990)
6. Kangas, T., Kukkala, P., Orsila, H., Salminen, E., Hännikäinen, M., Hämäläinen, T.D., Riihimäki, J., Kuusilinna, K.: Uml-based multiprocessor soc design framework. ACM Trans. Embed. Comput. Syst. 5(2), 281–320 (2006)
7. Kumar, S., Aylor, J., Johnson, B., Wulf, W.: Object-oriented techniques in hardware design. Computer 27(6), 64–70 (1994)
8. Lukovic, S., Fiorin, L.: An automated design flow for NoC-based MPSoCs on FPGA. In: 19th IEEE/IFIP Intl. Symposium on Rapid System Prototyping (RSP 2008), pp. 58–64 (June 2008)
9. Lyonnard, D., Yoo, S., Baghdadi, A., Jerraya, A.: Automatic generation of application-specific architectures for heterogeneous multiprocessor system-on-chip. In: Design Automation Conference (DAC 2001), pp. 518–523 (2001)
10. Meier, M., Engel, M., Steinkamp, M., Spinczyk, O.: LavA: An open platform for rapid prototyping of MPSoCs. In: 2010 Int. Conf. on Field Programmable Logic and Applications (FPL 2010), Milano, Italy, pp. 452–457. IEEE Computer Society Press (2010)
11. Roth, R., Ramanathan, D.: A high-level hardware design methodology using c++. In: 4th High Level Design Validation and Test Workshop, pp. 73–80 (1999)
12. Schirmeier, H., Spinczyk, O.: Tailoring infrastructure software product lines by static application analysis. In: 11th Int. Software Product Line Conference (SPLC 2007), pp. 255–260. IEEE Computer Society Press (2007)
13. Schirmeier, H., Spinczyk, O.: Challenges in software product line composition. In: 42nd Hawaii Int. Conf. on System Sciences (HICSS 2009), pp. 1–7. IEEE Computer Society Press, Waikoloa (January 2009)
14. Tanenbaum, A.S.: Structured Computer Organization, 5th edn. Prentice-Hall, Inc., Upper Saddle River (2005)
15. Thiele, L., Bacivarov, I., Haid, W., Huang, K.: Mapping applications to tiled multiprocessor embedded systems. In: 7th Int. Conf. on Application of Concurrency to System Design (ACSD 2007), pp. 29–40 (2007)
16. Thompson, M., Nikolov, H., Stefanov, T., Pimentel, A.D., Erbas, C., Polstra, S., Deprettere, E.F.: A framework for rapid system-level exploration, synthesis, and programming of multimedia mp-socs. In: 5th Int. Conf. on Hardware/software Codesign and System Synthesis (CODES+ISSS 2007), pp. 9–14. ACM (2007)
17. Urban, M., Lohmann, D., Spinczyk, O.: Puma: An aspect-oriented code analysis and manipulation framework for C and C++. In: Katz, S. (ed.) Transactions on AOSD VIII. LNCS, vol. 6580, pp. 144–165. Springer, Heidelberg (2011)
18. Wallentowitz, S., Lankes, A., Zaib, A., Wild, T., Herkersdorf, A.: A framework for open tiled manycore system-on-chip. In: 22nd Int. Conf. on Field Programmable Logic and Applications (FPL 2012), pp. 535–538 (2012)
19. Xiong, Z., Zhang, M., Li, S., Liu, S., Chao, Y.: Virtual embedded operating system for hardware/software co-design. In: 6th Int. Conf. on ASIC. ASICON, vol. 2, pp. 939–943 (2005)

uBuild: Automated Testing and Performance Evaluation of Embedded Linux Systems

Fabio Erculiani, Luca Abeni, and Luigi Palopoli*

DISI – University of Trento, 38123 Povo, Trento, Italy
fabio.erculiani@gmail.com, luca.abeni@unitn.it, palopoli@disi.unitn.it

Abstract. This paper describes uBuild, a novel tool designed to support the automated execution of repeatable and controlled tests of embedded Linux systems. This is useful for continuous integration purposes, and to evaluate the impact of various design and implementation options on the system's performance. uBuild allows the designer to build the embedded system image from scratch, by compiling all the needed software from the source code and by even building the needed cross-compilation toolchain if required. It provides deterministic control on the configuration options used to build the cross-compilation toolchain, the Linux kernel, the system libraries, and all the programs. In this way, the effects of each option can be tested and evaluated in isolation.

Keywords: Embedded Systems, Continuous Testing, Performance Evaluation.

1 Introduction

The recent developments in embedded computing devices and related technologies (sensing and battery technologies, etc...) are creating the premises for a pervasive diffusion of small computing systems that directly interact with the physical environment in many ways. This is reflected in the increasing importance of consumer electronics, which has become one of the most important drivers of the global economy. Smartphones, tablets, smart glasses are a few example of commercial breakthroughs. These devices operate in close interaction with their users offering an easy and intuitive access to their computing abilities and connectivity. Home automation, automotive and even fashion industries are example application areas where a massive penetration of these transformative devices is expected to introduce changes of unprecedented radicality.

At the heart of this new generation of embedded systems are Systems Chip (SoC) devices. Their evolution has transformed traditionally "low-power" devices into out-and-out computing units, whose power matches the one of Personal Computers of a generation ago. The gap of computing power between high end

---

* The research leading to these results has received funding from the European Union Seventh Framework Programme (FP7/2007-2013) under grant agreement n ICT-2011-288917 "DALi - Devices for Assisted Living".

E. Maehle et al. (Eds.): ARCS 2014, LNCS 8350, pp. 123–134, 2014.

embedded devices and PC is expected to be closed in a few years time horizon [3]. As a result, different authors observe a slow but steady decrease of the PC sales [6] and establish a clear connection of this commercial trend with the increased performance of modern embedded systems.

The constant growth of embedded systems computing power is being reflected on the complexity of the software that they execute. And of course a great (computational) power comes with great responsibility (in meeting the increased expectations of users on the functionality of embedded devices). This emphasises the role of the Operating System (OS) layer to facilitate the integration of complex functionalities and to optimally manage the system resources. As a consequence, it is possible to notice an evident transition from custom solutions to solutions based on the Linux Kernel.

A reliable and well tested OS layer is certainly a desirable feature but it is not sufficient. At the same level of importance are software testing, performance and power consumption evaluation and optimisation. Generally speaking, there is a need for development cycles based on a sound scientific basis. For this reason, embedded software engineers are experimenting with new solutions to development, test and release that could help preserving the quality of software, in spite of the pressure for a quick time-to-market and of the complexity of the embedded functionalities.

This paper presents the design of uBuild, a new tool aimed at simplifying and automatising the development and test of Linux-based embedded systems. uBuild allows developers to exactly define the software to be installed on the system and to build the software from source, using a customised cross-development toolchain. Since the tool gives complete control over the specific software versions to be used, additional patches to be applied to the various programs, the various build options, and the configuration of the cross-compiler, it becomes possible to test and evaluate the impact of every single option on the global performance of the generated embedded system. uBuild is a tool developed from the grounds up, which could help meet the pressing requirements of modern Linux Based embedded software.

2   The Problem

The process of consolidating the development and testing of Linux-based embedded systems has already started, as shown by the proliferation of terms like *continuous testing and integration* or *tinderbox systems* [10,15,11,8].

However, such activities as continuous integration, testing and profiling, need some way to automate the build, test, and evaluation process [14], while maintaining a high degree of flexibility and configurability to test and compare different setups. For example, when trying to improve a piece of code or its execution speed through compiler optimisations or when trying to evaluate the impact of some configuration option on the system performance, developers are typically looking for a proof that corroborates their expectations. The performance gain of a change in the software configuration should be deterministic, and measurable in a reliable and repeatable way.

In some situations, the designer of an embedded system might want to test a large number of software implementations, each one with a few configuration changes (the used libraries or cross-compilation tools, the compiler flags, the kernel version or the scheduling algorithm, etc...), collect performance results, and compare them at the end.

In this context, the term "performance" is used in a generic way and might refer to the ability of the system to respect temporal constraints, to power consumption, or to other aspects which could be critical, for instance, in Linux operated wearable devices.

Current Linux-based embedded systems are generally based on well-defined Linux distributions [4], which impose serious limitations in the choice of the used software. For example, the distribution might provide packages only for a limited number of software versions, and it is not possible to change the build options. Hence, the only way to have control on the used software is to re-compile it from the source code following a tedious and error-prone process. This option has become impractical because the size of the test matrices used to asses the system qualities can quickly grow as the variables increase in quantity. Hence, manually building all of the system images to be evaluated is not feasible.

To understand the multi-dimensionality of the domain space to be explored, consider some of the questions that a developer or system designer might ask:

- Will the system benefit (in terms of memory footprint, power consumption, or real-time performance) from a specific compiler optimisation?
- Will a specific compiler optimisation cause stability issues or affect the performance?
- Will the system benefit from a proposed patch to the Linux kernel (implementing, for example, a more advanced and experimental scheduler [1,5] or reducing the kernel latencies [13])?
- Will the system perform better with a different set of libraries?
- Will the system perform better if compiled with a different ABI (Application Binary Interface)? For example, consider ARM hardfp (using a hardware FPU for floating point operations) vs softfp (emulating floating point operations in software)
- Will the system pass the regressions test suite if some configuration option is changed?

Unfortunately, generating a system image according to all the requirements mentioned above can be difficult [16], and there is no *one-size-fits-all* solution which fulfils all of these requirements without slowing down the software development process. This problem is increasingly affecting popular software components, as witnessed by the development speed of the Linux kernel [7].

uBuild tries to address the issues mentioned above by providing a simple, controlled, reproducible, and fast way to build from scratch embedded systems based on the Linux kernel. Moreover, uBuild allows to configure and change a large amount of different parameters and options: the cross compiler toolchain (binutils, libc [12], gcc, linux-headers) version and its required patchset, the bootloader version, the used Linux kernel, the userspace environment, the compiler or linker flags, etc. Hence, uBuild can speed testing and development up, by making tests both *reproducible* and *deterministic* so that various implementation options can be correctly evaluated and compared, understanding the impact of all the possible choices.

The problem of the explosion of the size of the test matrix (mentioned above) is mitigated by uBuild in two orthogonal ways. First, the declarative language used for its specification files supports pre-processor statements (like for instance `#include`) that make it possible to reduce the duplications when managing a large amount of files. Then, uBuild provides a build cache for the result of the compilation processes that allows the system to reuse the generated binaries in future builds. Such a cache subsystem works at the build target level and is cooperative: this means that the generation of cache keys is done cooperatively with build profile parameters ("`cache_env =`" statements.)

Finally, uBuild is free software, released under the GNU General Public License (GPL) and is downloadable from `http://github.com/lxnay/ubuild`.

3   The uBuild Architecture

To address the problems presented in the previous section, uBuild has been developed within the following requirements:

1. **Portability and Distribution independence**: uBuild must run on every Linux-based OS where Python and Bash are available. Buildroot[1] is the only similar software tool that aims to be as independent from the host OS as uBuild;
2. **Determinism:** uBuild must be able to generate embedded system images, with specific properties, in a deterministic and reproducible way. This makes it possible to generate large test matrices and compare the results in a reliable way;
3. **Scalability:** uBuild must support the generation of images on a large scale (in order to support large test matrices). Multiple uBuild instances processing different specification files should be able to run in parallel in order to leverage all the CPU, RAM and I/O resources available on a single system. Different specification files (build profiles), can be created using `#include` statements, so that the amount of shared code reduces the complexity of managing hundreds of files;
4. **Smart Caching:** each uBuild target is cached on its own (more on this later) in order to increase the likelihood that the same target, with the same properties, has been already built by uBuild. In order to increase the cache hit, a cooperative caching strategy has been designed: the uBuild target has to assist uBuild in the generation of a hash key used in cache lookups;
5. **Reduced root privileges (ab-)use:** uBuild is designed to be executed by non privileged users. There are however some operations that cannot be

---

[1] `http://buildroot.uclibc.org`

executed without root privileges, like for instance: `mkfs`, `mount`, `mknod` and `losetup`. In order to execute these, operations *uBuild scripts* use the `sudo` command (overridable through the environment variable `PRIV_AGENT`). While *Linux Capabilities* may also be a possible solution, they are not portable and they require a specific filesystem support and the executable to be "marked" accordingly.

To comply with the goals stated above, uBuild is based on an architecture organised in 3 main components:

1. A **builder**, that is responsible of parsing and validating the command line arguments, passing the specification files (containing build profiles) to the parser, managing the uBuild target cache, and executing the build plan through the *target controller*;
2. A **cache manager** (*uBuild cache* in Figure 1) that manages cache writes, reads and lookups in an atomic way;
3. A set of **build scripts**, that are used to effectively compile code (be it the cross compiler itself or the executables required by the target architecture). These scripts must be provided by the user and are divided into the actual executable scripts and the *build scripts library*. The latter contains set of shell functions that can be used to correctly interface to *uBuild-core*.

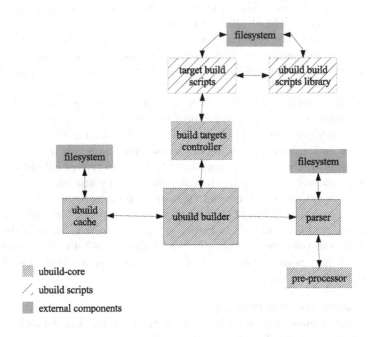

Fig. 1. The uBuild architecture diagram

Figure 1 shows the various uBuild components and their relationships. The first two components compose the **uBuild-core** and are written in Python, while the third one is written in Bash. With reference to the portability goal, it is worth noticing that uBuild-core is more portable than the uBuild scripts, since it only requires Python, while the uBuild scripts depend on Linux and use Linux specific tools.

The *build scripts* provided with the current uBuild codebase provide support for building embedded systems for the *BeagleBoard*, *BeagleBone* and *BeagleBone Black* in two different ABIs: `armhf` (ARMv7 hard floating point) and `armel` (older ARMv7 soft floating point).

uBuild configuration is based on *specification files* and *build profiles*. Strictly speaking, a specification file is a text file containing a build profile, but since there can only be one build profile per configuration file, both terms can be mixed without problems. Each build profile is composed of **global uBuild settings** (parameters that affect the whole uBuild build plan and its targets) and **uBuild targets** (the actual descriptors of what uBuild should try to build). The latter can either be a **cross compiler toolchain target** or a **package target** for the architecture that the profile builds for.

The global settings affect the execution of all the uBuild targets. Such settings can range from the name of the final filesystem image to the directories used by uBuild for downloading and compiling the sources. Without going too much into detail, it is safe to say that global settings are a way to declare shared environment variables (through bash-parseable environment files) or pre- and post-execution hooks. In other words, global settings allow to share pieces of information across all the defined uBuild targets.

Targets are executed in the order they are declared and behave in an *additive* way when declared multiple times. This enables the user to stack declarations on top of each other in a hierarchical fashion and to split them into separate files.

Note that uBuild specification files follow a declarative programming style. Declarative programming is *"a programming paradigm that expresses the logic of a computation without describing its control flow"* [9], leaving the *how* part of the problem to an implementation detail. Among the many advantages of a declarative language, there is certainly one that fits well into typical uBuild work scenarios: **static analysis** [2]. It is much easier to write a static analyser for a declarative language rather than for a compiled or even interpreted one.

uBuild targets are similar to `Makefile` targets for some aspects, but with some important differences. Like a `Makefile` target, a uBuild target is an individual entity that uBuild can reference to, containing a "build recipe". In other words, the content of a target is essentially a set of ordered statements that describe what uBuild is required to do, like for instance:

– read environment variables from a file
– use a given list of environment variables as part of the build cache lookup
– download the source code from a specified URL
– apply a set of patches

- call a build script
- build the source code inside a specified directory

On the other hand, a uBuild target differs from a `Makefile` target in the following ways:

- it is declarative (as previously explained)
- targets can be defined multiple times and the "recipes" are additive
- there is no way to define inter-target dependencies (this may change in future). Instead, targets are executed in the order they are declared
- caching doesn't happen through "timestamp magic" but rather through the **uBuild cache** subsystem, which is guaranteed to be atomic (for instance, by using syscalls exposed through `mkstemp(3)` and `rename(3)`).

Notice that previously a distinction between cross compiler toolchain targets and package targets has been pointed out. While they are all uBuild targets (and hence they are handled in the same way and undergo the same build plan), the former are expected to build a cross compiler (which is needed to build all the other packages) and are hence always executed before any package uBuild targets.

A uBuild target can expose an infinite number of build scripts and their arguments[2]. Similarly to uBuild targets, the build scripts are executed in the order as they are declared, using the environment variables read from the environment files defined in the same target.

Obviously, build scripts are not called in case of build cache hits. **uBuild-core** will take care of unpacking the cached data and placing it in the appropriate destination directory, which is determined by the nature of the defined target (either a *cross compiler toolchain build* target or a simple *package build* one).

The *uBuild cache* is probably the most interesting part of uBuild, since its beneficial effects have a great impact on the user. A well designed cache subsystem makes it possible to save huge amounts of time during *trial and error* or debugging phases, development, or performance testing. For this reason, the cache subsystem has been designed with these goals in mind:

- **Reliability**. The build cache must never generate corrupted cache objects or reuse stale data, unless a corruption in lower I/O layers happens.
- **Atomicity**. The build cache must handle cache objects in an atomic way, allowing for lock-less uBuild *processes parallelisation.*
- **Control**. The user must be able to control the way cache keys are generated, by defining a list of environment variables whose values become part of the (hashed) key.

A 160-bit hashing algorithm like `SHA-1` has been used for the uBuild cache, as its low collision probability makes it solid enough to be used as key for cache

---

[2] While in this context they are called "build scripts", uBuild only expects them to be executable and runs them through `execve(2)`: it is up to the kernel (with the shell interpreter as fallback) to determine the binary format through the `binfmt` subsystem.

objects. This is confirmed by the fact that SHA-1 is used for instance by git[3] to ensure the integrity of various types of internal objects and files.

While *uBuild-core* is very lightweight and most of the activity is carried out in the sample *build scripts* library and in the scripts written by the users, it plays an important role in solidly glueing everything together.

4   A Simple Example

As a simple example, uBuild has been used to evaluate the impact of some build options (ABI, CFLAGS, libc, etc...) on a simple signal processing application running on a BeagleBoard[4] (a small embedded board based on the ARMv7 Cortex-A8 32-bit architecture). In particular, uBuild has been used to answer the following questions:

- Is the new armhf ABI (using the hardware floating point unit) giving any real advantage in this scenario? Or maybe the old soft-floating point ABI avoids certain side-effects that could degrade the performance?
- Given the criticality of the task, is the gcc -O1 optimisation level enough? Is -O2 reliable enough? And what about -O3?
- Can the entire system be compiled with these CFLAGS? Or is this setting going to hit any compiler bug affecting runtime execution?
- Does the compiler auto-vectorisation (gcc -ftree-vectorize) provide any advantage? Does vectorisation actually work when it is supposed to?
- Do CPU specific optimisations (-mcpu=cortex-a8) have any impact on the application performance?

Notice that although it is possible to answer all these questions without uBuild, the time taken to correctly and reliably setup "by hand" a test framework shaped around this problem and the risk to taint the results in unpredictable ways is non-trivial. Hence, uBuild has been used to generate a test matrix in order to compare the results obtained with the various options. The uBuild specification files have been adapted by introducing a set of 7 different build flags that could help to determine the best configuration. A reference build using the optimisation level -O0 is used to verify if the compiler is doing its job correctly, and the other 6 builds use -O1 -mfpu=vfp, -O2 -mfpu=vfp, -O2 -mfpu=neon, -O2 -mfpu=neon -ftree-vectorize, -O3 -mfpu=neon, and -O3 -mcpu=cortex-a8 -mfpu=neon. The test software is compiled by defining a new build target inside the build profile and CFLAGS are swapped through global environment files. Finally, since both the hardfp and softpf ABI had to be tested, the total number of different build flags combination grew up to 14. It is easy to realise how this number can potentially grow very quickly, since the number of subsets of a set composed by n elements is is $O(2^n)$. Of course, assumptions and simplifications can be made in order to avoid to test less interesting scenarios.

---

[3] Git, the stupid content tracker - http://git-scm.com/
[4] http://www.beagleboard.org

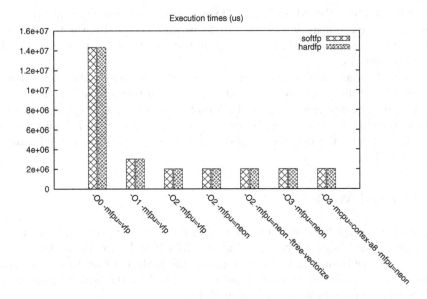

Fig. 2. test results of the 14-ways benchmark of armhf, armel and different CFLAGS. The Y axis reports the execution time, in microseconds.

Each build profile is stored in a file and in order to avoid "code" duplication it is possible to leverage the pre-processor features of the .spec language and use #include statements as explained in Section 3. Hence, the 14 specification files only contain one or more #include statement and an [ubuild] section hosting "env =" and "image_name =" statements.

Every generated image has been copied to microSD storage and configured to run on the target device that, after booting the Linux system, executes 10 iterations of the test and saves the processing time. Figure 2 shows the results obtained with this experiment.

The first important aspect of the results is that the "reference group" composed by the builds having CFLAGS="-O0" demonstrates that gcc correctly does what is asked to do in terms of optimisation. Hence, the whole testing pipeline seems to produce a correct outcome. A second apparent conclusion is that anything better than -O2 does not produce any relevant advantage. This could mean three things:

1. There are bottlenecks in the code that defy any compiler optimisations
2. The code is not complex enough or is already leveraging all the capabilities of the CPU
3. Code loops are too complex and the automatic vectorisation capabilities of the compiler is not working as expected. In this case, "gcc -ftree-vectorizer-verbose=n" could give some insights into why this happens.

Further analysis (based on "`gcc -ftree-vectorizer-verbose=n`") revealed that there were problems in how the `for` loops were designed in the test application, and this caused the auto-vectorisation feature of `gcc` to fail optimise code during compilation.

As a final observation, it is worth noting that the flexibility and configurability provided by uBuild does not come with big costs in terms of image size: while an embedded image generated by buildroot is about $7.2MB$ (plus a $2.8MB$ kernel), the size of a filesystem generated by uBuild is $9MB$ (and the kernel size is $3.6MB$). Hence, the flexibility and configurability provided by uBuild "costs" only $2.6MB$.

5   Related Work

In the open source field, it is possible to find several software solutions aimed at designing and building various kinds of embedded Linux-based OSs. All of these tools have been designed with very specific goals and sometimes targeting a very narrow audience. Besides, none of them tackles the family of problems addressed in the paper in the way uBuild does.

LTIB (Linux Target Image Builder)[5] has similar goals respect to uBuild, as it allows to build Linux-based filesystems for embedded devices. However, it uses a specific package manager (RPM) which can be unavailable on some host systems, and depends on a large number of software packages and libraries. uBuild, instead, is designed to be portable and to have a small number of dependencies (only a working C compiler, Python, and Bash).

Buildroot[6] is probably the most commonly used tool for building Linux-based embedded systems. Although a good tool for a wide variety of applications, buildroot comes with several limitations that make it hardly a good option for continuous integration and testing purposes. In particular, buildroot is strictly tied to a specific C library (uClibc) and does not allow to easily install packages that are not officially supported, or arbitrary versions of specific packages. Compiler flags tuning and patchsets handling are also not fully supported, and it is hard to maintain multiple configurations of the same system.

Cross Linux From Scratch (CLFS)[7] presents a different approach to building a Linux-based embedded system. As indicated in its official documentation, CLFS is "a project that provides you with step-by-step instructions for building your own customised Linux system entirely from source" . However, it does not provide most of the features needed by uBuild, such as the possibility to automate the system generation, an efficient build cache, etc...

Angstrom[8] is a Linux distribution based on the OpenEmbedded build framework[9], supporting a wide range of hardware architectures and offering an online

---

[5] http://ltib.org
[6] http://buildroot.uclibc.org
[7] http://www.cross-lfs.org
[8] http://www.angstrom-distribution.org
[9] http://www.openembedded.org

tool for generating and downloading custom "rootfs" images[10]. However, it does not provide much control on the software installed in the rootfs nor on the build options.

The Yocto project[11] is an "open source collaboration project that provides templates, tools and methods to help you create custom Linux-based systems for embedded products regardless of the hardware architecture". Hence, its main goal is to standardise the way embedded Linux images are generated by providing an open source development framework and compliance guidelines. However, as it happens with buildroot and Angstrom, the vertical architecture of Yocto does not help in building multiple variants of a system image containing different versions of the various packages, or using different patches and build flags (Yocto is a tool for creating Linux distributions and not something that can be easily used to assess a particular combination of *"input"* variables).

Portage[12] is a package management system specifically built for Gentoo Linux[13] that originally aimed at a good degree of operating system independence. However, recent versions of portage are not portable, and strictly depend on the host OS. Moreover, portage does not support cross compilation natively, which doesn't make it suitable to build embedded systems from scratch.

Many of the design choices taken in implementing uBuild have been consciously inherited from some of the software packages mentioned above. For example, while uBuild has different goals, it has to implement some sort of source-based package management system that builds source code, similarly to Portage. On the other hand, it uses a cross-compiler toolchain and install the generated binaries in a filesystem generated from scratch, similarly to buildroot and Angstrom/Yocto.

6 Conclusions

The process of evaluating and regression testing changes to an embedded system is, in general, expensive both in terms of time and money. Trial-and-error has always been the easiest way to evaluate benefits given by specific compile-time optimisations. Its complexity however, rapidly scales as the number of combinations to take into account grows, and with it, the risk of tainting the results with external, likely human, errors.

This paper presented a novel approach to performance evaluation and continuous testing of embedded Linux-based systems based on a tool, named uBuild, for the automated and controlled build of the embedded system image. uBuild is designed to offer an effective solution to the problems mentioned above, and relies on modern technological foundations: *declarative* configuration files, easy *extendibility* through shell scripts and *scalability* thanks to its efficient build cache.

---

[10] http://narcissus.angstrom-distribution.org

[11] https://www.yoctoproject.org

[12] http://www.gentoo.org/doc/en/handbook/handbook-x86.xml?part=2&chap=1

[13] http://www.gentoo.org

uBuild tries to ease and formalise the testing and performance evaluation process through a parametric "interface" that is specifically designed for generating multiple experimental scenarios, changing controlled sets of build parameters.

The determinism of the generated system images provides an effective framework for evaluating the performance benefits of specific compile options (for example, compile flags, linker flags) or specific patchsets.

References

1. Abeni, L., Buttazzo, G.: Integrating multimedia applications in hard real-time systems. In: Proceedings of the IEEE Real-Time Systems Symposium, Madrid, Spain (December 1998)
2. Chess, B., McGraw, G.: Static analysis for security. IEEE Security Privacy 2(6) (2004)
3. Detwiler, B.: Tabelts will replace pcs for many enterprise users (September 2011), http://www.techrepublic.com/blog/tr-dojo/tablets-will-replace-pcs-for -many-enterprise-users/
4. Dudak, J., Pavlikova, S., Gaspar, G., Kebisek, M.: Application of open source software on arm platform for data collection and processing. In: Proceedings of the 14th International Symposium MECHATRONIKA (2011)
5. Faggioli, D., Checconi, F., Trimarchi, M., Scordino, C.: An EDF scheduling class for the Linux kernel. In: Proceedings of the Eleventh Real-Time Linux Workshop, Dresden, Germany (September 2009)
6. Gartner, J.R., Meulen, R.V.D.: Gartner says worldwide pc, tablet and mobile phone combined shipments to reach 2.4 billion units in 2013 (April 2013), http://www.gartner.com/newsroom/id/2408515
7. Kroah-Hartman, G., Corbet, J., McPherson, A.: Linux kernel development: How fast it is going, who is doing it, what they are doing, and who is sponsoring it (2013 edition) (2013), http://www.linuxfoundation.org/publications/linux-foundation/who-writes-linux-2013
8. Lacoste, F.: Killing the gatekeeper: Introducing a continuous integration system. In: Proceedings of the Agile Conference (AGILE 2009), Chicago, IL (August 2009)
9. Lloyd, J.W.: Practical advantages of declarative programming. In: Proceedings of the Joint Conference on Declarative Programming, GULP-PRODE 1994 (September 1994)
10. Mitchell, D.J., Prince, T.: Automating build, test, and release with buildbot (2013), http://people.v.igoro.us/~dustin/buildbot-paper.pdf
11. Nimmer, J., Fallik, B., Martin, N., Chapin, J.: Continuous automated testing of sdr software. In: Proceedings of the 2006 Software Defined Radio Technical Conference (SDR 2006), Orlando, Florida (November 2006)
12. Plauger, P.J.: The standard C library, 1st edn. Prentice Hall PTR (1991)
13. Rostedt, S.: Internals of the rt patch. In: Proceedings of the Linux Symposium, Ottawa, Canada (June 2007)
14. Spinellis, D.: Software builders. IEEE Software 25(3) (2008)
15. Swartout, P.: Continuous Delivery and DevOps: A Quickstart Guide. Packt Publishing Ltd. (2012)
16. Weber, J., Rehkopf, A.: Description of a formalized approach to build reproducible linux images for a project-specific electronics platform. In: Proceedings of the 2nd International Conference on Adaptive Science Technology, ICAST 2009 (2009)

A Two-Tier Design Space Exploration Algorithm to Construct a GPU Performance Predictor

S. Ali Mirsoleimani[1], Ali Karami[1], and Farshad Khunjush[1,2,3]

[1] School of Electrical and Computer Engineering, Shiraz University, Shiraz, Iran
[2] Department of Electrical and Electronics Engineering, Hormozgan University,
Bandar Abbas, Iran
[3] School of Computer Science,
Institute for Research in Fundamental Sciences (IPM), Tehran, Iran
ali.mirsoleimani@gmail.com, {karami,khunjush}@cse.shirazu.ac.ir

Abstract. Graphics Processing Units (GPUs) have a large and complex design space that needs to be explored in order to optimize the performance of future GPUs. Statistical techniques are useful tools to help computer architects to predict performance of complex processors. In this study, these methods are utilized to build an effective performance prediction model for a Fermi GPU. The design space of this GPU is more than 8 million points. In order to build an accurate model, we propose a two-tier algorithm which builds a multiple linear regression model from a small set of simulated data. In this algorithm the Plackett and Burman design is used to find the key parameters of the GPU, and further simulations are guided by a fractional factorial design for the most important parameters. The generated performance model is able to predict the performance of any other point in the design space with an average prediction error between 1% to 5% for different benchmark applications. This accuracy is achieved by only sampling between 0.0003% to 0.0015% of the full design space.

1 Introduction

Computer architects try hard to design high performance microprocessors under restrictive power and technology constraints. The design space that has to be explored in order to evauate and find an optimal design is large. The recent trend towards many-core processors such as GPUs has aggravated this problem since interactions between various existing parameters occur.

Using cycle-accurate simulators such as GPGPU-Sim is a widely accepted solution for accurate performance evaluations of a GPU's micro-architecture [1]. It allows exploring the architecture design space through parameterization, i.e., running a simulation by changing simulator's parameters with a variety of proper benchmarks, in order to investigate the impact of an architecture feature or a novel design-idea. Unfortunately, with cycle-accurate simulators exploring the full design space requires long-running simulations that are frequently too costly. Therefore, architects need to restrict the number of design points that are evaluated.

E. Maehle et al. (Eds.): ARCS 2014, LNCS 8350, pp. 135–146, 2014.

Computer architects investigate the impact of GPU parameters such as cache size, latency, warp size as well as their interactions on performance by simulating different possible configurations of them. Simulating all possible configurations is really time consuming, therefore one can randomly generate and simulate some configurations [2]. However, this naive solution might involve unnecessary simulations because in GPU programming, a programmer does not necessarily use all the GPU features when optimizing their code. For example, one can omit shared memory, texture memory, or constant memory in writing a GPU program. A different approach is to explore the full design space systematically. For example, statistical-based experimental designs allow users to change the configurations of the simulator systematically and to investigate which GPU parameters have the greatest impact on performance. Therefore, it is desired to create a model of large micro-architectural design space from a small number of simulation samples. In our approach, we use statistical inference techniques to achieve this goal.

In this paper we propose to use statistical-based experimental designs for efficiently exploring the GPU design space. For this, we present a two-tier algorithm to prune the large GPU design space. The idea is to break up the exploration process into two steps to reduce the number of required simulations. In the first tier, the number of parameters may be large and the goal is to determine the relative effect of various parameters on the GPU performance. Therefore, the Plackett and Burman (P&B) design is used to explore the design space quickly and to prune the insignificant parameters in the design space. These parameters are not required to be included in further experiments. In the second tier, the number of parameters is reduced and we utilize a fractional factorial design to investigate the interactions between significant parameters. Using this technique we explore a small region of interest identified in the first tier.

The key contributions of this paper are:

1. Using the P&B design we prune the design space of a Fermi GPU architecture for 23 micro-architectural parameters. We find that this technique quickly shows GPU performance bottlenecks for each application, significantly decreasing the total number of required simulations to build a performance prediction model.
2. Using statistical experimental designs, a multiple linear regression model is constructed by sampling less than 0.0015% of design points from the full design space of 8M points. The proposed model achieves an average prediction error of less than 5%.

The remainder of this paper is organized as follows. Related work is presented in sect. 2. In sect. 3 and 4 statistical-base experimental designs and regression analysis are described. We give a brief background on GPU architecture in sect. 5 and our proposed algorithm is elaborated in sect. 6. In sect. 7, we describe our experimental methodology and setup. sect. 8 provides our experimental results and a detailed evaluation of the proposed model. Finally, we conclude the paper in sect. 9.

2   Related Work

Architectural design space exploration and performance modeling for GPUs have recently emerged as an interesting and important problem in computer architecture design. In contrast, the performance analysis for CPUs has a long history and there exist many methods for this purpose.

Lee et al. proposed a regression-based modeling approach to study the CPU design space [3]. Joseph et al. proposed an automatic iterative approach using a stepwise regression technique to automatically explore a CPU design space [4]. Their approach has been similar to ours. They also employ a regression technique and also achieve a good model accuracy with a small number of sampled simulations. Yi et al. [5] have explored significant micro-architectural parameters by conducting simulations based on the P&B design. However, their approach differs from our method in the way in which the P&B design is used. As the P&B design cannot quantify all the interactions between processor parameters, we use the P&B design to only identify significant parameters and then employ these parameters for performing further simulations.

In addition to studies of the CPU design, there have been a wide range of performance studies on GPUs from statistical to analytical methods. Jooya et al. [6] presented a method to optimize resource allocation in GPU architecture by using the P&B design to explore the design space of 4 GPU parameters. They formulate the problem as a constraint optimization problem. Jia et al. [2] proposed a design space exploration technique which simulates randomly selected design points from a GPU design space of 933K points. The design space is constructed from 10 GPU parameters. Next, they exploit the well-known stepwise regression technique to construct a performance model. Their model is trained with 0.03% of the full design space to predict any other design point with less than 1.1% error on average. Our work has some major differences. First, our design space has more than 8M points with 23 parameters and is based on the Fermi architecture. Second, instead of sampling design points randomly we choose them systematically using a novel algorithm. This approach causes a great reduction in number of required simulations for training the predictor model. Using this technique our method requires less than 0.0015% of the full design space to build accurate performance models.

3   Factorial Design

Factorial designs are frequently used in experiments involving several factors where it is necessary to study the joint effect of the factors on a response. In many cases, it is sufficient to consider the factors affecting the system at 2 high and low levels. A complete replicate of such a design requires at least 2^k observations which is called a 2^k factorial design or full factorial design. This kind of design is appropriate for studying the effects of GPU parameters, although the number of necessary simulations in the experiment increases geometrically due to large number of GPU parameters. For example, to study 10 parameters we require

$2^{10} = 1024$ runs in the experiment. Because each run is a time-consuming and costly simulation, it is not feasible to run many different simulations for the experiment.

As the full factorial design considers all relations among factors, the analysis takes a long time to investigate the design space. However, due to the sparsity-of-effects principle (i.e., the processor performance is usually dominated by main effects and low order interactions) [5][4] during early stages of the analysis, there is little interest in high-order interactions among different factors. Thus, a *fractional factorial* design, in which fewer runs is required, can be used to obtain information on the main effects and low-order interactions. In general, a full factorial design may be run in a $1/2^p$ fraction called a $2^{(k-p)}$ design. For example, a 1/4 fraction is called a $2^{(k-2)}$ design. Plackett and Burman [7] show how full factorial designs can be fractionalized in a different manner, to yield saturated designs where the number of runs is a multiple of 4, rather than a power of 2. This design has been named after them as the Plackett and Burman design.

3.1   The Plackett and Burman Design

We use a P&B design as a screening tool to determine which GPU parameters have the most effect on performance. Screening experiments are usually performed in early stages of a project when it is likely that many of the factors initially considered have little or no effect on the response. The factors that are identified as important are then investigated more thoroughly in subsequent experiments. The P&B design is efficient when we use design of experiments to learn as much as possible from the smallest amount of data.

In the P&B design, for each benchmark, the value of each parameter is given by a matrix. It requires as few as n runs to determine the main effects for k factors, where n is the next multiple of 4 greater than k. As an example, a P&B design with 11 factors and 12 runs is shown in Table 1. We have used "+1" and "-1" to denote the values of the high and low levels of a factor, respectively. The first row pattern determines the entire design. Each subsequent row is simply a circular right shift on the previous row. The final row is set to all "-1." Each row of this matrix represents a simulation configuration.

Running a benchmark for all the configurations, we measure a performance metric (PM) for each run. Then, the effect of each parameter is calculated by multiplying each parameter's value ("1" or "-1") to its corresponding PM value. The effect of each parameter is calculated by summing all of these products. For example, the effect of parameter D in 1 is computed as:

$Effect_D = 13 + (-14) + 18 + 22 + (-19) + 12 + (-23) + (-21) + (-15) + 14 + 20 + (-24) = -17$

The magnitude of the measured effect is used for ranking the parameters. The parameters that have higher ranks represent significant performance bottlenecks. It should be noticed that the P&B design does not reveal whether the effect of a parameter depends on another parameter. Therefore, we use it as a starting point for more detailed experimentation.

Table 1. Plackett and Burman matrix for 12 runs and 11 parameters

Run	A	B	C	D	E	F	G	H	I	J	K	PM
1	+1	+1	-1	+1	+1	+1	-1	-1	-1	+1	-1	13
2	-1	+1	+1	-1	+1	+1	+1	-1	-1	-1	+1	14
3	+1	-1	+1	+1	-1	+1	+1	+1	-1	-1	-1	18
4	-1	+1	-1	+1	+1	-1	+1	+1	+1	-1	-1	22
5	-1	-1	+1	-1	+1	+1	-1	+1	+1	+1	-1	19
6	-1	-1	-1	+1	-1	+1	+1	-1	+1	+1	+1	12
7	+1	-1	-1	-1	+1	-1	+1	+1	-1	+1	+1	23
8	+1	+1	-1	-1	-1	+1	-1	+1	+1	-1	+1	21
9	+1	+1	+1	-1	-1	-1	+1	-1	+1	+1	-1	15
10	-1	+1	+1	+1	-1	-1	-1	+1	-1	+1	+1	14
11	+1	-1	+1	+1	+1	-1	-1	-1	+1	-1	+1	20
12	-1	-1	-1	-1	-1	-1	-1	-1	-1	-1	-1	24
Effect			-17									

4   Multiple Linear Regression

Regression analysis is a statistical technique for modeling and investigating the relationships between one dependent variable (response variable) and one or more independent variables in a given design space [8]. This technique can be utilized to predict a GPU performance based on the values of micro-architectural parameters.

Many applications of regression analysis involve situations in which there are more than one independent variable. A regression model containing more than one independent variable is called a multiple linear regression model. For example, a system with one response variable y and k independent variables $x_j, j = 1, 2, ..., k$ can be modeled as:

$$y = \beta_0 + \beta_1 x_1 + \beta_2 x_2 + ... + \beta_k x_k + \epsilon \tag{1}$$

where parameters $\beta_j, j = 0, 1, 2, ..., k$ are the regression coefficients and ϵ is a random error term. The term linear is used because (1) is a linear function of the unknown parameters β_j. This model describes a hyperplane in the k-dimensional space of the independent variables x_j.

A multiple linear regression may also be used to model the interactions between independent variables. An interaction between two variables can be represented by a cross-product term in the model, such as:

$$y = \beta_0 + \beta_1 x_1 + \beta_2 x_2 + \beta_{12} x_1 x_2 + \epsilon \tag{2}$$

4.1   Transformation

It has been shown that a non-linear function can be expressed as a linear model by using a suitable transformation of response variables. For example, Joseph et al. [4] show that such transformations might result in response surfaces that are more linear and easier to fit for CPU processors. On the other hand, it has been shown that GPU micro-architectural parameters and their interactions exhibit strong and highly nonlinear impacts on the performance of applications [2]. Therefore, we consider to apply a proper transformation to map from a non-linear space to a linear one. For this, several transformations such as $1/y$, $log(y)$ and $\sqrt{y}$ have been examined and the $log(y)$ transformation exhibits the best performance among them. We use this transformation to linearize the GPU design space.

4.2   Prediction

Once the performance prediction model is determined, to analyze the accuracy of predictions made by the model, for each benchmark an independent test set of 1000 design points are randomly selected from full design space. They are simulated to measure their actual performance. These 1000 samples are different from those used for constructing the model. The predicted performance for each of these points is measured using the constructed performance model, then using (3), the prediction error (PE) for each of them is calculated. The reported average and maximum errors, are the mean and maximum across all 1000 tests.

$$PE = |(predicted - Actual)/Actual| * 100\% \tag{3}$$

5   GPU Architecture

GPUs are processors with hundreds of processing cores which provide high throughput and high memory-bandwidth. The building blocks of a GPU architecture are streaming multiprocessors (SMs). A Fermi-based multiprocessor GPU leverages a SIMT (Single-Instruction, Multiple-Thread) architecture and includes 32 SIMD (Single-Instruction, Multiple-Data) Streaming Processors (SPs). A SM executes a group of 32 threads concurrently, called a warp [9]. Each SM consists of 64 KB of SRAM that can be partitioned between the L1 cache and a shared memory. The GPU also contains 64 KB of read-only constant cache and 4 texture units backed by 12 KB of texture cache. A Fermi-based GPU includes a 384-bit memory interface divided into 6 independent 64-bit partitions. Each partition has two 32-bit GDDR5 DRAMs. This arrangement supports up to a total of 6-GB of DRAM memory [9]. There exist two types of memories: off-chip and on-chip memories. The off-chip memories, which are the largest but slowest memories, include global, constant, and texture memories which are shared among all threads. The off-chip memories contain large amount of spaces with high latency. The Fermi-based GPU architecture provides two levels of caches (i.e., L1 and L2 caches) to exploit data locality within each SM which can be leveraged to hide the latency of global memory transactions. This architecture also includes four more types of on-chip caches for each SM named *Instruction*, *Local*, *Constant*, and *Texture*.

6   Proposed Model Construction Algorithm

Algorithm 1 shows our model construction procedure for predicting GPU performance. This procedure takes k parameters, ranges of parameters value r, model prediction error threshold t, and number of tries i as its inputs. This algorithm has two tiers:

Tier 1 Screening: This step of the algorithm reduces the maximum number of parameters in the design space to only those which have significant effects on GPU performance. Therefore, we just need to focus on points in the design space that are touched by these parameters. This is really important because not all GPU candidate parameters are necessary to adequately model GPU performance.

A P&B design is constructed for k GPU candidate parameters. For each row of the P&B matrix, we modified the configuration file of the simulator and ran a simulation. The performance metric for each run is collected. Afterwards, we

---

Algorithm 1. Two-tier design space exploration algorithm

Require: Parameters $p_1, p_2, ..., p_k$
Require: Ranges of parameters value $r_1, r_2, ..., r_k$
Require: Prediction error threshold t
Require: Number of tries i
Require: Test set size S
Require: Initial number of important parameters m
  1: Create an initial P&B design for k parameters and X experiments
  2: Simulate all the experiments in the design and measure the performance metric y for all of them

  3: **for** Each $p \in p_1, p_2, ..., p_k$ **do**
  4:      **for** $j = 1$ to number of experiments in X **do**
  5:          Effect(p)=$\sum(X_{jp}y_j)$
  6:      **end for**
  7: **end for**
  8: Sort the parameters based on their effect
  9: Randomly choose S design points from full design space as test set
 10: Simulate all the points in the test set and measure the actual performance metric for them
 11: Select m most important parameters
 12: $n = 1$
 13: **while** APE $\leq t$ or $n \leq i$ **do**
 14:      **if** $m \leq 7$ **then**
 15:          $p = 0$
 16:      **else**
 17:          $p = \log_2(2^m/128)$
 18:      **end if**
 19:      Create a $2^{(m-p)}$ factorial design for m parameters
 20:      Simulate all the experiments in the design and measure the performance metric for all of them
 21:      Obtain a multiple linear regression model L using a stepwise regression technique
 22:      Measure the average prediction error of s design points in test set using model L
 23:      $APE = 0$
 24:      **for** Each $s \in$ test set **do**
 25:          $APE+ = |(predict(s)byL - actual(s))/actual(s)|$
 26:      **end for**
 27:      $APE/ = S$
 28:      $m+ = 1$
 29:      $n+ = 1$
 30: **end while**
 31: **return** L as the final model

---

rank the parameters based on their importance. The sorted parameters resulting from this tier are stored to be used in the subsequent tier of the algorithm.

Tier 2 Modeling: In this phase the algorithm attempts to build the most accurate prediction equation. Once the sorted parameters are available, a fractional factorial design is constructed using m most important parameters. The value of m can be any number from 1 to the number of parameters. If the value of m was greater than 7, then the algorithm calculates the value of p in such a way that no more than 128 simulations are required. For each row of the newly created design matrix we run a simulation and compute the performance metric.

Once the performance measurements for all rows are available, the algorithm tries to build a multiple linear regression model using a stepwise regression method. This is the most widely used variable selection technique for model construction [8]. Then constructed model L is used to measure the average of predict error of the design points in the test set.

This procedure repetitively selects the next $m + 1$ significant parameters to build a new performance model until a specific prediction error threshold is met or the maximum number of tries i is passed.

7   Experimental Setup

We use some applications with reasonable execution time from GPGPU-Sim [1] and Rodinia [10] benchmarks. The selected applications are listed in Table 2. In this study, a cycle-level GPU PTX-ISA simulator, GPGPU-Sim [1], is chosen to run the benchmarks. The simulation results are reported as instruction per cycle (IPC). This is the performance metric which is used as response variable. We implemented Algorithm 1 by using *STATISTICA*, a software environment for statistical analysis, which takes the required inputs and completed simulation experimental data, and performs the propose model construction algorithm by providing accurate coefficient estimates.

Table 2. Benchmark programs

Suit	Name	Abr.	Description
GPGU-Sim	3D Laplace Solver	LPS	3D Laplace equation solver
	Ray Tracing	RAY	Graphics rendering of lighting effects
	StoreGPU	STO	Sliding-window-based MD5 calculation
	Coulombic Potential	CP	Calculate Coulombic potential in molecular dynamics
	Breadth First Search	BFS	Breadth-first search on a graph
Rodinia	Back Propagation	BP	Training weights in a layered neural network
	Breadth First Search	BFS_r	Breadth-first search on a graph
	Gaussian Elimination	GS	Linear system solver using Gaussian elimination
	Hot Spot	HS	Microprocessor thermal modeling on a 2D grid
	Needleman Wunsch	NW	Parallel Needleman-Wunsch algorithm for DNA sequencing

Table 3 lists 47 micro-architectural parameters and their value ranges. We have configured the simulator based on these values. Among them 24 parameters are held constant in our experiments. The design space for other 23 parameters has 8,388,608 unique design points. We select the high and low values of our parameters based on findings in several other studies, including [2] [1] [10]. All parameters are chosen considering the NVIDIA Fermi GTX 480 GPU. Those parameters that are held constant in the experiments are shown. Due to the simulator constraints, the L2 block size is set to 256 bytes.

Table 3. Micro-architectural parameters and their value ranges

Parameter	Abr.	Fix	Unit	Low	High
Instruction Cache Size/SM	il1_size	No	KB	1	32
Instruction Cache Associativity	il1_assoc	No	way	2	4
Instruction Cache Block Size	il1_bsize	No	byte	32	256
Instruction Cache Repl. Policy	il1_rep	Yes	type	LRU	
L1 Data Cache Size/SM	dl1_size	No	KB	8	64
L1 Data Cache Associativity	dl1_assoc	No	way	8	32
L1 Data Cache Block Size	dl1_bsize	No	byte	128	256
L1 Data Cache Repl. Policy	dl1_rep	Yes	type	LRU	
L2 Data Cache Size	dl2_size	No	KB	64	256
L2 Data Cache Associativity	dl2_assoc	No	way	8	32
L2 Data Cache Block Size	dl2_bsize	Yes	byte	256	256
L2 Data Cache Repl. Policy	dl2_rep	Yes	type	LRU	
L2 Data Chache Latency	dl2_lat	No	cycle	60	240
Texture Cache Size/SM	tl1_size	No	KB	1	32
Texture Cache Associativity	tl1_assoc	No	way	2	4
Texture Cache Block Size	tl1_bsize	No	byte	32	256
Texture Cache Repl. Policy	tl1_rep	Yes	type	LRU	
Constant Cache Size/SM	cl1_size	No	KB	1	32
Constant Cache Associativity	cl1_assoc	No	way	1	4
Constant Cache Block Size	cl1_bsize	No	byte	16	128
Constant Cache Repl. Policy	cl1_rep	Yes	type	LRU	
Shared Memory Number of Banks	shmem_nbanks	No	num	16	64
Shared Memory Size/SM	shmem_size	Yes	KB	48	
Number of Memory Controller	n_mem_ctrlr	Yes	num	4	8
Number of DRAM Chips / Controller	n_chips	Yes	num	2	
DRAM Clock Frequency	dram_freq	Yes	MHz	1848	
DRAM Scheduler Queue Size	dram_sched_qsize	No	num	8	32
DRAM Bus Width	dram_buswidth	Yes	bytes	4	8
DRAM type	dram_type	Yes	type	GDDR5	
DRAM Latency	dram_latency	No	cycle	50	200
Core Clock Frequency	core_freq	Yes	MHz	700	
SIMD Pipeline Width	simd_width	No	num	16	64
Number of Blocks / SM	n_blocks	No	num	1	16
Number of Register / SM	n_registers	No	num	16384	65536
Number of Threads / SM	n_threads	No	num	768	2048
Number of Scheduler / SM	n_sched	No	num	1	4
Number of register banks	n_reg_banks	Yes	num	8	32
Topology	topo	Yes	type	butterfly	
Routing	rout	Yes	type	Destination tag	
Virtual Channels	vc	Yes	count	1	
VC Buffer Size	vc_bufsize	Yes	byte	8	
Flit Size	f_size	Yes	byte	32	

8 Experimental Results

8.1 Screening Results

Table 4 shows the results of the screening tier with parameter values shown
in Table 3. This table shows the ranks of 23 parameters for all benchmarks.
As shown, the ranks of the parameters of different benchmarks are completely
different. Therefore, In the screening step, the most important GPU parameters
for each benchmark are found. Using these parameters we can build an accurate
model with minimum number of simulations.

The parameters which have the lower average ranks are significant across most
of the benchmarks. In other words, the high rank parameters are the biggest
performance bottlenecks in the GPU and determine the execution time of a
benchmark. Therefore, they should be included in further experiments in order
to build the performance model.

The effect of each benchmark on GPU performance can be defined as the
performance bottlenecks when running that application. For example, for *BFS*
and *BFS_r*, since the *dl1_size* ranked first among parameters, the performance
of memory accesses is the most limiting factor. For benchmarks that utilize large
amounts of memory, the *dl2_lat* will be likely a performance bottleneck. On the
other hand, for a computation-intensive benchmarks, the *simd_width* may be a
performance bottleneck.

Table 4. P&B design result for all GPU parameters

Parameters	BFS	LPS	RAY	STO	CP	BP	BFS_r	GS	HS	NW	Avg. Rank
n_blocks	4	1	3	1	2	1	8	6	4	4	3.40
dl2_lat	2	11	7	9	4	8	2	1	7	1	5.20
simd_width	12	2	2	3	1	2	14	3	1	16	5.60
shmem_nbanks	5	4	4	4	5	4	22	18	3	10	7.90
dram_lat	18	3	6	8	10	3	13	8	6	5	8.00
n_sched	14	5	8	7	6	7	10	7	9	8	8.10
dram_sched_qsize	13	6	11	14	9	5	5	4	10	9	8.60
il1_bsize	9	13	13	5	7	11	6	2	23	3	9.20
n_registers	11	8	5	6	11	6	9	17	2	17	9.20
dl1_size	1	12	14	12	20	12	1	9	13	11	10.50
il1_size	17	18	1	2	23	18	12	12	5	2	11.00
tl1_bsize	10	9	9	10	17	9	15	23	14	19	13.50
dl2_size	6	22	19	21	12	14	4	20	19	6	14.30
cl1_assoc	21	14	15	15	13	15	18	5	21	7	14.40
dl1_bsize	3	15	23	19	8	21	3	19	18	22	15.10
dl2_assoc	22	10	16	22	16	13	23	11	8	13	15.40
n_threads	16	7	21	23	18	10	17	16	12	15	15.50
tl1_assoc	7	21	20	16	14	22	7	22	16	14	15.90
dl1_assoc	19	16	12	11	22	20	21	10	17	12	16.00
tl1_size	15	23	10	13	19	19	19	13	11	18	16.00
il1_assoc	8	20	17	18	15	16	11	21	15	23	16.40
cl1_size	20	19	18	17	3	17	20	14	22	20	17.00
cl1_bsize	23	17	22	20	21	23	16	15	20	21	19.80

Table 5. Summary of average and maximum of prediction error

Suit	m	# of Sim.	BFS (%)		LPS (%)		CP (%)		STO (%)		RAY (%)	
			Avg.	Max	Avg.	Max	Avg.	Max	Avg.	Max	Avg	Max
	5	32	1.73	14.34	3.67	13.24	4.64	25.70	6.62	23.82	8.56	42.89
GPGPU-Sim	6	64	--		3.66	13.35	3.53	24.24	6.35	18.35	8.48	42.91
	7	128	--		3.05	13.56	3.39	23.16	4.96	18.16	7.37	30.50
	8	128	--		2.65	7.39	3.38	22.70	4.86	18.60	5.85	31.81
			BP		BFS_r		GS		HS		NW	
			Avg.	Max	Avg.	Max	Avg.	Max	Avg.	Max	Avg.	Max
	5	32	4.30	11.94	2.95	11.58	2.56	20.75	7.71	33.40	3.19	10.91
Rodinia	6	64	3.67	9.23	2.84	11.39	2.06	20.75	7.19	33.95	1.78	10.61
	7	128	2.61	8.79	2.82	11.25	1.74	20.83	6.17	27.23	--	
	8	128	--		--		--		5.72	27.61	--	

8.2 Modeling Results

Our model construction algorithm builds a performance prediction model with minimum number of simulations. Table 5 reports the maximum number of parameters in the model, required simulations, the average prediction error, and the maximum prediction error for each benchmark. In order to construct the performance model for each benchmark the prediction error threshold is set to t=2, and the number of tries is set to i=3. In the case of undesirable accuracy one additional try is run for some benchmarks.

We observed that, the constructed model for GS, NW, and BFS can predict the performance with an average error of less than 2%. To reach this level of accuracy we just need to simulate 128, 64, and 32 points, respectively. The model for LPS, CP, BP, and BFS_r is able to predict with an average error of 3% or less than that using just 128 simulations. The average errors of the model for RAY, STO, and HS are about 5% and less than that. As can be seen, our method does not need more than 128 simulations.

As mentioned in sect. 2, the most similar work to ours is [2]. Although our design space is completely different and almost 8 times larger, a comparison between these two approaches reveals interesting results. In [2], they required 300 simulations to construct their model with average prediction error of about 1% for all of the benchmarks. However, our algorithm only needs less than 128 simulations to build a model with average prediction errors between 1% to 5% for different benchmarks. It is also important to consider the maximum error of prediction. In [2], the maximum error is about 50% when the number of simulations is less than 100. In our approach, the maximum error of the model among all of the benchmarks is 42%, when there are just 32 simulations, and it can be reduced to 31% by having 128 simulations.

9 Conclusion

In this paper a two-tier algorithm has been proposed for design space exploration and constructing a performance model for a GPU design space. Our method presents useful techniques in terms of pruning insignificant parameters on GPU performance when running an application. In the first tier of the algorithm, the Plackett and Burman design is used for pruning the design space, and in the second tier a fractional factorial design is utilized to investigate the interactions between the most effective parameters. Our approach reduces the number of required simulations for building an accurate performance model significantly (128 out of 8M). In future work, we plan to increase the levels of parameters value to more than 2 in order to investigate the effectiveness of our approach on larger design spaces.

Acknowledgment. This work was supported in part by School of Computer Science, Institute for Research in Fundamental Sciences (IPM) under grant number CS1391-4-03.

References

1. Bakhoda, A., Yuan, G.G.L., Fung, W.W.W.L., Wong, H., Aamodt, T.M.: Analyzing CUDA workloads using a detailed GPU simulator. In: 2009 IEEE International Symposium on Performance Analysis of Systems and Software, ISPASS 2009, pp. 163–174. IEEE (April 2009)
2. Jia, W., Shaw, K.A., Martonosi, M.: Stargazer: Automated Regression-Based GPU Design Space Exploration. In: IEEE International Symposium on Performance Analysis of Systems and Software, ISPASS (2012)
3. Lee, B., Brooks, D.: Accurate and efficient regression modeling for microarchitectural performance and power prediction. In: Proceedings of the 12th International Conference on Architectural Support for Programming Languages and Operating Systems, vol. 40, pp. 185–194. ACM (October 2006)
4. Joseph, P., Vaswani, K., Thazhuthaveetil, M.: Construction and Use of Linear Regression Models for Processor Performance Analysis. In: The Twelfth International Symposium on High-Performance Computer Architecture, pp. 99–108. IEEE (2006)
5. Yi, J., Lilja, D., Hawkins, D.: Improving computer architecture simulation methodology by adding statistical rigor. IEEE Transactions on Computers 54(11), 1360–1373 (2005)
6. Jooya, A., Baniasadi, A., Dimopoulos, N.J.: Efficient design space exploration of GPGPU architectures. In: Caragiannis, I., Alexander, M., Badia, R.M., Cannataro, M., Costan, A., Danelutto, M., Desprez, F., Krammer, B., Sahuquillo, J., Scott, S.L., Weidendorfer, J. (eds.) Euro-Par Workshops 2012. LNCS, vol. 7640, pp. 518–527. Springer, Heidelberg (2013)
7. Plackett, R., Burman, J.: The Design of Optimum Multifactorial Experiments. Biometrika 33(4), 305–325 (1946)
8. Montgomery, D.C., Runger, G.C.: Applied Statistics and Probability for Engineers, 5th edn. John Wiley & Sons (2010)
9. NVIDA: Whitepaper NVIDIA's Next Generation CUDA Compute Architecture: Fermi (2009)
10. Che, S., Boyer, M., Meng, J., Tarjan, D., Sheaffer, J.W., Lee, S.H., Skadron, K.: Rodinia: A benchmark suite for heterogeneous computing. In: 2009 IEEE International Symposium on Workload Characterization IISWC 2009(c), pp. 44–54 (2009)

A Sensor Network Architecture
for Urban Traffic State Estimation
with Mixed Eulerian/Lagrangian Sensing
Based on Distributed Computing

Edward Canepa, Enas Odat, Ahmad Dehwah, Mustafa Mousa,
Jiming Jiang, and Christian Claudel

King Abdullah University of Science and Technology, Thuwal 23955, Saudi Arabia
`firstname.lastname@kaust.edu.sa`

Abstract. This article describes a new approach to urban traffic flow
sensing using decentralized traffic state estimation. Traffic sensor data is
generated both by fixed traffic flow sensor nodes and by probe vehicles
equipped with a short range transceiver. The data generated by these
sensors is sent to a local coordinator node, that poses the problem of
estimating the local state of traffic as a mixed integer linear program
(MILP). The resulting optimization program is then solved by the nodes
in a distributed manner, using branch-and-bound methods. An optimal
amount of noise is then added to the maps before dissemination to a
central database. Unlike existing probe-based traffic monitoring systems,
this system does not transmit user generated location tracks nor any
user presence information to a centralized server, effectively preventing
privacy attacks. A simulation of the system performance on computer-
generated traffic data shows that the system can be implemented with
currently available technology.

1 Introduction

Traffic congestion is an increasing concern in large urban areas of the world,
and is expected to become worse as global traffic demand increases. While traffic control methods such as ramp metering, adaptive speed limits and demand
response could solve the problem to a certain extent, such methods require as
an input accurate traffic density, velocity and flow estimates.

In the recent years, probe vehicles (*i.e.* vehicles containing speed and/or position sensors) have emerged as a possible solution to the traffic monitoring
problem. Probe sensing offers the potential for low cost sensing (in contrast
to expensive fixed traffic sensor networks), in particular when sensing relies on
existing devices (for instance smartphones), see for instance [24]. Nevertheless,
all current probe-based traffic monitoring systems require users to send their
location data to a centralized server, which carries high risks of user privacy intrusion whenever the location data servers are attacked. It should be noted that
even anonymous location tracks can yield substantial information on users [17],

E. Maehle et al. (Eds.): ARCS 2014, LNCS 8350, pp. 147–158, 2014.

which can be correlated with social network data to identify user identity based on their tracks. Such privacy risks are one of the main reasons preventing the large-scale implementation of cheap transceivers and positioning devices on all vehicles (despite the considerable societal benefits), specially since the recent PRISM revelations.

Several attempts to address the user privacy issues in probe-based traffic monitoring systems have been made [18]. All techniques either modify the sampling characteristics [14] (locations of samples, sampling rate) or attempt to obfuscate the real data trace by either removing data points or adding fake data points (or noise). A spatial sampling method called *virtual trip lines* (VTLs) is proposed in [15], to prevent users from sending their data whenever they are close to locations that could help identify them (home, workplace). However, this method is not applicable for traffic monitoring in urban environments since most urban areas are either workplaces or accommodations. Another obfuscation method is shown in [21], but the same article shows that generating fake data to hide real location tracks is challenging, even with aggregated statistical data.

The above privacy issues can only addressed at the system level if the system estimates the traffic flow conditions in a decentralized manner, since a central server receiving user data (even temporarily) would be a primary target for a privacy attack. In this article, we propose a new heterogenous sensor network architecture for traffic flow sensing in which user-generated data is processed by the nodes of the sensor network, possibly together with data generated by existing traffic sensors, to generate traffic estimates directly. By construction of this system, no information related to the presence of any user located outside of the radio range of a cluster (of configurable size) can be inferred.

This article is organized as follows. We present the sensing paradigm in section 2, including the distributed computing aspect of the system. We then study the privacy properties of the resulting system in section 3, with an analysis of the possible privacy attack scenarios. We then present in section 5 an ongoing wireless sensor network implementation (with currently no distributed computing algorithms implemented), with an associated simulation of the performance of the system.

2   Sensing Paradigm

2.1   Current Architecture of Probe-Based Traffic Sensing Systems

Probe-based traffic sensing systems follow typical sensor network architectures, in which data generated by sensors is sent to a centralized server for processing or display [22]. Traffic speed and/or density maps are the end product for the user, and the basis of all other location-based services such as travel time estimation or optimal routing. The architecture of such systems is illustrated in Figure 1.

One of the major drawbacks of such systems is the fact that the ID proxy server holds privacy sensitive information regarding the users. Privacy of users is at risk even when data is anonymized [17], therefore even the input database of the system can contain privacy sensitive data. While some systems [22] attempt

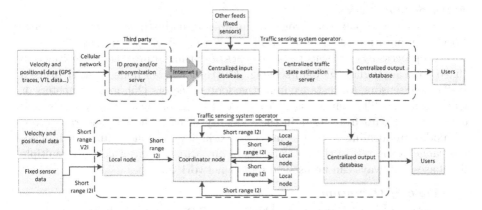

Fig. 1. Traffic monitoring systems architectures
Up: current systems. The data generated by users is sent to a proxy server for obfuscation/anonymization . The resulting data is then sent to an input database that also collects data from the existing fixed sensor infrastructure (if it exists). The resulting data is the fused with traffic flow models (a process sometimes referred to as *data assimilation*) to generate traffic maps. The resulting estimates are sent to an output database, which is queried by the users.
Down: proposed system. In the proposed system, traffic estimation is integrated to the wireless sensor network, which computes the traffic maps in each cluster using distributed computing. The resulting traffic maps are then forwarded to an output database.

to solve the privacy problem using data obfuscation or specific spatial sampling strategies [15], it is important to note that none of these strategies can guarantee that user privacy is preserved in all situations. In particular, no sampling strategy can prevent the identification of the approximate path whenever only one user is present in a given geographical area (the extent of which depends on the vehicle speed and the sampling rate).

Since user location and velocity information is required by the model to build the traffic maps, and since a centralized server handing user data can always be a target of attacks, the above privacy issues can be solved only if the information about the user location and velocity is used locally. This implies that the traffic state estimation process, which consists in fusing traffic flow data with traffic flow models, can only be done locally (for instance by the sensor nodes themselves). In this approach, privacy-critical information (location tracks) are not sent to a centralized location, and remain in a small (configurable) area around the probe vehicle.

2.2 Proposed System Architecture

Our proposed system consists in an heterogenous wireless sensor network, connected to a centralized output database. The database itself can directly be queried by the clients, or feed other on-demand location based services such as optimal routing or travel time estimation.

Fixed Sensor Nodes

The sensor nodes play three roles: communication (in the wireless sensor network), computation (distributed traffic inference, vehicle positioning, fixed sensor data processing) and sensing. Two types of sensing approaches exist: Eulerian (fixed) or Lagrangian (mobile) sensing. *Eulerian sensing* nodes consist in fixed traffic flow sensors, for instance inductive loop detectors [25], magnetometers or traffic cameras. The remaining nodes are called *Lagrangian sensing* nodes, and collect traffic data from users in their vicinity using a short range transceiver. All nodes are forming a wireless mesh network. The output database is in wireless range of the rest of the network. As in any wireless sensor network multiple databases/gateways can be used to reduce network load.

Principle of Operation

The network of fixed nodes is divided into clusters. In a given cluster, the nodes form a subnetwork (for traffic estimation purposes) to compute the local traffic conditions. Clusters can communicate between each other, though the only data sent by a cluster to another is anonymized traffic maps. A local coordinator node is chosen in each subnetwork.

Probe vehicles broadcast their location and/or speed information to surrounding Lagrangian sensing nodes, which temporarily store this data as well as network connectivity data (RSSI, CRC). All location (if any), speed and connectivity data is forwarded to the local coordinator node. If no positional information is available to probe vehicles, the coordinator node estimates the corresponding vehicle positions in the road network using inputs from surrounding nodes. Vehicle mapping can be done through a variety of methods, for example using RSSI data.

In addition to the data transmitted from local Lagrangian sensing nodes, the coordinator receives traffic data generated by Eulerian sensor nodes in the subnetwork.

Since traffic data is sparse and of different nature, reconstructing the state of traffic everywhere requires the combination of available data with traffic flow models, a process sometimes referred to as *data assimilation*. In our present case, we consider all incoming traffic data during the time window $[t - \Delta t, t]$ to estimate the traffic state at time t. The data assimilation method used in this article is outlined in the subsequent sections.

While no user information is directly present in this traffic map, it may nonetheless reveal user presence in some circumstances. To make the system completely privacy preserving, one needs to obfuscate the presence of users in the resulting maps (a problem that all traffic monitoring systems have, irrespective of their internal mechanisms). Such methods are detailed in section 3.

The anonymized density maps are then forwarded by other clusters to a central database for dissemination to the users, using multi-hop communication.

3 User Privacy Analysis

3.1 Threat Model

In this article, we assume that attackers can compromise any part of the system, that is, any individual node, any local coordinator, and any output database.

3.2 Properties of the System

By construction, no vehicle track information can be obtained beyond the radio range of the cluster in which the vehicle lies. Thus, an eavesdropper can "track" a vehicle's position only if he/she can listen to all clusters in the path of the vehicle. While such a distributed attack is theoretically possible, it is very costly and impractical, requiring the deployment of listening nodes in all clusters (which have independent encryption keys).

3.3 Privacy Attacks and Countermeasures

Compromising a Local Coordinator. Since all information in a cluster is handled by the local coordinator, the worst-case attack is to compromise it to obtain the position or velocities of all vehicles in the cluster (though these positions remain anonymous). Other attacks would result in partial knowledge of the position of vehicles in the radio range of the attacker.

This type of attack can be countered in two ways. First, the size of a cluster can be made arbitrarily small, to minimize the extent of the privacy intrusion. There is a tradeoff though, as smaller size will yield less accurate results for the estimation process due to the uncertainty in the estimated boundary conditions.

Another strategy is to change the coordinator node in the cluster periodically, using a scheduler or according to other constraints such as energy or bandwidth. Thus, an attacker compromising a coordinator would have limited knowledge (in time) of the presence of vehicles. Since it cannot be inferred which node will be a coordinator in advance (for instance if the scheduling is random), an attacker would have to physically compromise all nodes in a cluster to guarantee an access to the vehicle positions.

Possible Attacks. Based on these results, an attacker that wants to reidentify the track of a given vehicle has to compromise either all nodes in the path of the vehicle, or all coordinators in all clusters in the path of the vehicle. Thus, the system is only vulnerable to distributed privacy attacks (distributed eavesdropping).

Given the cost of such an attack (installing transceivers around all nodes, and breaking the encryption keys of all clusters), it is probably easier for an attacker to implement its own monitoring network to listen to vehicle communications directly. The system would be vulnerable to this type of attack, though an additional wireless sensor network deployed in a city would probably be detected sooner or later through its radio emissions.

Compromising an Output Database. By compromising an output database (there may be one or many output databases for the complete network), an attacker can only gain access to anonymized traffic maps (since these are the only information sent to the databases), which are also public.

While no track information from a cluster is not propagated beyond its radio range, traffic maps are propagated beyond each cluster to reach a gateway. Thus, the privacy of the user is maintained only if the problem of reconstructing trajectories from traffic maps (speed and/or density maps) does not yield a unique solution. Different anonymization strategies are possible to increase the number of solutions to the previous problem. One of the possible strategies could be the use of k-anonymity techniques [19] to determine the optimal level of noise to apply, in order to guarantee that a user is indistinguishable from others.

Note that while inferring vehicle positions from traffic maps is theoretically possible from any traffic map, it is difficult for two main reasons: low accuracy of current traffic systems, and security through obscurity from traffic providers. A wireless sensor network should not rely on security through obscurity as it is relatively easy to access one node (the code is identical in all nodes) and decompile its code.

4   Distributed Computing for Traffic State Estimation

The data assimilation scheme is based on the seminal *Lighthill Whitham Richards* [20] (LWR) traffic flow model, a first order scalar conservation law, with triangular flux function. It is here based on a decomposition of the solutions using the inf-morphism property of the solutions to the *Hamilton Jacobi* equation from which the LWR model is derived [8,9]. Using this decomposition, we write the problem of estimating traffic density on a section of road as a mixed integer linear program (MILP) [6]. The solution to the MILP correspond to a vector of current traffic densities, which can be interpreted as a traffic density map.

4.1   Input Data

Specifically, on each segment of road, the input data can take any of the following forms.

**Definition 41 *[Affine initial, boundary and internal conditions]* ** *Let us define* $\mathbb{K} = \{0, \ldots, k_{\max}\}$, $\mathbb{N} = \{0, \ldots, n_{\max}\}$ *and* $\mathbb{M} = \{0, \ldots, m_{\max}\}$. *For all* $k \in \mathbb{K}$, $n \in \mathbb{N}$ *and* $m \in \mathbb{M}$, *we define the following functions, respectively called initial, upstream, downstream (boundary) and internal conditions:*

$$M_k(t,x) = \begin{cases} -\sum_{i=0}^{k-1} \rho(i)X \\ -\rho(k)(x-kX) \text{ if } t=0 \\ \quad \text{and } x \in [kX, (k+1)X] \\ +\infty \qquad \text{otherwise} \end{cases}$$

$$\gamma_n(t,x) = \begin{cases} \sum_{i=0}^{n-1} q_{\text{in}}(i)T \\ +q_{\text{in}}(n)(t-nT) \text{ if } x=\xi \\ \quad \text{and } t \in [nT, (n+1)T] \\ +\infty \qquad \text{otherwise} \end{cases}$$

$$\beta_n(t,x) = \begin{cases} \sum_{i=0}^{n-1} q_{\text{out}}(i)T \\ +q_{\text{out}}(n)(t-nT) \\ -\sum_{k=0}^{k_{max}} \rho(k)X \text{ if } x=\chi \\ \quad \text{and } t \in [nT, (n+1)T] \\ +\infty \qquad \text{otherwise} \end{cases}$$

$$\mu_m(t,x) = \begin{cases} L_m + r_m(t - t_{\min}(m)) \\ (\text{if } x = x_{\min}(m) \\ +\frac{x_{\max}(m)-x_{\min}(m)}{t_{\max}(m)-t_{\min}(m)}(t-t_{\min}(m)) \\ \quad \text{and } t \in [t_{\min}(m), t_{\max}(m)]) \\ +\infty \qquad \text{otherwise} \end{cases}$$

The LWR model [20] is encoded by the following Hamilton-Jacobi [9] partial differential equation:

$$\frac{\partial \mathbf{M}(t,x)}{\partial t} - \psi\left(-\frac{\partial \mathbf{M}(t,x)}{\partial x}\right) = 0 \tag{1}$$

The function $\psi(\cdot)$ defined in equation (1) is the *Hamiltonian*. The B-J/F [4,13] solutions to equation (1) are fully characterized by a *Lax-Hopf* formula [3,8], which was initially derived using the control framework of viability theory [2]. We assume that the Hamiltonian is piecewise affine and continuous [12]:

$$\psi(\rho) = \begin{cases} v_f\rho & : \rho \in [0, k_c] \\ w(\rho - \kappa) & : \rho \in [k_c, \kappa] \end{cases} \tag{2}$$

4.2 Traffic State Estimation Using Mixed Integer Linear Programming

We consider a set of block boundary conditions 41, with unknown coefficients. Let us call V the vector space of unknown coefficients. Our measurement data (from the data set) constraints the possible values of these coefficients. Such constraints are called *data constraints*. Similarly, the PDE model also constraints the possible values of the unknown coefficients. Such constraints are called *model constraints*. An important and nontrivial result of [10] is that all these constraints are explicit. The extensive list of all constraints can be found in [6,7], though we do not write them in this article for compactness. The main result is the following:

Fact 42 [Mixed integer linear inequality property] *The model constraints [7] are mixed integer linear in the variables* $\rho(1), \rho(2), \ldots, \rho(k_{\max}), q_{\text{in}}(1), \ldots,$ $q_{\text{in}}(n_{\max}), q_{\text{out}}(1), \ldots, q_{\text{out}}(n_{\max}), L_1, \ldots, L_{m_{\max}}$ *and* $r_1, \ldots, r_{m_{\max}}$.

The proof of this proposition is available in [7].

Similarly, the unknown coefficients of the initial, boundary and internal conditions have to satisfy data constraints to be compatible with the observations. The data constraints express the fact that the true values of the initial, boundary and internal conditions coefficients should be within the bounds of the sensor measurement errors (which are known).

Hypothesis 43 [Data constraints] *In the remainder of our article, we assume that the data constraints are linear in the unknown coefficients of the initial, boundary and internal conditions.*

Different important and practical choices of error models that yield linear data constraints are available in [6]. Among all possible choices, the L_1 norm of the initial (or final) densities is a good candidate to obtain a sparse density map.

In the remainder of this article, we define y as the decision variable of the problem, containing the continuous variables $\rho(1), \rho(2), \ldots, \rho(k_{max})$, $q_{in}(1), \ldots,$ $q_{in}(n_{max}), q_{out}(1), \ldots, q_{out}(n_{max})$, $L_1, \ldots, L_{m_{max}}$ and $r_1, \ldots, r_{m_{max}}$, with additional integer variables representing continuity constraints.

Using the above equations, the set of possible traffic scenarios compatible with the data and the model can be written as $\{y | Ay \leq b \text{ and} Cy \leq d\}$. To select a solution among all possible choices, we choose a linear function of y, which can represent for instance the minimal travel time or the maximal average density at the current time. We can also look for sparse solutions by minimizing the L_1 norm of y. All of these examples boil down (modulo additional slack variables) to *Mixed Integer Linear Programs* (MILPs):

$$\text{Min. } c^T y$$
$$\text{s. t. } \begin{cases} Ay \leq b \\ Cy \leq d \end{cases} \tag{3}$$

We refer the reader to [11] for examples of choices of linear objectives relevant to traffic state estimation.

4.3 Distributed Computing Principle

MILPs can be parallelized [1,16] using parallel branch and bound methods. In the present case, the coordinator will coordinate the computation of the solution to the MILP, sending branches to explore to other nodes in the cluster, under a tree topology. See [1] for an example of implementation of a parallel MILP solver. Note that the attribution of tasks is *dynamic*. Once a node has found a better optimal solution, it will broadcast its results (multi-hop communication will be used if the nodes are not all in radio range) to the remaining nodes so only branches with possibly optimal candidates can be explored.

Once the MILP is solved (if it is not solved by the deadline, then the most optimal current solution can be used in lieu of the optimal solution), the coordinator node "anonymizes" the map by adding an optimal amount of noise (if the map "reveals" the location of an user) and then sends the resulting traffic map to an output database (through other clusters). The general principle is illustrated in Figure 2.

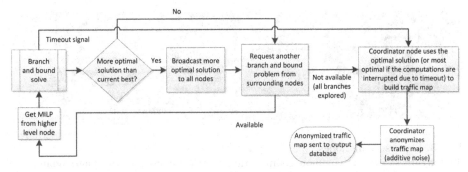

Fig. 2. Distributed computing process used by the proposed system

5   Implementation

We now present an ongoing implementation of a distributed-computing based traffic sensing system, as well as a simulation of the performance of the deployed system.

5.1   Computational Platform

In order to minimize power consumption while allowing distributed computing to be performed, we designed a new hardware platform around a 32-bit `ARM Cortex M4` normally operating at 168 MHz. The platform draws its energy jointly from a solar panel and a rechargeable $Li - FePO_4$ battery. It is designed to be OTA (over-the-air programming) capable. The current implementation of this platform is illustrated in Figure 3.

The STM32F407 microcontroller (MCU) includes a 1 Mbyte Flash memory and 196 KBytes of data RAM. It supports up to seventeen timers, 24 channels for analog to digital conversion and two 12-bit DACs. With embedded real-time memory accelerator, multi-AHB bus matrix and two dual-port DMA controllers, a maximal performance of 1.25DMIPS/MHz (Dhrystone million instructions per second per MHz) can be achieved.

5.2   Fixed Eulerian and Lagrangian Sensor Nodes

For this application, we also developed fixed traffic flow sensors that can sense both traffic and urban flash flooding (a secondary application of this system, which is out of the scope of this article). Each node is capable of monitoring traffic flow on two adjacent traffic lanes, as well as detect the presence and accurately measure the level of water in case of flooding. Measurements rely on two arrays of remote temperature (Melexis MLX90614) sensors (using passive infrared detection), as well as one ultrasonic rangefinder (MaxBotix MB7066), as illustrated in Figure 3. All sensors are digitally connected (SMBus and serial respectively) to a fixed transceiver node (described above) which generates traffic measurement data. .

 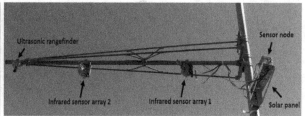

Fig. 3. Fixed sensing nodes
This figure shows the common computational platform used in the Lagrangian and
Eulerian sensor nodes (left), as well as an Eulerian sensor node deployed on KAUST
campus (right).

5.3   Mobile Transceivers

Mobile transceivers equipping vehicles are a key component of the proposed
system, and will initially consist in dedicated low-cost modules, though they can
piggyback on future V2V systems [5].

5.4   Simulated Performance of the System

Since the system is not fully functional yet (due to porting an OS and developing
libraries for the OTA and for the MILP solver), we simulate the performance of
an actual system using traffic data generated by the PTV VISSIM[23] microsim-
ulator. We simulate a small road network consisting of 10 roads. Owing to the
fact that the boundary conditions between links are known in some instances
(for instance when the traffic light in a section is red), we decompose the traffic
estimation problem into smaller scale subproblems involving 4 roads only, as
illustrated in Figure 4. We consider a time horizon of 5 seconds and two internal
conditions (obtained from vehicle position data), two boundary conditions and
one initial condition (which can be the previous estimate) per road. On our 5
minutes of simulated data, The computational time required to solve it on an
Imac with an Intel i5@2.5GHz varies between 25 ms and 65 ms, which translates into between 1 second to 3 seconds on our prototype experimental platform
(using the Coremark benchmark, and assuming a similar computational efficiency
between both platforms). On the simulated examples, the MILPs have between
44 and 49 variables, and between 177 and 196 constraints.

Since there exists an overhead for transmitting data (during the branch and
bound process) and for the traffic sensing activities themselves, we expect that
1-2 nodes would be required to reliably estimate the traffic on these four roads,
or equivalently that 4 nodes would be required for the complete set of 10 roads,
which covers an area of 0.15 km^2, making this system an inexpensive traffic
sensing solution.

 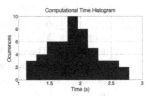

Fig. 4. Screenshot of the simulated transportation network
Left: we consider a subnetwork of four roads (in red), and compute 50 consecutive traffic estimation problems (5s time horizon).
Right: distribution of simulated computational times on the ARM-based platform.

6   Conclusions

This article presents a new wireless sensor network architecture for estimating traffic conditions in an urban environment based on distributed computing. Provided that the traffic estimation is distributed among a set of local nodes, we show that no user track information is sent beyond the radio range of this cluster, thereby preventing inference attacks on user location tracks. An ongoing implementation is briefly discussed, as well as a simulation of the system's performance. Future work will deal with the implementation of this system on the new ARM-based computational platform developed in our lab.

Acknowledgments. We would like to thank Guodong Li (KAUST) for his CAD design of the traffic sensor system, Sergio Favela (MS, KAUST) for his help writing the embedded code and Ehsan Wariach (PhD, U. Groningen) for his help on Eulerian sensor data processing.

References

1. Alonso, J., Schmidt, H., Alexandrov, V.N.: Parallel branch and bound algorithms for integer and mixed integer linear programming problems under PVM. In: Bubak, M., Waśniewski, J., Dongarra, J. (eds.) PVM/MPI 1997. LNCS, vol. 1332, pp. 313–320. Springer, Heidelberg (1997)
2. Aubin, J.-P.: Viability Theory. Systems and Control: Foundations and Applications. Birkhäuser, Boston (1991)
3. Aubin, J.-P., Bayen, A.M., Saint-Pierre, P.: Dirichlet problems for some Hamilton-Jacobi equations with inequality constraints. SIAM Journal on Control and Optimization 47(5), 2348–2380 (2008)
4. Barron, E.N., Jensen, R.: Semicontinuous viscosity solutions for Hamilton-Jacobi equations with convex Hamiltonians. Communications in Partial Differential Equations 15, 1713–1742 (1990)
5. Biswas, S., Tatchikou, R., Dion, F.: Vehicle-to-vehicle wireless communication protocols for enhancing highway traffic safety. IEEE Communications Magazine 44(1), 74–82 (2006)
6. Canepa, E.S., Claudel, C.G.: Exact solutions to traffic density estimation problems involving the LWR traffic flow model using MILPs. In: Proceedings of the 15th IEEE ITSC Conference, Anchorage, AK (September 2012)

7. Canepa, E.S., Claudel, C.G.: Spoofing Cyber Attack Detection in Probe-based Traffic Monitoring Systems using MILP. In: Proceedings of IEEE ICNC, San Diego, CA (January 2013)
8. Claudel, C.G., Bayen, A.M.: Lax-Hopf based incorporation of internal boundary conditions into Hamilton-Jacobi equation. Part I: theory. IEEE Transactions on Automatic Control 55(5), 1142–1157 (2010), doi:10.1109/TAC.2010.2041976.
9. Claudel, C.G., Bayen, A.M.: Lax-Hopf based incorporation of internal boundary conditions into Hamilton-Jacobi equation. Part II: Computational methods. IEEE Transactions on Automatic Control 55(5), 1158–1174 (2010), doi:10.1109/TAC.2010.2045439.
10. Claudel, C.G., Bayen, A.: Convex formulations of data assimilation problems for a class of Hamilton-Jacobi equations. SIAM Journal on Control and Optimization 49, 383–402 (2011)
11. Claudel, C.G., Chamoin, T., Bayen, A.M.: Solutions to estimation problems for Hamilton-Jacobi equations using Linear Programming. In: Submitted to IEEE Transactions on Control Sytems Technology (2010)
12. Daganzo, C.F.: A variational formulation of kinematic waves: basic theory and complex boundary conditions. Transporation Research B 39B(2), 187–196 (2005)
13. Frankowska, H.: Lower semicontinuous solutions of Hamilton-Jacobi-Bellman equations. SIAM Journal of Control and Optimization 31(1), 257–272 (1993)
14. Gruteser, M., Grunwald, D.: Anonymous usage of location-based services through spatial and temporal cloaking. In: Proceedings of the 1st International Conference on Mobile Systems, Applications and Services, pp. 31–42. ACM (2003)
15. Hoh, B., Gruteser, M., Herring, R., Ban, J., Work, D., Herrera, J.C., Bayen, A.M., Annavaram, M., Jacobson, Q.: Virtual trip lines for distributed privacy-preserving traffic monitoring. In: MobiSys 2008, Breckenridge, CO (2008) (to appear)
16. Kitakami, H., Hara, H., Yamanaka, H., Miyazaki, T.: Performance evaluation for parallel mixed-integer linear programming system. Optimization Methods and Software 3(4), 257–272 (1994)
17. Krumm, J.: Inference attacks on location tracks. In: LaMarca, A., Langheinrich, M., Truong, K.N. (eds.) Pervasive 2007. LNCS, vol. 4480, pp. 127–143. Springer, Heidelberg (2007)
18. Krumm, J.: A survey of computational location privacy. Personal and Ubiquitous Computing 13(6), 391–399 (2009)
19. Le Ny, J., Pappas, G.: Privacy-preserving release of aggregate dynamic models. In: Proceedings of the 2nd ACM International Conference on High Confidence Networked Systems, pp. 49–56. ACM (2013)
20. Lighthill, M.J., Whitham, G.B.: On kinematic waves. II. A theory of traffic flow on long crowded roads. Proceedings of the Royal Society of London 229(1178), 317–345 (1956)
21. Peddinti, S.T., Saxena, N., Birmingham, A.L.: On the limitations of query obfuscation techniques for location privacy. In: International Conference on Ubiquitous Computing (2011)
22. Work, D., Blandin, S., Tossavainen, O., Piccoli, B., Bayen, A.: A distributed highway velocity model for traffic state reconstruction. Applied Research Mathematics eXpress (ARMX) 1, 1–35 (2010)
23. http://www.vissim.de/
24. http://traffic.berkeley.edu/
25. http://pems.eecs.berkeley.edu

From Smart Clothing to Smart Table Cloth: Design and Implementation of a Large Scale, Textile Pressure Matrix Sensor

Bo Zhou, Jingyuan Cheng, Mathias Sundholm, and Paul Lukowicz

Embedded Intelligence
German Research Center for Artificial Intelligence (DFKI)
{bo.zhou,jingyuan.cheng,mathias.sundholm,paul.lukowicz}@ dfki.de

Abstract. We describe the design and implementation of an unobtrusive, cheap, large scale, pressure sensor matrix that can be used for a variety of applications ranging from smart clothing, through smart furniture, to an intelligent table cloth or carpet. The specific functionality and with it most of the complexity lies in the electronics and the processing software. We propose a scalable, modular architecture for such electronics, describe a prototype implementation, and present the results of its application to three different scenarios.

Keywords: large scale data acquisition system, pressure sensor matrix, wearable and ubiquitous computing.

1 Introduction

Human activity recognition with ubiquitous sensors is a well established research area [1]. While, over time, a variety of sensor modalities have been proposed and evaluated, there are still many applications that are limited by the quality and reliability of information sources. In particular, the trade-off between the effort involved in the instrumentation of the environment and the amount of information provided by the system remains a key issue.

In this paper, we describe our research on unobtrusive, high density, high sample rate textile pressure sensor matrices. As described in Section 2, the actual sensor matrix can be produced cheaply by printing arrays of conductive lines on an elastic, high resistance material. The resulting device is essentially a piece of textile that can be used for a broad range of applications: from smart clothing through smart furniture to an intelligent table cloth or carpet (see Figures 5,6,7). The specific functionality and, with it, most of the complexity lies in the electronics and the processing software (following the concept of "textile-based wearable sensing as an app" [2]). Thus, given envisioned sensor densities of several points per cm^2 and sensor area of up to several m^2, a core problem is how to realize the required read-out electronics with appropriate sensitivity and refresh rates.

Related Work and Paper Contributions. Different pressure sensor matrices with flexible and thin features have already been proposed and demonstrated.

E. Maehle et al. (Eds.): ARCS 2014, LNCS 8350, pp. 159–170, 2014.

Table 1. Overview on Existing Digital Pressure Matrix

application	modality	node amount	analogue precision	refresh rate
chair user posture [4]	resistive matrix	42x84	8-bit	6Hz
bed sleeper vital signs and posture[5] [6]	resistive matrix	16x16	unspecified	12Hz
shoes gait analysis [7]	opto-electronic	64 nodes	14-bit	1.8kHz
cushion user posture [8]	resistive matrix	16x16	unspecified	10Hz
commercial surface pressure mapping [9]	resistive matrix	32-by-32	discharging capacitor[a]	1kHz
driver comfort [10]	capacitive matrix	10x10	10-bit	100Hz
humanoid robotics	resistive EIT[b]	16[c]	unspecified	24Hz

[a] Discharging a capacitor is a low-end alternative to using an ADC. [11]
[b] Electrical Impedance Tomography, a technique to reversely estimate the resistance distribution of a conductive material only from the rim. [12]
[c] This number is only the physical electrodes; the calculated pressure mapping has higher resolution but is not specified by the authors.

A brief overview is given in Table 1, from which, it is easy to see, that current approaches are limited by the sampling electronics to raise the resolutions, conversion bits and refresh rates comprehensively. In [3], Bränzel, etc. recognize people and objects by sensing the pressure distribution in a room based on optical interference, where transparent glass floor with a large space underneath the testing room is required by the camera, using the camera to solve the hardware limits. Clearly such a solution involves much more installation effort than carpet-like textiles. Compared to the existing systems summarized above, the contribution of our work lies in a general hardware architecture topology which is:

– *large-scale.* The modularized hardware's complexity grows with n while the matrix's channel number grows with n^2. (detailed in Section 3) With existing hardware, the maximum channel number can be more than 10^6;
– *high pixel (analogue) and temporal (scanning rate) resolution.* Recent studies have shown high precision pressure sensor helps reveal subtle activities(e.g. four pressure force sensors under chair's leg can distinguish not only user's postures but also activities like nodding or moving the mouse. [13]). We thus choose 24-bit analogue-digital converters (ADCs) rather than low-end 10-bit integrated ADCs, the structural separation between the digital and analogue modules can minimize noise level;
– *suitable for a broad range of applications.* As demonstrated in Section 4, our system provides relevant information in applications ranging from on-body sensing through a smart table cloth to carpet-like structures.

In the paper, we first describe the basic sensing principle (Section 2). We then outline a generalized, scalable, adaptive architecture for the driver electronics (Section 3). This includes concepts for dynamic reconfiguration and data

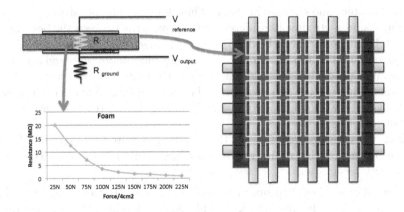

Fig. 1. Sensing Principle

compression schemes to reduce the data transmission load and facilitate real-time processing. It also encompasses a detailed analysis of the scalability in terms of size and sampling rate on the basis of existing off-the-shelf components. In Section 5 we then describe our first prototype implementation of the system and discuss performance results in three different scenarios (smart carpet for exercise monitoring, smart table cloth and wearable posture monitoring).

2 Textile Pressure Sensor Matrix

The general principle of our textile pressure sensor matrix is shown in Figure 1. The basis is a large area of a material that has high resistivity that can be locally reduced by applying vertical pressure. The force/resistance curve for the foam material used in the tablecloth example in Section 5 is shown in the bottom left part of Figure 1. Other materials can have steeper or gentler slopes and different regions of operation. For large body area wearable applications, material flexibility and 'feel' is also an important consideration.

Once an appropriate material has been selected, an array of conductive lines is attached to (or printed on) the upper and the lower side in such a way that the lines on the lower side are perpendicular to the lines on the upper side (as shown on the right side of Figure 1). Thus, at every intersection of two lines, a sensing element, as shown in the top left part of Figure 1, is generated. Each sensing element can be read out by measuring the resistance between the respective horizontal and vertical line.

3 Processing Architecture

3.1 Design Requirements

The concept of a large scale pressure sensor matrix as information source for activity recognition is motivated by the insight that many activities are determined by physical contact and changes in shape. Thus, for example, physical exercises (eg. push-ups, sit ups etc) involve different contact patterns between the body and the ground. Having a meal can be described by the placement and changes of weight of objects caused by food being moved from one plate to another and eaten, pressure being applied when cutting something on the plate, and the position of hands and arms. Body motion and posture can be acquired from changes in the pressure distribution between the body and tightly fitting clothes (e.g. as muscle expand on contraction).

From the above considerations, the following requirements can be identified for the processing electronics required for large scale sensing matrices suitable for activity recognition:

- *Spacial resolution.* Appropriate pixel density is essential for recognizing shapes of objects (feet, furniture legs, etc.) placed on relevant surfaces (floor, tables). In general a resolution in sub-cm range is desirable. Higher density clearly will offer more details; however, it also significantly increases data amount, so that a good tradeoff must be found.
- *Measurement sensitivity and dynamic range.* Studies such as [14] and [13] show that subtle difference in weight and weight distribution contain important information about user activities. In general a sensitivity well below 100g with a measurement range of well over a typical body weight ($\simeq$100kg) is required.
- *Sample rate.* Since not only identifying objects, but also recognizing activities is of interest, sufficient scanning rate must be appropriate for typical human motions, which is described as around 10Hz to 50Hz, according to relative studies.[15]
- *Scalability.* A key advantage of the proposed sensor system is the fact that the same basic textile structure can be used in a wide variety of applications. Obviously the core matrix structure scales well and different sized matrices can be easily combined to form large, complex systems. However this implies that the control and evaluation must also scale with respect to scanning rate, driving load and supported data rates. Thus, system sizes up to a mega-pixel (1024x1024) are conceivable in many applications.

3.2   Architecture

Based on the specifications discussed above, to achieve a large scale, high analogue precision, large channel amount system, we propose an architecture described in Figure 2. In this chapter the system design considerations will be discussed in details.

First of all, the sensor matrix is in fact constructed by intersecting two sets of parallel wires (X and Y). The sensor node between each conjunction can be abstracted as a block with an enable input, pinned to the corresponding Y wire, and an analogue output, connected to the X direction. During the scanning procedure, one Y wire is powered each time, enabling the nodes with the same Y to generate outputs on the X wires. A complete frame is done by sweeping the

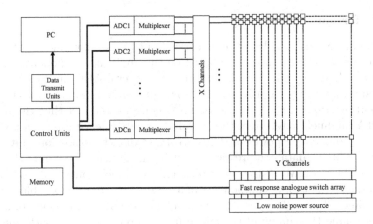

Fig. 2. Matrix Data Acquisition System Architecture

Y axes to address all the sensor nodes. As an example to illustrate the amount of data that needs to be processed, we consider a 128-by-128 system.

High analogue precision always requires low noise level. To achieve this we separate the digital and analogue parts and equip the analogue part with ultra low noise power supply ICs. The Y electrodes are separated from the digital part by fast analogue switches. The addressing sequence can be implemented by several layers of demultiplexers; however, in our architecture, a single IC with sufficient I/O pins is chosen to simplify the printed circuit board (PCB) and facilitate complex control and scanning strategies.

The X electrodes need to be connected to ADC input channels for sampling; we choose single channel high precision ADCs for the flexibility in building the structure. In general it is impractical to have a dedicated ADC channel for each X line. Therefore, we put analogue multiplexers in front of the ADC to route analogue signals. To route 128 channels into one ADC input using existing devices requires at least one base layer of four 32-to-1 multiplexers and a second level layer of 4-to-1 multiplexers, which in turn increases noise and settling time. The settling time increase applies to every sample and thus has a big influence on the scanning rate. Our approach uses a hybrid combination of ADC-multiplexer blocks to balance performance and cost: each block includes one ADC and a 32-to-1 multiplexer as the front end, and four of these blocks can cover 128 channels.

A master control unit coordinates the scanning sequence, reads out the ADC sampling result, processes data and sends the data to the computer. The control units including the master unit and the demultiplexer unit are FPGAs, with a high number of I/Os and the capability to process the data from multiple ADC-multiplexer blocks simultaneously. The data transmission method is flexible. Available options include: a serial port, Universal Serial Bus, Gigabit-Ethernet, Peripheral Component Interconnect Bus, etc. The choice should be made based on the actual data bandwidth and the complexity of developing the local drivers on the computer.

3.3   Performance Limits

In the following part, a calculation is carried out to see how much spatial resolution our architecture can achieve based on the analogue components commercially available today. Since on the X direction, several ADC-multiplexer blocks operate simultaneously, in principle, the analogue sampling timing does not limit the resolution. However in practice we must consider the fact that the product of X and Y channels determines the overall data rate in each frame and, with it, the required processing power of the control and data transmission unit (in the case that on-board data compression is not implemented). Assuming the ADC-multiplexer blocks have 32-to-1 multiplexers, each block controls $32 \times Y$ nodes. Figure 3 shows the timing components of a single ADC-multiplexer block within a frame. Since the blocks operate in parallel, the timing components of a single block determine the timing of the entire frame. Looking at the performance of currently available off the shelf components we have the following:

– high performance ADCs (24 bit, $2.5MHz$ output sample rate, $100dB$ Signal-to-Noise ratio) with a $2500ns$ complete sample-conversion cycle (T_{ADC});
– high speed analogue switch with $T_{Yon} = T_{Yoff} = 10ns$ at the Y channels;
– high speed 32-to-1 analogue multiplexers with $T_{Xon} = T_{Xoff} = 30ns$ on and off times at the X channels.

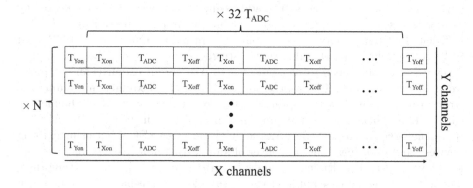

Fig. 3. ADC-Multiplexer block timing components

Thus, to maintain a maintain a 50Hz scanning rate the following constraint should hold:

$$[m \times 2560ns + 20ns] \times N \times R < 1s,$$

$m = 32$, multiplexer input channels;
$R = 50$, scanning rate;
N: Y channels.

The maximum integer value of N meeting this constraint is 244. With 8 blocks, a 255-by-244 matrix can be configured. From the above constraint, the Y channel limit N increases with less analogue multiplexer input channels m. Therefore

Table 2. Scalability – small to large scale designs with the same architecture

	Small (Prototype)	Medium	Large	Tessellation
Scale	32 × 32	128 × 128	1024 × 1024	16 × 255 × 244
Multiplexer	32-to-1	32-to-1	8-to-1	32-to-1
ADC-MUX blocks	1	4	125	128
Refresh rate	>50Hz	50Hz	47Hz	50Hz
ADC precision	16-bit	24-bit	24-bit	24-bit
demultiplexer controllers I/Os	32	128	1024	16 × 244
Data rate (uncompressed)	100kB/s	2.4MB/s	141GB/s	16x9.1MB/s

more ADCs are needed to achieve higher spacial resolutions. This structure can fully utilize the ADC sampling time.

3.4 Scalability

From the constraint in section 3.3, having $m = 8$ and $N = 1024$ will result in $R < 47.6$. That is to say, using 8-to-1 analogue multiplexers and having 1024 Y channels, the system will still have a scanning rate of 47Hz. With 125 ADC-multiplexer blocks, the system can scale up to 1024-by-1024, i.e. mega-pixel level. Another alternative for scaling is to tesselate a big matrix with several intermediate-sized systems as submodules, in which case, there is the option to process the data either centrally, distributedly or in a hybrid fashion. Tessellation with distributed data processing in theory can unlock the scale limit, because it is essentially a duplication of the base system. Table 2 summarizes the above mentioned scalability of the architecture.

3.5 Dynamic Reconfiguration and Data Compression Schemes

As described above, our architecture scales well with respect to the timing limits of the analogue components. However, from Table 2 it can be seen that data rates generated by the system will become a bottleneck as the scale of the system goes up. Even though PCIe interfaces can now deliver speeds up to 128 Gbps (Gen3) [16], there is still consideration of power consumption, system size and etc. Luckily, there is significant potential to reduce the data rate. The uncompressed data from matrix shares great similarity with gray-colored video ($1024 \times 1024@50Hz$ vs. $1280 \times 720@25Hz$) in:

- *temporal redundancy.* Most of the human activities are of low frequencies ($< 20Hz$), so there is similarity from frame to frame.
- *spatial redundancy.* There is similarity between adjacent channels. And more importantly, for pressure matrix is the ratio of triggered to un-triggered

channels. Taking a carpet covering a $3 \times 3m^2$ living room with 3 people for example, when the people are standing or walking around, maximum 6 feet $(30 \times 10cm^2)$ are triggering the carpet, which, for 1024×1024 resolution, means 200 channels, uncompressed data-rate 30kB/s. The information about furniture, which are stable, can be sent as a base-frame from time to time.

- *statistical redundancy.* The distribution of 24-bit codes are not the same. For everyday activity recognition, subtle activities which result in small signals (e.g. move head/hand, walk around, cooking) are much more likely to happen than activities with big pressure distribution change (run, drag big furniture, roll about on the floor).

With FPGA included already in the architecture, first-step compressions such as applying a threshold to remove the un-triggered channels can be done for each ADC in parallel. This may bring even further advantage: reducing power consumption. Because the process of scanning each channel is controlled by FPGA, combined with parameters feed back to FPGA from on-line processing software, the scanning rate for un-triggered channels can be dropped to a much lower value. (E.g. a program detecting human feet and only the area of possible next step is scanned at a high speed.)

We would like to mention that our paper puts emphasize on the hardware architecture. For that we explain here only the potential of data compression. How to modify and implement existing compression methods for image and video to the pressure matrix lies in our future work.

4   Implementation and Results

4.1   Prototype Hardware

To test the architecture and demonstrate the capability of the sensor matrix we made out of low cost materials, a prototype of 32-by-32 channels with 16-bit ADC precision was built. The prototype's hardware structure is shown in Figure 4. It is not exactly the same as the architecture described in Section 3, but the overall structure falls into the architecture. The ADC with 32-to-1 multiplexer is integrated in a micro-controller; since the ADC precision does not require ultra low noise power on the Y channels, the FPGA I/O pins are connected directly to the Y channels.

The sensor matrix is made by attaching two perpendicular arrays of electrode stripes (aluminium foil on fiber-glass reinforced polypropylene tape) on two sides of flexible resistive material sheets, of which the volume resistance changes with the deformation caused by pressure. We use two different materials to represent carpet and cloth separately. The spacial distance on X and Y directions between pixels is $30mm$ for the former and $20mm$ for the latter.

4.2   Results and Application Examples

We have used the prototype to acquire and analyse signals in three scenarios that were already mentioned in the paper: (1) physical exercise, (2) a 'smart

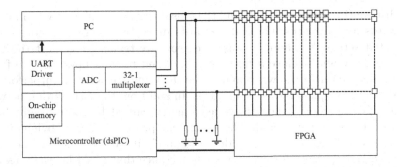

Fig. 4. Prototype System Structure

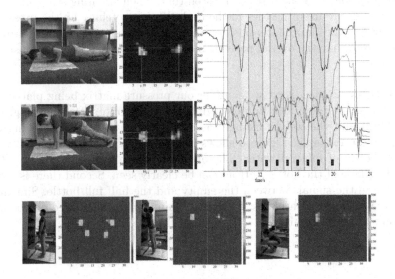

Fig. 5. Prototype Experiment Result: push-ups on the top, reaching shelves on the bottom)

tablecloth' and (3) sensing body shape changes with tight fitting garments. These scenarios represent a broad rang of applications with different requirements with respect to resolution and fore sensitivity. Since the focus of this paper is on sensing system design, not on activity recognition, we refrain from doing actual recognition (which is subject of future work). Instead, we focus on demonstrating that our system can acquire signals that reflect the differences between relevant situations and actions.

Detecting Physical Exercise with a Mat. We consider a person exercising on the floor. Specifically Figure 5 shows the signals acquired when doing push-ups with hands on the smart mat made of our sensor matrix. It can be seen that the force distribution between hands and the sensor matrix is different when moving downwards and upwards. On a downwards move the forces are more evenly distributed across the hand, because the arms are trying to support the body against gravity and achieve a fluent speed. When moving upwards, the forces are more focused near the waist joint since the arms are actively outperforming against gravity to push the body upwards. In addition, the distribution between the left and the right hands shows asymmetry caused by more weight being placed on the dominant hand. The movement process is more obvious in the dynamic data of several marked nodes in Figure 5. It can be seen that the signal contains a clear pattern for every push up instance that could be easily used to for counting.

On the bottom of Figure 5 the same system is used to detect a person reaching diferent locations of a shelf. It can be seen that, when standing still, the signals show the pressure from the toes to the heel. When stretching up the pressure is focused on the toes, in the low position the pressure is spread out on the soles of the feet. Note that the overall pattern is distinctly different from the push ups.

Smart Table Cloth. Next we consider our pressure matrix being placed on a table as a 'smart tablecloth' to detect different types of objects (plates, glasses, bottles etc) and the weight changes associated with their content being consumed. As an example, Figure 6 shows the signal produced by an empty and half full bottle of mineral water. The observation can be made. First, in both cases the shape of the bottle bottom can be clearly seen. Second there is a clear difference in the signals between the empty and the half full bottle. Similar results were achieved with plates, bowls etc. Hands and arms placed on the table also show distinct signals.

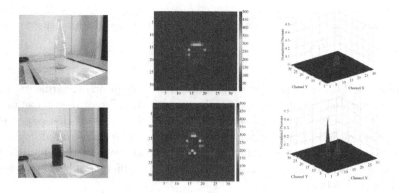

Fig. 6. Prototype Experiment Result: table cloth

Wearable Sensing. To investigate the suitability of the proposed system for on-body sensing, the matrix previously used for table cloth has been first wrapped around the users upper and lower arm. The resulting signal is shown in Figure 7 a) and b). It can be clearly seen that the signals differ significantly for a straight and flexed elbow.

Second, we have placed the matrix in the trousers on the buttock to compare the signals for different sitting situations. Figure 7 shows the signals obtained from sitting on a chair and leaning on the edge of a table. Again a clear difference can be seen.

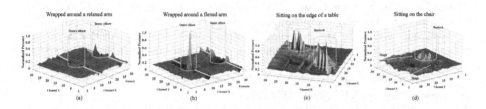

Fig. 7. Prototype Experiment Result: wearable scenarios

5 Conclusion

The main conclusion from the work presented in this paper is that large scale textile pressure matrix that produce information relevant to a variety of context recognition tasks is feasible. In particular we have shown that, using existing commercial components, system sizes of up to 1024x1024 (1 million individual sensors) are feasible with sample rates of up to 50Hz.

As a next step, we are currently working on demonstrating the actual recognition of different activities (e.g. distinguishing different exercises and counting repetitions). In parallel a larger version of the system will be deployed on the floor of the social area of our lab in a long term experiment.

Acknowledgments. This work was partially supported by the collaborative project SimpleSkin under contract with the European Commission (#323849) in the FP7 FET Open framework. The support is gratefully acknowledged.

References

1. Chen, L., Hoey, J., Nugent, C., Cook, D., Yu, Z.: Sensor-based activity recognition. IEEE Transactions on Systems, Man, and Cybernetics, Part C: Applications and Reviews 42(6), 790–808 (2012)
2. Cheng, J., Lukowicz, P., Henze, N., Schmidt, A., Amft, O., Salvatore, G., Troster, G.: Smart textiles: From niche to mainstream. IEEE Pervasive Computing 12(3), 81–84 (2013)

3. Bränzel, A., Holz, C., Hoffmann, D., Schmidt, D., Knaust, M., Lühne, P., Meusel, R., Richter, S., Baudisch, P.: Gravityspace: Tracking users and their poses in a smart room using a pressure-sensing floor. In: CHI 2013, Paris, France, April 27-May 2 (2013)
4. Tan, H., Slivovsky, L., Pentland, A.: A sensing chair using pressure distribution sensors. IEEE/ASME Transactions on Mechatronics 6(3), 261–268 (2001)
5. Kortelainen, J., van Gils, M., Parkka, J.: Multichannel bed pressure sensor for sleep monitoring. In: Computing in Cardiology (CinC 2012), pp. 313–316 (2012)
6. Lokavee, S., Puntheeranurak, T., Kerdcharoen, T., Watthanwisuth, N., Tuantranont, A.: Sensor pillow and bed sheet system: Unconstrained monitoring of respiration rate and posture movements during sleep. In: 2012 IEEE International Conference on Systems, Man, and Cybernetics (SMC), pp. 1564–1568 (2012)
7. De Rossi, S., Lenzi, T., Vitiello, N., Donati, M., Persichetti, A., Giovacchini, F., Vecchi, F., Carrozza, M.: Development of an in-shoe pressure-sensitive device for gait analysis. In: 33rd Annual International Conference of the IEEE EMBS (2011)
8. Xu, W., Huang, M.C., Amini, N., He, L., Sarrafzadeh, M.: ecushion: A textile pressure sensor array design and calibration for sitting posture analysis. IEEE Sensors Journal 13(10), 3926–3934 (2013)
9. Sensor Product INC.: Tactilus real-time surface pressure mapping technology
10. Marenzi, E., Lombardi, R., Bertolotti, G.M., Cristiani, A., Cabras, B.: Design and development of a novel capacitive sensor matrix for measuring pressure distribution. In: 2012 IEEE Sensors Applications Symposium, SAS (2012)
11. Holtek Semiconductor INC.: Using an i/o port pin as an a/d converter input
12. Holder, D.S.: Electrical impedance tomography:methods, history and applications. Institute of Physics (2004)
13. Cheng, J., Zhou, B., Sundholm, M., Lukowicz, P.: Smart chair: What can simple pressure sensors under the chair's legs tell us about user activity? In: Ubicomm 2013 (2013)
14. Adami, A.M., Hayes, T.L., Pave, M.: Unobtrusive monitoring of sleep patterns. In: Proceedings of the 25th Annual International Conference of the IEEE EMBS (2003)
15. Wilde, A.G.: An overview of human activity detection technologies for pervasive systems, Department of Informatics University of Fribourg, Switzerland (2010)
16. Vienne, J., Chen, J., Wasi-ur Rahman, M., Islam, N., Subramoni, H., Panda, D.: Performance analysis and evaluation of infiniband fdr and 40gige roce on hpc and cloud computing systems. In: 2012 IEEE 20th Annual Symposium on High-Performance Interconnects (HOTI), pp. 48–55 (2012)

Performance Isolation Exposure in Virtualized Platforms with PCI Passthrough I/O Sharing

Andre Richter, Christian Herber, Holm Rauchfuss,
Thomas Wild, and Andreas Herkersdorf

Institute for Integrated Systems, Technische Universität München,
Arcisstr. 21, 80290 Munich, Germany
{andre.richter,christian.herber,holm.rauchfuss,
thomas.wild,herkersdorf}@tum.de
http://www.lis.ei.tum.de

Abstract. PCI Passthrough is an x86 virtualization technology that enables low overhead, high performance I/O virtualization. It is an established technology in server and cloud computing environments and a promising technology for sharing I/O devices in future Cyber Physical Systems that consolidate mixed-criticality applications on multi-core CPUs. In this paper, we show that current implementations of x86 PCI Passthrough are prone to Denial-of-Service attacks. We demonstrate that attacks can be launched from within Virtual Machine environments and affect the performance of *every* I/O device on the interconnect. This means that malicious or malfunctioning applications inside Virtual Machines can impair the I/O performance of co-residential Virtual Machines. For example, attacking an SR-IOV capable Gigabit Ethernet NIC causes its TCP throughput to drop by 326 Mbit/s; latencies for reading 32 bit words from the NIC increase by over 650%. We investigate which hardware parameters influence the impact of such attacks and introduce three protection approaches.

Keywords: Performance Isolation, Virtualization, Passthrough I/O.

1   Introduction

A current research challenge in Cyber Physical Systems (CPS) is the enablement of multi-core processor platforms for the consolidation of multiple, independent software applications [8] [7]. Parallel execution on a multi-core processor introduces concerns regarding performance and risks regarding safety and security, because they have to share resources like memory, caches and I/O devices. In order to prevent consolidated applications running on a multi-core from interfering with each other, spatial and temporal isolation of the shared resources is mandatory. This is especially important for future mixed-criticality CPS systems, where applications with different real-time requirements are consolidated, e.g. safety-critical driver-assist and high data volume Infotainment applications. At the same time, the overhead of isolation mechanisms should impair the performance of individual applications only as little as possible.

E. Maehle et al. (Eds.): ARCS 2014, LNCS 8350, pp. 171–182, 2014.

Virtualization of computing resources is a promising approach for solving these challenges [10]. Spatial isolation of memory is nowadays enforced via hardware virtualization extensions, which ensure that co-residential Virtual Machines (VMs) do not spy on or corrupt each other's memory. These hardware extensions have low overheads and are available in modern, commercial off-the-shelf (COTS) processors and chipsets. On the x86 platform, for example, processors provide MMUs with virtualization extensions for isolating CPU-to-memory transactions, while virtualization-enabled IOMMUs isolate I/O-to-memory transactions.

Besides isolation, IOMMUs also help to solve the problem of efficiently sharing I/O devices for virtualized applications running on a multi-core. They enable VMs to directly communicate with PCI(e)-connected I/O devices, without any involvement of the Hypervisor. This is called direct device assignment or, on x86 platforms, PCI Passthrough. Utilizing PCI Passthrough also allows to make use of the PCI Express Single Root I/O Virtualization (SR-IOV) technology. SR-IOV enables a single physical PCIe device to offer several hundred Virtual Functions (VFs), each of which can be directly assigned to a distinct VM. SR-IOV offloads routines for virtualizing I/O devices into the target device's hardware. This makes PCI Passthrough with SR-IOV the currently best performing I/O virtualization approach [2], because in contrast to emulation [12] and paravirtualization [1] approaches, the computation of isolation and I/O device virtualization routines are offloaded into hardware accelerators. This minimizes processor overhead and therefore boosts I/O virtualization performance. Additionally, PCI Passthrough and SR-IOV technologies are nowadays widely deployed in server and cloud computing environments. This ensures that virtualization extensions and (IO)MMU enforced spatial separation are quite mature and tested in currently available x86 COTS hardware.

However, besides superior performance and low processor overhead, PCI Passthrough has yet-to-be-solved problems regarding temporal isolation [6], because multiple VMs running on different cores share a single bus for accessing their assigned I/O devices or VFs. Current PCI Passthrough setups have no instance that monitors access to shared devices, because the datapath of PCI Passthrough bypasses the Hypervisor. Therefore, no control instance is present that may block exhaustive access to them.

In this paper, we demonstrate the severeness of this lack of temporal isolation. We show how it can be exploited in order to significantly degrade the performance of co-residential VMs and the host system: We present how Denial-of-Service attacks on an SR-IOV capable Gigabit Ethernet NIC cause its TCP throughputs to drop by 326 MBit/s and how latencies for reading 32 bit words from the NIC to increase by over 650%. We investigate why PCI Passthrough setups are prone to such attacks and propose three different approaches for tackling the presented problems.

The remainder of this paper is organized as follows: Section 2 explains the evaluation methodology, experimental setup and threat model. Section 3 presents results of our experiments. Section 4 proposes protection approaches. Section 5 reviews related work. Finally, Section 6 concludes this paper.

2   Experimental Setup and Threat Model

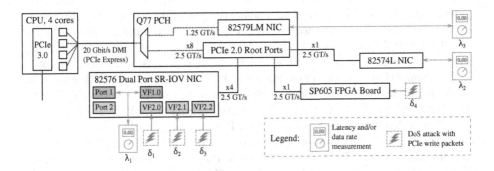

Fig. 1. Block diagram of virtualization platform

For our experiments, we utilized an advanced x86 platform that was chosen for providing the latest generation of hardware virtualization accelerators. An overview is depicted in Figure 1. An Intel DQ77MK Motherboard is equipped with a Core i7-3770T CPU (2.5 GHz, 4 physical cores, 8 logical cores with HyperThreading enabled) and 32 GB of RAM. The proprietary 20 Gbit/s Direct Media Interface (DMI) 2.0 connects the CPU to the Q77 Platform-Controller-Hub (PCH), which provides access to the platform's PCIe 2.0 subsystem.

PCIe is a serial, point-to-point, packet-switched interconnect. A connection between two PCIe devices is called a link. A link's bandwidth is determined by its number of lanes, the encoding on the physical layer and the physical layer bit rate. The latter is always given in GigaTransfers per second (GT/s). For example, PCIe 2.0 uses 8b/10b encoding, which means a four lane connection with a speed of 2.5 GT/s (x4, 2.5GT/s) can move $2.5 \cdot 4 \cdot (8/10) = 8\,Gbit/s$ in one direction.

The Q77 hosts three PCIe 2.0 Root Ports, one featuring four lanes (x4), while the other two provide one lane (x1), respectively. Each lane has a rate of 2.5 GigaTransfers per second (GT/s). The Q77 also integrates an 82579LM Gigabit Ethernet NIC, which mimics a PCIe interface so it can be accessed easily with standard drivers. However, the connection is only capable of providing a speed of 1.25 GT/s [4]. Another Gigabit Ethernet NIC, the 82574L, is soldered onto the Motherboard and connected to one of the x1 Root Ports. The x4 Root Port is connected to a PCIe slot where we put in an SR-IOV capable, dual port gigabit Ethernet extension card with an Intel 82576 controller. Each of the controller's ports can provide up to seven VFs. We configured the card to use one VF (VF1.0) for Port 1, and three VFs (VF2.X) for Port 2. The remaining x1 Root Port is equipped with a Xilinx SP605, a PCIe board housing a Spartan 6 FPGA. We use this board as a target for standard read/write operations. Its purpose will be discussed in detail in Section 3.2. The PCIe 3.0 controller embedded onto the CPU will be discussed in Section 3.3.

On the software side, the host system is running Ubuntu 12.10 with the KVM Hypervisor. Each guest VM uses the same Ubuntu version and kernel as the host and is assigned 4096 MB of RAM.

2.1   Threat Model

Our attack scenarios assume that the virtualization platform hosts several VMs concurrently. Each VM is pinned on a dedicated physical core with HyperThreading disabled. This is because we do not want two VMs running on the same core to influence each other's performance. Additionally, we needed this partitioning for accurate latency measurements, which will be explained in subsection 2.2.

We assume that an attacker overtakes VMs by gathering root privileges inside the VMs operating system, which enables him to install his own device drivers. An overtaken, malicious VM is either directly assigned to a Virtual Function of the SR-IOV NIC or to the SP605 via PCI Passthrough. In order to compromise performance of the host system and co-residential VMs, the attacker will abuse the directly assigned PCIe device by launching a Denial-of-Service attack on one of the device's Memory Mapped I/O (MMIO) resources. Accessing MMIO resources of a device means that the CPU reads from or writes to registers or other forms of memory that are located on the device.

Malicious VMs launch a MMIO DoS attack against its PCI Passthrough device by removing the device's standard driver and inserting a Linux kernel module that contains an attack method. This DoS attack method is realized with a for-loop that floods the PCIe device with 32 bit write packets. We chose write packets for flooding because a PCIe write is, in contrast to a PCIe read, a so called *posted* transaction. This means that a write transaction does not wait for an acknowledge or any other type of response. Therefore, write packets can be generated with a very high rate. The generation rate is only constrained by the CPU clock, which is 2.5 GHz in our case.

2.2   Evaluation Methodology

To quantify the impact of DoS attacks on the performance of co-residential VMs and the host system, we measured two indicators:

Latencies for PCIe 32 bit reads are a general metric of a DoS attack's impact on the interconnect level. Latency is measured by counting the time it takes from requesting a word from the PCIe device until the response with the respective data arrives at the requesting CPU core. To realize this, we extended our Linux kernel module for launching the MMIO DoS attacks with a latency measurement function. The function utilizes the Linux kernel's `readl()` instruction, which reads a 32 bit word from the target device. Time is counted using the CPU's Time Stamp Counter (TSC) register like described in [9]. There is one TSC per core available. Latency results presented in this paper are always the average of one million samples. HyperThreading has been disabled in order to prevent that an active measuring thread is pushed from its core, which would cause erroneous results. To get consistent and reproducible results, we disabled SpeedStep and TurboBoost technologies. Otherwise, the frequency of the CPU cores would have varied depending on the current thermal conditions and the workload of other cores.

TCP and UDP throughputs of the multiple NICs of our hardware platform are the second set of indicators used in the following experiments. They directly depend on the read/write latencies of the PCIe devices, but give a better idea of a DoS attack's impact on standard I/O workloads in a computer system. Additionally, it is easier to put network throughput benchmarks in context than raw read/write latencies of interconnects. Network throughputs were measured with the `netperf` tool between our virtualization platform and a dedicated PC. We used standard TCP and UDP stream tests (1500 Byte Ethernet Frames) without any additional parameters.

3 Results

This Section presents three experiments we conducted in order to evaluate the impact of MMIO DoS attacks, including the respective results and conclusions.

3.1 Experiment 1: Attacking SR-IOV Virtual Functions

SR-IOV capable PCIe devices are built with the intention to be shared between multiple, potentially untrusted virtual machines. The 82576 NIC used in our hardware platform represents such a commercially available device. It features two disjunct gigabit Ethernet ports, each of which may be shared by up to eight Virtual Functions, respectively. The PCIe board on which the 82576 controller resides is designed to operate both Ethernet ports at full speed simultaneously (x4, 2.5 GT/s). Our `netperf` tests showed 941 Mbit/s for TCP stream tests and 961 Mbit/s for UDP stream tests for both ports in concurrent operation.

If the same Ethernet port is used by two VMs at the same time, e.g. one VM assigned to VF2.0 and one VM assigned to VF2.1, the resulting throughput for each VM halves. For 3 VMs it divides by three, and so on. Given the premise that all VMs attached to a VF are non-malicious and use the standard driver for the VF, throughput of Port 1 is never influenced by usage of Port 2, no matter how many VMs are accessing Port 2 concurrently.

In the following experiment, we want to show that malicious guests can have a huge impact on the throughput of co-residential VMs. Therefore, we first measured latencies and TCP throughput for VF1.0 (compare Figure 1, λ_1) when the rest of the system is idle. The results, 941 Mbit/s TCP throughput and a latency of 1.58 µs, shall serve as the baseline measurements and are depicted in the "none" column of Figure 2. The remaining columns show how latency and throughput of VF1.0 are impaired by MMIO DoS attacks on VFs2.X of disjunct Ethernet Port 2. Results are depicted for a single DoS attack $A = \{\delta_1\}$ and concurrent attacks $A = \{\delta_1, \delta_2\}$ and $A = \{\delta_1, \delta_2, \delta_3\}$. Each DoS attack δ_x was launched from within a VM running on a dedicated core and targeted its respective VF2.X (compare Figure 1).

The results show that a single DoS attack (δ_1 on VF2.0) from one malicious VM suffices to force a TCP throughput drop from 941 to 684 Mbit/s for VF1.0, which is allocated to a different physical Ethernet port than the DoS target. A second DoS attack (δ_2 on VF2.1) which is launched concurrently from an additional VM causes the TCP throughput to drop further down to 615 Mbit/s. A third attack does not result in an additional performance drop.

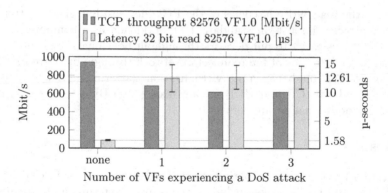

Fig. 2. Latency for 32 bit reads and TCP throughput for VF1.0 of the 82576 NIC while one or more VFs of the 82576 NIC experience MMIO DoS attacks

The reason for these performance drops lies within the architecture of PCIe interconnects. The CPU cores of the malicious VMs are able to produce write packets at a rate much higher than the 82576 NIC can consume them. Eventually, this leads to a congestion in the ingress buffers of the 82576 NIC. PCIe flow control mechanisms then pass on the backpressure to the next device in the PCIe hierarchy, and so on. This congestions builds up through the Q77 PCH until it reaches the CPU itself. This is also visible from the latencies shown in Figure 2, which increase from 1.58 µs for an idle system to 12.61 µs. This increase of 689% is the actual reason for the TCP throughput drop. With latencies of 12.61 µs , it is no longer possible to transfer data at near 1 Gbit/s volumes to and from the PCIe device.

That the congestion during DoS attacks spreads over the whole PCIe interconnect can be shown by exchanging the NIC for which the TCP throughputs are measured. Therefore, the 82574L and 82579LM NICs (compare λ_2 and λ_3 in Figure 1) were used for measuring TCP throughputs, one at a time. Both NICs are connected at different locations of the PCIe tree, compared to the DoS target (82576 NIC). Figure 3 compares the results of the new measurements to the previously measured throughputs of the 82576's VF1.0

The results show that the congestion spreads over the whole PCIe interconnect, because all three NICs suffer from throughput degradation. In comparison to VF1.0 of the 82576 NIC, the other NICs perform worse. Throughputs drop to 506 Mbit/s for the 82574L and 325 Mbit/s for the 82579LM. The observed gaps result from the different link speeds at which the NICs are connected to their PCIe ports. These link speeds define the time it takes to transfer an Ethernet frame to the NIC. As mentioned in Section 2, a PCIe link's data bit rate R_{data} is calculated from the number of lanes n_{lanes}, the physical layer bit rate R_{phys} and the encoding on the physical layer: $R_{data} = n_{lanes} \times R_{phys} \times encoding$.

Table 1 shows these parameters for the three NICs (also depicted in Figure 1), together with the calculated time T_{trans} it takes to transfer a 1500 Byte Ethernet Frame. As one can see, the 82576 NIC has 4.5 µs and 10.5 µs faster transfer times

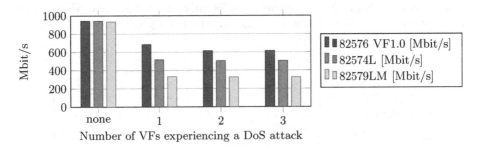

Fig. 3. TCP throughputs of the three NICs of the test system while one or more VFs of the 82576 NIC experience a MMIO DoS attack

Table 1. Transfer time for a 1500 Byte Ethernet Frame

NIC	n_{lanes}	R_{phys}	enc	R_{data}	T_{trans}
82576	x4	2.5 GT/s	8b/10b	8 Gbit/s	1.5 μs
82574L	x1	2.5 GT/s	8b/10b	2 Gbit/s	6.0 μs
82579LM	x1	1.5 GT/s	8b/10b	1 Gbit/s	12 μs

than the 82574L and 82579LM, respectively. This means that the overall delay for the NICs is the sum of the DoS-caused latency and the transfer time T_{trans} of the NIC's PCIe link. Consequently, the overall latencies for the three NICs differ, which results in the diverse throughput drops.

3.2   Experiment 2: Influence of the DoS Target's Processing Speed

In our second experiment, we measured how the processing speed of the device under attack influences the system's performance drop. To do so, we used a SP605 FPGA board to implement a standard PCIe endpoint. We designed the logic on the FPGA to be able to dynamically adjust the time it takes to process an incoming PCIe write packet. The minimum time the SP605 achieves is 112 ns. Processing time is modified by artificially keeping the write busy signal of the ingress port on **high**. This triggers the PCIe flow control mechanism to stop sending more packets to the SP605, which eventually leads to the congestion build-up on the PCIe interconnect. To quantify the impact of the different processing times, the following measurement series has been conducted:

1. The SP605 was attached to a VM via PCI Passthrough.
2. Packet processing times varied from 112 ns to 7.15 μs.
3. For each processing time, the VM executed a MMIO DoS attack on the SP605 device (see δ_4, Figure 1).
4. During the DoS attack, the latency for reading from the 82576 NIC was measured.

We chose the 82576 NIC for measuring, because out of the three NICs in our test system, it is the most advanced and has the fastest link speed. The results are depicted in Figure 4.

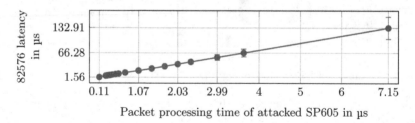

Fig. 4. Latency degradation for reading 32 bit words from the 82576 NIC while the SP605 experiences a MMIO DoS attack

They show a linear dependency between the processing time of the DoS target and the latency for reading from the 82576 NIC. This is because the PCIe packets which request a data word from the 82576 NIC must traverse many buffers and their respective slots which are also traversed by the DoS packets flowing to the SP605 device. This follows that, in the congested case, a packet can only advance one buffer slot further on its way to the endpoint after the DoS target has processed a packet. Therefore, the additional flight time of a packet, in the case of a fully congested interconnect, depends on two characteristics:

– The number of buffer slots shared with the DoS packets.
– The DoS target's processing time of a PCIe packet.

How the different processing speeds of the DoS target translate to network throughput degradation is shown in Figure 5.

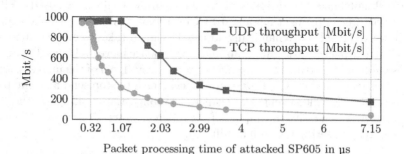

Fig. 5. TCP and UDP throughput degradation of the 82576 NIC while the SP605 experiences a MMIO DoS attack

The results show UDP and TCP throughputs of the 82576 NIC during a DoS attack on the SP605 as a function of the packet processing time of the attacked

SP605 device. TCP throughput is experiencing a drop for packet processing times greater than 320 ns, while UDP throughput sees a degradation for times greater than 1.07 μs. TCP is more affected by DoS attacks because of its protocol nature. Besides packets carrying the actual payload, additional SYN and ACK packets need to be transferred, which are also affected by the congestion on the interconnect. UDP, on the other hand, is a fire and forget protocol where every packet contains payload.

3.3 Experiment 3: Influence of the Path to the DoS Target

Our third experiment shows the influence of buffers and switching circuitry on the path from the CPU to the DoS target. Therefore, we put the 82576 SR-IOV NIC into the CPU slot, which connects to the PCIe 3.0 controller that is integrated into the CPU (compare Figure 1). As PCIe 3.0 is backwards compatible, the NIC runs with the same speed (x4, 2.5 GT/s) as in the Q77 slot.

Similar to Experiment 1 in Section 3.1, latencies for VF1.0 were measured for the idle case, as well as for one, two and three VMs attacking their respective VFs2.X. The results are shown in Figure 6, where they are compared to the results of the 82576 NIC residing in the Q77 slot (aka results of Experiment 1).

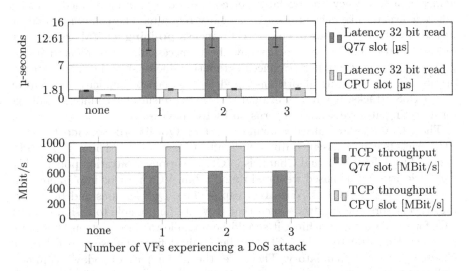

Fig. 6. Latency for 32 bit reads and TCP throughput for VF1.0 of the 82576 NIC while one or more VFs of the 82576 NIC experience MMIO DoS attacks. Results distinguished by the utilized slot (Q77 or CPU).

The results show, that for the idle case, the CPU slot is already faster than the Q77 slot (0.7 μs vs. 1.58 μs). Both latencies suffice to saturate a Gigabit link. However, when experiencing MMIO DoS attacks, the CPU slot is less impaired than the Q77 slot. Latencies for the CPU slot increase up to 1.81 μs. This is still fast enough for Gigabit Ethernet, but a 10 Gigabit connection would most likely experience a drop in throughput. This experiment shows that a shorter path to the I/O device (less buffers and switching circuitry) lowers the impact of DoS attacks. However, we still observe an increase in latencies by 157% (compare to the 698% increase from Experiment 1).

4   Protection Approaches

The three experiments conducted in Section 3 demonstrated that the impact of MMIO DoS attacks mainly depends on three key factors:

- The production rate of PCIe packets of the attacking CPU/core, aka frequency of the core.
- The consumption rate of the PCIe device targeted by a MMIO DoS attack.
- Switching circuitry and buffers on the path to the DoS target.

In the following, we present three approaches for tackling these weak points of current PCI Passthrough implementations. Each approach aims at a different component involved in the CPU to I/O device path.

Modern x86 CPUs support performance monitoring through built-in performance counters. They are available per core and can be programmed to count different events, like cache-misses or memory requests. The counters could be utilized by the Hypervisor to enforce **I/O-access policing** for VMs running on different cores. Similar approaches have been successfully implemented in the past, e.g. for mitigating performance degradation due to shared caches or memory [5][14]. The policing algorithms could be designed to implicitly prevent or detect DoS attacks. It must be evaluated if there are suitable counters available for detecting abusive access patterns on PCI(e) devices.

The PCIe standard already defines a set of **Quality-of-Service** features. PCIe packets can be assigned different Traffic Classes (TCs). These TCs can be assigned to different Virtual Channels (VC) via various arbitration policies, like fixed priority or time based weighted round robin. VCs must be implemented as dedicated physical buffers. With the help of these QoS features and by adapting Hypervisors and hardware such that it would be possible to assign distinct TCs for each Virtual Machine, it should be possible to enforce strong temporal isolation. Unfortunately, the PCIe standard only defines the use of one Virtual Channel (VC0) as mandatory. Therefore, the major part of today's commercially available hardware only employs a single buffer for ingress and egress ports. It should be evaluated how multiple VCs and available arbitration schemes could be leveraged to enforce temporal isolation.

Experiment 2 showed that the impact of a DoS attack depends on the DoS targets processing speed, given that the interconnect is faster than the packet production rate of the CPU. This has been shown in Figure 5, where performance drops for gigabit Ethernet emerged only for processing times that are slower than a certain threshold. Therefore, it is possible to employ countermeasures into the endpoint device. Like mentioned in [3], a **DoS detection** inside the I/O device could identify possibly harmful access patterns. If such a pattern is detected, the endpoint can discard these packets as fast as possible, which lowers the impact of the DoS attack. At the same time, the device reports the DoS attack's source via an interrupt to the Hypervisor. The latter can then take appropriate countermeasures, e.g. by shutting down the attacking VM.

5   Related Work

We are not aware of previous work that quantifies the impact of MMIO DoS attacks on the PCIe interconnect. However, other attacks relevant to PCI Passthrough have been demonstrated.

In [13], software attacks against Intel's VT-d IOMMU are demonstrated. They allow to break out of a Xen driver domain by generating specially crafted Message Signaled Interrupts with a PCI Passthrough device. Interrupt Remapping technology, which is available on recent hardware, can be used to prevent the demonstrated attacks if set up properly.

In [11], two possibilities for circumventing VT-d protection are presented. I/O devices with reconfigurable hardware could be used to spoof another device's source-id. These IDs are used by the VT-d IOMMU to identify a device's access rights to the system's memory regions. Supplying wrong device IDs enables a VM to compromise memory of co-residential VMs or the host. A second attack scenario describes the exploitation of PCI-to-PCI Express bridges with modified peripheral hardware. This attack requires physical access to the system.

6   Conclusion and Outlook

In this paper, we demonstrated that current, commercially available x86 virtualization solutions utilizing PCI Passthrough are vulnerable to MMIO Denial of Service attacks from malicious VMs. Three experiments with our test system showed how these attacks exploit the lack of temporal isolation in modern x86 setups. As a result, the performance of co-residential VMs and the host is impaired, because performance of every I/O device connected to the interconnect degrades significantly. Our findings are relevant to server and cloud computing environments, where PCI Passthrough and SR-IOV are established and deployed technologies, as well as for future CPS systems that aim to consolidate mixed-criticality applications on multi-core CPUs.

We are currently investigating and evaluating the presented protection approaches. First results showed that performance counters in modern Intel CPUs may be capable of detecting abusive access to PCIe I/O devices. Simulations with QoS enabled PCIe switches promise a strong temporal isolation between different VMs. Furthermore, we are investigating additional attack vectors like programming DMA engines of PCI Passthrough devices to execute DoS attacks or exploiting hardware bugs of PCI Passthrough devices. Such attacks might also require new/different approaches for countermeasures.

Acknowledgments. This work was funded within the project ARAMiS by the German Federal Ministry for Education and Research with the funding IDs 01|S11035. The responsibility for the content remains with the authors.

References

1. Barham, P., Dragovic, B., Fraser, K., Hand, S., Harris, T., Ho, A., Neugebauer, R., Pratt, I., Warfield, A.: Xen and the art of virtualization. In: ACM SIGOPS Operating Systems Review, vol. 37, pp. 164–177. ACM (2003)
2. Dong, Y., Yang, X., Li, J., Liao, G., Tian, K., Guan, H.: High performance network virtualization with sr-iov. Journal of Parallel and Distributed Computing (2012)
3. Dong, Y., Yu, Z., Rose, G.: Sr-iov networking in xen: architecture, design and implementation. In: Proceedings of the First Conference on I/O Virtualization, pp. 10–10. USENIX Association (2008)
4. Intel: Intel 7 series / c216 chipset family platform controller hub (pch) datasheet (2012)
5. Jing, W.: Performance Isolation for Mixed Criticality Real-time System on Multicore with Xen Hypervisor. Master's thesis, Uppsala University, Department of Information Technology (2013)
6. Kotaba, O., Nowotsch, J., Paulitsch, M., Petters, S.M., Theiling, H.: Multicore in real-time systems–temporal isolation challenges due to shared resources. In: Workshop on Industry-Driven Approaches for Cost-effective Certification of Safety-Critical, Mixed-Criticality Systems, WICERT (2013)
7. Navet, N., Monot, A., Bavoux, B., Simonot-Lion, F.: Multi-source and multicore automotive ecus-os protection mechanisms and scheduling. In: International Symposium on Industrial Electronics-ISIE 2010 (2010)
8. Nowotsch, J., Paulitsch, M.: Leveraging multi-core computing architectures in avionics. In: 2012 Ninth European Dependable Computing Conference (EDCC), pp. 132–143 (2012)
9. Paoloni, G.: How to benchmark code execution times on intel ia-32 and ia-64 instruction set architectures. White paper. Intel Corporation (2010)
10. Reinhardt, D., Kaule, D., Kucera, M.: Achieving a scalable e/e-architecture using autosar and virtualization. In: SAE World Congress (2013)
11. Sang, F.L., Lacombe, E., Nicomette, V., Deswarte, Y.: Exploiting an i/ommu vulnerability. In: 2010 5th International Conference on Malicious and Unwanted Software (MALWARE), pp. 7–14. IEEE (2010)
12. Sugerman, J., Venkitachalam, G., Lim, B.H.: Virtualizing i/o devices on vmware workstation's hosted virtual machine monitor. In: Proceedings of the General Track: 2002 USENIX Annual Technical Conference, pp. 1–14 (2001)
13. Wojtczuk, R., Rutkowska, J.: Following the white rabbit: Software attacks against intel vt-d technology (2011)
14. Zhuravlev, S., Blagodurov, S., Fedorova, A.: Addressing shared resource contention in multicore processors via scheduling. In: ACM SIGARCH Computer Architecture News, pp. 129–142. ACM (2010)

3D DRAM and PCMs in Processor Memory Hierarchy

Krishna Kavi[1], Stefano Pianelli[2], Giandomenico Pisano[2],
Giuseppe Regina[2], and Mike Ignatowski[3]

[1] University of North Texas, Denton, Texas, USA
[2] University of Pisa, Italy
[3] Advanced Micro Devices, Austin, Texas, USA

Abstract. In this paper we describe and evaluate two possible architectures using 3D DRAMs and PCMs in the processor memory hierarchy. We explore using (a) 3D DRAM as main memory with PCM as backing store and (b) 3D DRAM as the Last Level Cache and PCM as the main memory. In each of these configurations, since the proposed main memories are significantly faster than today's off-chip 2D DRAMs for main memory and either flash memory based SSDs or magnetic hard drives for secondary storage, we will introduce hardware assistance for virtual to physical address translation and to speed up page-fault handling.

We use Simics, a full system simulator and benchmarks from both SPEC 2006 and OLTP suites to evaluate our designs. Our experiments measure energy consumed and execution performance; we use CACTI for obtaining energy and latency values for our memory configurations.

Index Terms: Memory hierarchy, 3D DRAMs, PCM, set-associate addressing, energy modeling, memory latency modeling.

1   Introduction

The purpose of this paper is to investigate different alternatives for using 3D DRAMs and PCMs in the memory hierarchy. More specifically, we will explore the following organizations:

a). 3D DRAM as main memory (we call this CMM) and PCM as secondary memory

b). 3D DRAM as Last Level Cache and PCM as main memory (we call this LLC).

Since 3D stacked DRAMs offer much lower access latencies (and higher bandwidths) than off-chip 2D DRAMs, and PCMs offer similar advantages over other technologies for secondary memory, we will assume hardware assistance for virtual to physical address translation, as well as different ways of viewing pages and how page faults are handled. Our feeling is that traditional memory management that relies on several levels of page tables for translating virtual addresses to physical addresses will effectively defeat the advantages of the new technologies. Moreover, since the time needed to transfer pages between PCM and 3D DRAM will be significantly less than

E. Maehle et al. (Eds.): ARCS 2014, LNCS 8350, pp. 183–195, 2014.
© Springer International Publishing Switzerland 2014

that for transferring pages between magnetic disk drives and 2D DRAMs, kernel intervention leading to process context switches on page faults should be minimized.

In this paper we will evaluate our memory organizations and associated hardware needed to achieve our objective; we use execution performance and energy consumption as evaluation metrics. We use several different benchmarks drawn from both SPEC 2006 and OLTP suites, and vary benchmark mixes running on different cores in a multicore system. We use Simics, a full system simulator for our simulations, and CACTI for evaluating latencies and power requirements for our organizations.

The rest of the paper is organized as follows. In the next section we will review research that is very closely related to ours. In Section 3, we will describe the underlying hardware components for our memory architectures. Section 4 shows the results obtained using CACTI models for 3D DRAM memories along with the additional hardware structures (primarily SRAMs) and PCM memories. Using values for access latencies and power taken from CACTI simulations, we evaluate our memory organizations for executing various benchmarks. The experimental setup is described in Section 5. Section 6 analyzes the results.

2   Related Works

There are several methods used for stacking two or more dies: wafer-to-wafer bonding, die-to-die bonding and die-to-wafer bonding with different kinds of overlays. We will assume die-to-die technology with face-to-face overlays [7]. Stacking technology allows for the reduction of wire lengths by introducing vertical connections between dies called *Through Silicon Vias* (TSV) [6]. 3D stacked DRAMs appear to be an obvious way to take advantage of the new technology, and overcome memory access delays [8][9]. By using high capacity DRAM dies and using several die-to-die connections we can greatly reduce memory access latencies and increase bandwidths [10][11]. Several studies have shown that 3D DRAM memory may also reduce energy consumed by applications while improving performance, particularly when the memory layers are organized as *True 3D* [12]. In a *True 3D DRAM* organization, the $N-1$ upper layers contain only DRAM bit-cells. Layer 1 contains only the control logic such as sense amplifiers, row decoders, row buffers etc. In true 3D organization, ranks and banks of DRAM cross multiple layers to reduce the length of data paths and increase clock frequencies. In our work we assume that all the extra logic such as SRAMs needed for our cache like indexing, row buffers, and other components of a memory controller, are placed on the same logic layer (i.e. layer 1). In fact since layer 1 is dedicated to these functions we feel that it should have more than adequate area to accommodate our requirements. We use CACTI to model True-3D organization and obtain latencies and energy values for our memory organizations.

Qureshi et. al., [1] have studied the use of PCMs as main memory with a small 2D DRAM as a buffer to both speedup accesses and reduce write-backs to PCM. In particular, they focused their work to study the effect of overall system performance by adding PCM as a complement to the DRAM memory. The DRAM buffer is organized similarly to a hardware cache that is not visible to the OS, and is managed by the

DRAM controller. In our study, however, we evaluate different memory organizing using 3D DRAM and PCM in the memory hierarchy. The study by Lee, et. al., [13] is similar to that of Qureshi [1], in that they also use PCM as a replacement to DRAM as main memory. Like Qureshi, Lee uses small DRAM based buffers between last level caches and PCM, to reduce the amount of data written back to PCM. However, Lee studies the use of multiple DRAM buffers instead of a single DRAM based cache.

Our previous studies [16] have provided an organization and named it Cache Main Memory (CMM). The idea behind the CMM organization is that, since 3D DRAMs have lower latencies and higher bandwidths, allowing them to appear both as cache and as main memory can be advantageous. This duality makes the memory perfect either for operations that are more efficient if they use cache like addressing (fast address translation) or for operations that require main memory like organization (DMA, shared pages, OS management of memory). Our previous studies were limited since: (a) they did not provide details on the hardware needed, (b) they did not provide results on energy consumption, (c) they used access latencies for 3D DRAM and PCM memories that were simplistic and rely on average values, and (d) benchmarks did not seem to fully stress the memory architectures. In this paper we have addressed these limitations.

There have been other studies that are aimed at improving performance of PCM-based memory system and reduce the amount of data written back to PCMs [2][3] [4], [13]. These approaches are orthogonal to our studies since they can be applied within our organizations.

3   Foundation of the Architecture

The cache like indexing mentioned above with CMM [16] designs allows us to minimize the number of levels of page tables needed by the OS for translating virtual addresses to physical addresses. We assume that OS will use one or two levels of page tables and map a *large* virtually addressed region (or segment) to a *smaller* physical region (segment) in main memory. We assume that a virtual segment has k pages but physical segments contain fewer than k pages – pages in a virtual segment compete for pages in a physical segment similar to cache lines (see Figure 1).

In this paper we assumed 1024 pages per virtual segment, and use 64 pages per physical segment. The sizes of virtual and physical segments can be varied based on the size of the main memory, the number of page tables that must be looked up during translation and the number of tag bits needed for cache-like addressing of pages in a segment. SRAM structures store the virtual page numbers associated with pages that are currently in these physical pages. We use set associative search through the sets belonging to a physical segment to find the desired page. Once found, the newly obtained physical address is stored in TLB for future accesses; to further speedup the translation TLBs are used. Using larger virtual segments will require more tag bits.

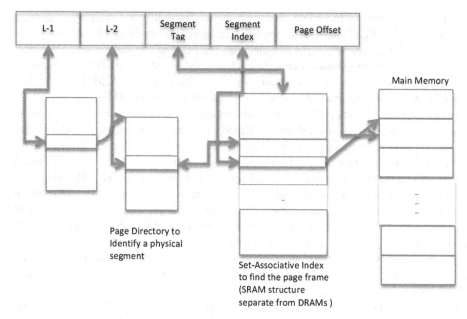

Fig. 1. Cache Like Indexing for Virtual Address Translation

3D-DRAM as LLC

In a configuration reported in this paper we explore using 3D DRAM as LLC (instead of SRAM based caches), and PCM as main memory. 3D DRAM as last level cache should be distinguished from traditional SRAM based caches. 3D LLC are divided into two components:

1. One component built with SRAM logic, which implements cache-like indexing and holds tags (usually on the logic layer of the 3D organizations).
2. The other component is implemented with DRAM logic and stores the actual data contained in LLC

For very large DRAMs when used as LLC, the number of lines of data in LLC will be large and thus the number of SRAM entries will also be very large. However, note that most SRAM based level 3 caches in current processors require a large portion of a chip (as much as 50%). Since we eliminate the traditional SRAM based level 3 cache, we feel that the saved area can be used to build a SRAM to hold the tags for DRAM based LLCs.

The actual data contained in the LLC will be located in the 3D DRAM. The SRAM location with matching tags will be used as an index into DRAM to find the desired data. When using 3D DRAM as LLC, the size of a single memory line is set to 1024 bytes, or 8 times larger than a typical cache line. The underlying memory controller will transfer data equivalent to a cache line to $L2$ caches.

PCM

When 3D DRAM is used as LLC, PCM will be used as main memory and we propose to use the same virtual to physical address translation described previously with the CMM organization for accessing PCM pages (Figure 1). This requires SRAM based tag structure (as with CMM organization described previously). For PCM as main memory configuration, the internal organization of PCM is similar to a DRAM organization using ranks, banks and row buffers.

4   Cacti Models

We modeled SRAM, PCM and 3D DRAM memories using CACTI (in particular we used CACTI-3DD [15] to simulate 3D DRAMs), in order to obtain very accurate design parameters for estimating delays and power requirements of the components used in our architectures. More specifically we obtain values for: *memory access times, cycle times, area and dynamic power.* We used all these parameters taken from CACTI within our simulations for obtaining execution performance results and overall energy consumed by benchmark applications. We explored different sizes and associatives for TLBs and as can be seen from Figure 2, a 2048 entry 8-way associative TLB provides a good compromise between performance and energy consumed by TLB hardware.

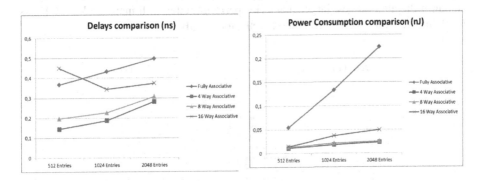

Fig. 2. TLB latencies and Power requirements

In addition, we use SRAM structure to contain tags representing (partial) physical addresses of currently resident physical pages (see Figure 1). The size of the SRAM depends on the size of the main memory, since a tag is stored in SRAM for each main memory page. SRAM is also used when 3D DRAM is used as the Last Level Cache. The size of the SRAM depends on the number of cache line in 3D DRAM. We use 8-way associativity. Figure 3 shows the results for different SRAM sizes -- x-axis represents DRAM sizes for which SRAMs contain tags.

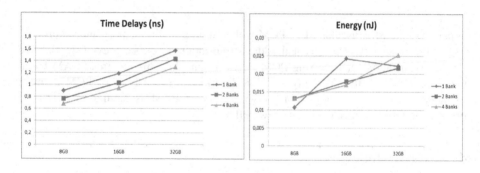

Fig. 3. Evaluation of SRAM latencies and Energy

We also used CACTI to model 3D DRAM. We chose 8, 16 and 32 GB for our DRAMs, but varied the number of ranks and banks. The number of channels has been fixed to 1. This choice actually penalizes the memory parallelism but it also provide a very simple entry-level 3D-DRAM for the *True-3D* configuration. We decided to use 4 ranks similar to the research described in [8] and [12]. The number of banks and the number of dies have been varied in our experiments (see Figure 4). All the results indicate designs with 8 dies (8 layers of DRAM cells) are not the best choice for our organization: they consume more energy and cause longer latencies. We notice that among 4 die alternatives, larger memories perform better with more banks: 16 banks for 8 GB, 32 banks for 16 GB and 64 banks for 32 GB.

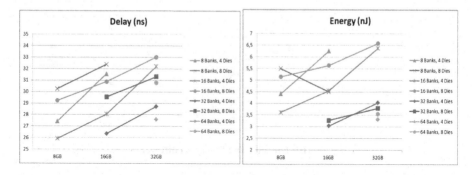

Fig. 4. CACTI models for 3D DRAM

Initially we explored available CACTI extensions for modeling PCM, such as the NVSim [17]. However this tool proved to be not useful for our study because it only simulates PCM at a bank level while we needed to simulate a complete PCM memory device with multiple banks. So we followed the work of Qureshi [1]. Basically, if we use a PCM with x GB, its delays and energies will be 4 times those of a 2D-DRAM with x/4 GB capacity

5   Experimental Setup

To simulate the different memory architectures we described in this paper we used Wind River Simics, a full system simulator. Simics includes several tools and modules that can be used to model user-defined architectures and components. Since we are only studying memory subsystem, the module of interest to us is the G-Cache. This module was originally designed to simulate simple caches but can easily be expanded to simulate any memory hierarchy.

We used benchmarks from SPEC 2006 and OLTP suites. Since we used a 4-core $x86 - 64$ "Hammer" system in our simulations, we created several benchmark mixes (mixes of 4 benchmarks each) to test our architecture as shown in Table 1 and Table 2. We will refer to each mix of 4 benchmarks by the name given in the first column of the table[1].

For L-1 and L-2 caches we used the same configurations as those of [16]. Per core L-1 caches are 32KB, 128 byte lines and use 4 way associative; per cores L-2 caches are 256KB, 8-way associative and 128byte lines.

Baseline

In order to evaluate the efficiencies of our proposed organizations we defined a generous baseline system. The system includes an *infinite* 2D DRAM for main memory. Thus it does not encounter page faults. However the system relies on slower 2D technology. The latencies and the energies modeled are taken from commercially available DDR3 DRAMs with 1GB for each bank. Also the baseline uses traditional 4K pages (unlike 32KB pages used for 3D DRAM organizations of our work) and relies on multiple levels of page tables for virtual to physical address translation. It uses a finite sized TLB and thus can encounter penalties on TLB misses. We modeled the baseline with TLB miss penalties using data for commercial systems using AMD processors. We felt that using a very generous baseline allows us to see the true benefits of new memory technologies.

Table 1. SPEC 2006 Benchmark Mixes

Mix Name	Bench 1	Bench 2	Bench 3	Bench 4	Total (GB)
Gobmk	Gobmk	Hmmer	H264Ref	Gromacs	0.046
Gamess	Gamess	Sphinx3	Tonto	Namd	0.027
Sjeng	Sjeng	Libquantum	Leslie3d	Astar	0.192
Omnetpp	Omnetpp	Astar	Calculix	Gcc	0.140
Milc	Milc	Wrf	Zeusmp	Soplex	0.866
Zeusmp	Zeusmp	Leslie3d	Gcc	CactusADM	0.718
GemsFTD	GemsFDTD	Mcf	Bwaves	CactusADM	2.262
Mcf	Mcf	Zeusmp	Milc	Bwaves	1.656

---

[1] Thus when we say 'Gobmk' or any other benchmark name, are actually referring to corresponding mix and not a single benchmark application.

Table 2. OLTP Benchmark Mixes

Mix Name	Bench1	Bench2	Bench3[2]	Bench4	Total (GB)
Auction Mark	Auction Mark	Auction Mark	Sjeng	Stream	20 ÷ 25
Seats	Seats	Seats	Sjeng	Stream	20 ÷ 25
Tatp	Tatp	Tatp	Sjeng	Stream	20 ÷ 25
Epinions	Epinions	Epinions	Sjeng	Stream	20 ÷ 25

6   Results and Analysis

A). CMM (3D DRAM as Main Memory)

In the first memory organization (or CMM that uses 3D DRAM as main memory) we used different TLB configurations (capacities and associativity). Charts 1 and 2 depict results obtained with the tested configurations, compared to the baseline, using SPEC2006 benchmark mixes. *For these experiments, we used a 8GB 3D DRAM since the memory footprints for SPEC2006 benchmarks is relatively small. We explored larger 3D DRAM sizes for OLTP benchmarks.* Although the baseline consists of an infinite 2D DRAM, the baseline does not always outperform our CMM. There are several reasons for this. First, the benchmarks used have finite memory footprints, often smaller than the 3D DRAM configurations we used - thus infinite 2D DRAM offers no special advantage. Second, conventional off-chip 2D DRAMs are significantly slower than 3D DRAMs. And baseline uses 4 KB pages (compared to 32 KB in 3D DRAM). This requires more frequent accesses to TLB and page tables for address translations.

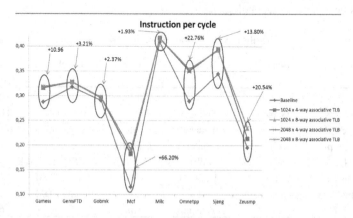

Chart 1. IPC - SPEC 2006 for CMM architecture (using different TLB configurations)

---

[2] We used Sjeng and Stream benchmarks along with OLTP in these mixes to represent server environments that may be presented with large footprint applications along with heavy processing load benchmarks.

It appears that for CMM (3D DRAM as main memory), 8-way 2048 entry TLB performs better than other configurations. *In subsequent experiments we will use this TLB configuration.* The chart shows that on average, this configuration performs 18% *better than the baseline.*

Let's now look at energy consumed. Although the baseline configuration contains infinite DRAM, in order to estimate power values for the baseline (infinite 2D DRAM) we used sizes that are comparable to the 3D DRAM used in CMM organization. Looking at the Chart 2, it should be noted that even under this assumption (finite energy consumption), our CMM system has comparable performance in terms of energy requirements for SPEC2006 mixes. *And most interestingly, TLBs and SRAM structures needed for CMM consume less than 1% of the energy used by the CMM memory system (detailed data not included in this paper, but similar observation can be made from Chart 8).*

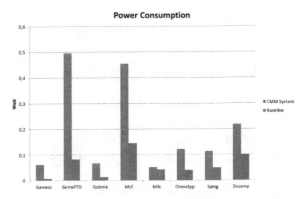

Chart 2. Energy Consumption - SPEC 2006 for CMM architecture (using 2048 8-way TLB)

OLTP benchmarks are characterized by a large memory footprint, in the order of $20 - 25\,GB$, and represent Cloud applications. As can be expected, for these applications the baseline's infinite DRAM becomes advantageous and outperforms our CMM (see Chart 3). And within CMM, lager memory footprint applications perform better with larger TLBs (Chart 3 shows data for different TLB sizes). Note that having a large 3D DRAM is not always beneficial - in some cases the longer latencies associated with larger 3D DRAMs can defeat the larger capacity (unless more than 4 dies are used; we used 4 dies). This can be seen when 32 GB 3D DRAM is used (which is more than sufficient to fully contain the OLTP benchmarks) the performance, in terms of IPC is worse than the baseline. It should be noted that while baseline does better than CMM, the performance differences are not significant. In reality a practical 2D DRAM based system will face several additional delays due to page faults.

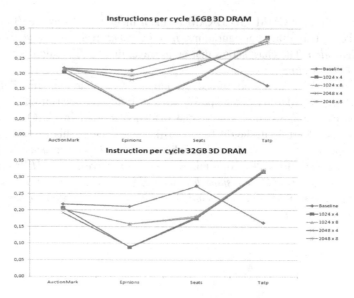

Chart 3. IPC - OLTP for CMM architecture

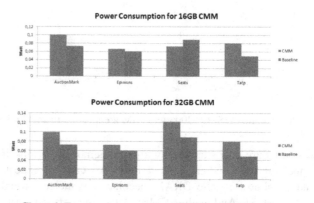

Chart 4. Energy consumption – OLTP for CMM architecture

Let's now consider energy performance for OLTP benchmarks. Chart 4 confirms what was stated before: even though CMM power consumption is still greater than the baseline, the values are within comparable range; in some cases, CMM actually has lower energy values than the baseline. Note that the baseline energy values are based on 2D DRAM sizes that are comparable to our 3D DRAM sizes used in CMM. If the baseline included a magnetic disk as a backing store, the power requirements for that configuration would be significantly greater than that for our organizations.

B). 3D-DRAM as Last Level Cache (LLC)

Charts 5 and 6 clearly show that our configuration that uses 3D DRAM as LLC and PCM as main memory outperforms the baseline configuration (with infinite 2D DRAM).

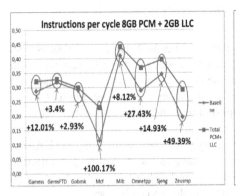

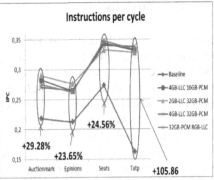

Chart 5. IPC for SPEC 2006 for LLC   **Chart 6.** IPC for OLTP for LLC

The execution performance gains are particularly impressive for mcf (SPEC2006) and Tatp (OLTP)[3]. The average performance gains for SPEC2006 benchmark mixes are **+27.30%** and **+45%** for the OLTP mixes. An observation that should be emphasized from the data shown above is that using larger than **2 GB** 3D DRAM for LLC shows insignificant performance improvements, regardless how large the PCM is. This may be in part because of our system, which has only 4 cores and the nature of these benchmark programs. Our experiments show that **2 GB** 3D DRAM as LLC and **32 GB** PCM as main memory is the best choice.

Looking at Charts 7 and 8, the significant energy consumed in this configuration is due to the 3D DRAM (as LLC), but the energy consumed increases only marginally when the size of the DRAM is doubled. This allows us to choose, depending on our needs, the best alternative: for instance a greater last level cache may be more useful when the application can use more cache capacity, or use smaller caches to save energy and cost of the system.

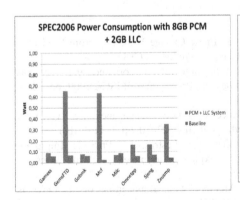

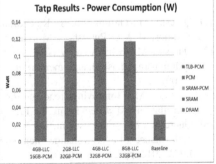

Chart 7. Power consumption for SPEC 2006   **Chart 8.** Power consumption for OLTP

---

[3] Note these names refer to benchmark mixes and not single benchmark.

7   Conclusions

Memory wall, which refers to the disparity of speeds between processors and memories, is still a major problem limiting the performance that can be achieved with modern processor technologies. Some new memory technologies may alleviate this problem to some extent. They include 3D DRAM memories and Phase Change Memories. These technologies present opportunities and challenges when they are included in processor memory hierarchy.

In this paper we explored two different memory organizations for using 3D DRAMs and PCMs. Each configuration has associated advantages and disadvantages, differing in execution performance, energy consumed and cost. Our goal is to provide initial data that may guide choices on how these new technologies can be used.

3D DRAM as LLC configuration, with PCM as the main memory, achieves best results in terms of execution times, but consume more energy than the other configuration. This is due to larger SRAMs needed to store tags for a large LLC (we separate the tags form DRAM and store them in SRAM for fast access to tags).

The CMM (3D DRAM as main memory and PCM as secondary memory) configuration require higher execution times than the previous case, but require lower energies. This is expected because CMM uses a longer path to its data using larger pages; at the same time, we needed smaller SRAMs. In this configuration, SPEC2006 benchmarks mixes achieve reasonably comparable results as the baseline, since they exhibit smaller memory footprints, unlike OLTP benchmarks where CMM performs worse than the baseline.

Acknowledgement. This work is supported in part by the NSF Net-Centric I/UCRC, AMD and other industrial members

References

[1] Qureshi, M., Gurumurthi, S., Rajendran, B.: Phase Change Memory – from Devices to Systems. M. & C. Publishers, Morgan & Claypool Publishers (2011)
[2] Qureshi, M., Srinivasan, V., Rivers, J.A.: Scalable high performance main memory system using phase change memory tecnology. In: Proceedings of ISCA 2009, pp. 24–33 (2009)
[3] Qureshi, M.: Improving read performance of phase change memories via write cancellation and write pausing. In: Proceedings of HPCA 2010, pp. 1–11 (2010)
[4] Quereshi, M., Franceschini, M., Jagmohan, A., Lastras, L.: PreSET: Improving performance of phase change memories by exploiting asymmetry in write times. In: ISCA 2012, pp. 380–391 (2012)
[5] Wulf, W.A., McKee, S.A.: Hitting the Memory Wall: Implications of the Obvious. Computer Architecture News 23(1), 20–24 (1995)
[6] Lau, J.: Through-Silicon Vias for 3D Integration. McGraw-Hill Professional (2012)
[7] Lecarpentier, G., Vos, J.D.: Die 2 Die Bonding, SET S.A.S. (Smart Equipment Technology), 131 Impasse Barteudet, 74490 Saint Jeoire, France & IMEC, Kapeldreef 75, Leuven B-3001, Belgium (2012)

 [8] Loh, G.: Computer architecture for Die Stacking. In: International Symposium on VLSI Technology, Systems and Applications, Hsinchu, Taiwan, pp. 1–2 (2012)

 [9] Liu, C.: Bridging the processor-memory gap with 3D IC technology. IEEE Design and Test, 564–565 (2005)

[10] Sun, H.: 3D DRAM design and application to 3D multicore systems. IEEE Design & Test of Computers, 36–46 (2009)

[11] Weis, C.: Design space exploration for 3D-stacked DRAMs. In: Proceedings of DATE-11 (2001)

[12] Loh, G.: 3D-Stacked Memory Architectures for Multi-core Processors. In: 35th International Symposium on Computer Architecture, ISCA 2008, pp. 453–464 (2008)

[13] Lee, B.C., Ipek, E., Mutlu, O., Burger, D.: Architecting phase change memory as a scalable dram alternative. Sigarc Comput. Archit. News 3(37), 2–13 (2009)

[14] Barr, T., Cox, A., Rixner, S.: Translation caching: skip, don't walk (the page table). In: ISCA 2010, Saint-Melo, pp. 48–59 (2010)

[15] Wilton, S.J.E., Jouppi, N.: CACTI: an enhanced cache access and cycle time model. IEEE Journal of Solid-State Circuits 31(5), 677–688 (1996)

[16] Sherman, J., Kavi, K., Potter, B., Ignatowski, M.: A Multi-core Memory Organization for 3-D DRAM as Main Memory. In: Kubátová, H., Hochberger, C., Daněk, M., Sick, B. (eds.) ARCS 2013. LNCS, vol. 7767, pp. 62–73. Springer, Heidelberg (2013)

[17] Xiangyu, D., Cong, X., Yuan, X., Norman, P.J.: NVSim: A Circuit-Level Performance, Energy, and Area Model for Emerging Nonvolatile Memory. IEEE Transactions on Computer-Aided Design of Integrated Circuits and Systems 31(7), 994–1007 (2012)

A Service-Oriented Architecture for Virtualizing Robots in Robot-as-a-Service Clouds

Anis Koubaa

Prince Sultan University, Riyadh, Saudi Arabia
CISTER/INESC-TEC, ISEP, Polytechnic Institute of Porto, Porto, Portugal
COINS Research Group, Riyadh, Saudi Arabia
akoubaa@coins-lab.org

Abstract. Exposing software and hardware computing resources as services through a cloud is increasingly emerging in the recent years. This comes as a result of extending the service-oriented architecture (SOA) paradigm to virtualize computing resources. In this paper, we extend the paradigm of the SOA approach to virtualize robotic hardware and software resources to expose them as services through the Web. This allows non-technical users to access, interact and manipulate robots simply through a Web browser. The proposed RoboWeb system is based on a SOAP-based Web service middleware that binds robots computing resources as services and publish them to the end-users. We consider robots that operates with the Robotic Operating System (ROS), as it provides hardware abstraction that makes easier applications development. We describe the implementation of RoboWeb and demonstrate how researchers can use it to interact remotely with the robots. We believe that this work consistently contributes to enabling remote robotic labs using the cloud paradigm.

Keywords: Cloud Robotics, Service-Oriented Architecture, SOAP, Web Services, Robot Operating System (ROS), Remote Robotic Labs.

1 Introduction

Cloud robotics have been attracting a lot of interest in the last three years [1–5]. In a general sense, this emerging paradigm consists in integrating cloud computing concepts and other Internet Web-centered technologies to leverage converged infrastructures and shared services for robotics [6]. Cloud robotics are very promising to be the most effective way to create and monitor robotic applications, in particular for service robots, in different fields including security and surveillance, remote robotic labs, and home and industrial automation. Indeed, on the one hand, robots will be able to go beyond their limited processing capabilities and take profit from Internet computing resources. On the other hand, robots can be accessed anywhere and anytime through Web interfaces. Several recent works have proposed different designs and implementations for cloud robotics [2, 4, 7, 6, 8]. With reference to these works [1], the robotic cloud

E. Maehle et al. (Eds.): ARCS 2014, LNCS 8350, pp. 196–208, 2014.

can play two different roles. The first role is to act as a *virtualization middleware*, where service-oriented technologies are used to build virtual environments of robotic ecosystem through Web services, which allow the users to access the robots through Web browsers and Internet utilities. The virtualization of robotic ecosystem through Web services contributed to offering the Robot as a Service (RaaS) model [1, 7]. For instance, in [1], the authors designed and implemented an service-oriented framework of RaaS model for both Windows and Linux operating systems using Web 2.0 technologies and complies with common service and development platforms standards. The second role that the robotic cloud plays is *computations offloading*, which consists in migrating intensive computations and processing tasks from the robot to the cloud computing infrastructure [9, 2]. This is particularly interesting for mobile robots that might have low computation and energy capabilities to perform computationally-intensive tasks, such as 3D localization and mapping, image processing, object recognition, etc. For instance, in [9], the authors proposed a cloud robotics system for recognizing and grasping common household objects by sending 2D images captured by the robot to the cloud, which returns semantic information about the object.

In this paper, we consider the design and implementation of a cloud robotics system of the first category, i.e. virtualization layer. Indeed, the idea of this work is triggered by our need to develop a remote robotic lab to allow different students and researchers outside the University and/or abroad to access and use our robotic platforms located in Saudi Arabia. Our main objective is to make our robots accessible through the Internet for authorized users through Web browsers. We would like to allow students and researchers to access, manipulate, interact and perform experiments with robots living behind the "cloud". For this purpose, we devised a service-oriented framework based on SOAP Web services for mapping hardware and software robotic resources as *services* and publish them to the end-users as Web services. We considered robots operating with the Robotic Operating System (ROS) [10], which also provides an abstraction layer, at the level of the operating system, of the hardware resources of the robots. The main advantage of ROS is that it allows to manipulate sensor data of the robot as a labeled abstract data stream, called topic, without having to deal with hardware drivers. Several previous works have also proposed different architecture for cloud robotics and remote robotic labs, which we present and discuss their advantages and limitations in details in Section 2, and we clarify the difference of our proposed system as compared to other existing systems.

The remainder of this paper is as follows. Section 2 surveys the most relevant works on cloud robotics and discusses their contributions to the field. Section 3 describes the system and software architecture of the RoboWeb system starting from requirements specification to system design. In Section 4, we present the implementation, deployment and experimentation with the RoboWeb system and we demonstrate its features. Section 5 concludes the paper and discusses future works.

2   Related Works

The concept of cloud robotics has been increasingly expanding since the last three years. Basically, the cloud robotics research trend can be roughly classified into two categories: (*i.*) using cloud for virtualizing robotic resources (e.g. [1, 7]), (*ii.*) using cloud for offloading heavy computations from the robot to the cloud (e.g. [9]). In what follows, we present the most relevant works over the past four years in the increasing chronological order of their publications dates.

In [1], the authors exploited the Service Oriented Architecture (SOA) technology to design and implement a prototype of the Robot as a Service (RaaS) cloud computing model. The design complies with the common service standards, development platforms, and execution infrastructure, following the Web 2.0 principles and participation. The authors also demonstrated through experiments that their system is effective, flexible, and portable.

DAvinCi was proposed in [2] as a cloud computing software framework for service robots. The goal of this system is to offload intensive workloads from the onboard robots' resources to a backend cluster system in the cloud. The idea was to investigate the possibility of parallelizing the execution some complex robotic algorithms, and applied it to the FastSLAM algorithm as a proof of concept. The DAvinCi architecture was implemented using the open source Hadoop cluster and ROS as messaging framwork for the robotic ecosystem. The deployment did not consider network latencies and delays, which turns the results limited to ideal operational conditions.

In [11], the authors designed a robot cloud center to overcome the limitation in capacity, versatility and extensibility of robotic applications, and to meet the diverse requirements of the end-users requesting robot resources according to their demand. They also designed a Robot Resources Scheduler to minimize the task execution cost while still meeting the end-users requirements. Robot scheduling simulation proved that robots, especially whose cost-capability density is low, can be used more efficiently with the scheduler. In [12], the authors have proposed the RSi Research Cloud (RSi-Cloud) that seamlessly integrates robotic services with the Internet.

In [4], the authors described their vision of cloud robotics and proposed different possible architectures to address the constraints faced by current networked robots. The motivation of the work was to allow the robots to share information and computation resources among each other and cooperate through the cloud to acquire new knowledge and behaviors. The cloud artchitecture design takes into account two types of communication paradigms namely the machine-to-machine (M2M) communications among participating robots, and the machine-to-cloud (M2C) communications between the robots and the cloud. The authors also proposed three elastic computing models for cloud robotics, namely the peer-to-peer model, proxy-based model and the clone-based model.

In [13] and [7], the authors made interesting extensions to the ROS middleware, namely *rosjs*, which is a JavaScript library for ROS that exposes the robot functionalities as web services, and *rosbridge*, which is a light weight protocol that exposes robot sensor data and controllers, through web sockets accessible anywhere over the Internet, and provides security mechanisms and runtime tools for remotely manipulating the robots. Similarly to one of the objective of our work, The rosjs and robridge were proved to enable remote laboratories, and a prototype was implemented and tested for monitoring iRobot Create and PR2 robots. The difference with our work is that our approach is based on a SOAP-based service oriented archirtcture, which represents a complementary solution to rosjs and rosbridge.

3   RoboWeb System Architecture

In this section, we describe the system architecture and the software development process of the RoboWeb system. We start by specifying the functional and non-functional requirements of RoboWeb, then, we describe the system architecture and software design. RoboWeb differs from existing systems in that it leverages SOAP-based Web services for building the virtualization layer of the cloud robotic infrastructure.

3.1   Requirements Specification

As a research group installed in Saudi Arabia at Al-Imam Mohamed bin Saud University and Prince Sultan University, we have several robotic platforms including four Turtlebot robots, two Wifibot Lab robots, two unmanned aerial vehicles (UAVs), namely the AscTec Pelican and AscTec FireFly, which are cutting-edge and expensive robotic technologies, and several other sensor and robotic devices. Our objective is to allow our students and researchers abroad or from outside the University during non-working hours to access and use the robots in a ubiquitous and seamless way, i.e. anywhere and anytime, through the Internet. This lead us to design a service-oriented cloud robotics system, namely RoboWeb.

Basically, the idea of RoboWeb is to develop a service-oriented middleware that plays the role of the virtualization layer. This layer binds software and hardware robotic resources as Web services allowing authorized users to subscribe to the published services of interests, through which they can "play" with the robots. Two Web services options were possible: SOAP approach or the RESTful approach. We had to make a milestone decision at this point. Finally, we have opted for the SOAP approach for several reasons. First, SOAP provides a well-structured transctional model between the client (service subscriber) and server (service publisher) that allows to define a contract between both ends. Indeed, in contrast to SOAP, REST is basically an architectural style based on the HTTP protocol rather than a SOA middleware as it is the case with SOAP Web services. Second, SOAP Web services enables the definition of composable and complex Web services in contrast to REST. This is an important requirement in the design of RoboWeb as we need to take advantage of the flexibility of the SOAP approach to define different service/abstraction layers, which help achieving virtulization more effectively.

With respect to robots to be supported by the system, we considered robotic platforms operating with ROS. The adoption of ROS has several advantages. First, ROS is a free and open-source middleware for robots that acts as a meta operating system and builds a hardware abstraction layer. This makes the programming of ROS-enabled robots much easier as software developers will not have to deal with hardware drivers and interfacing. In fact, ROS already provides comprehensive and well-structured libraries and drivers for several robots and sensor devices, and publishes sensor data (camera frames, laser range data, IMU data, motors speeds, etc.) simply as labeled data streams called *topics*. Second, the control of robots through Web services will be much easier when ROS is used as the Web server will only have to deal with topics rather than with hardware resources. Indeed, ROS provides another level of resources virtualization at the operating system level. Third, ROS complies with component-based software development, which makes ROS-based system modular, extensible and flexible. This is particularly important as architectural design since services can be mapped to software components making easier their composition, addition and removal.

We also derived the following four (most important) non-functional properties for the RoboWeb system:

- **Service-Orientation:** This is the most important requirement in our system as we need to map any robotic resource or operation as a service. The SOA approach allow to easily extends the capabilities and functionalities of the system by dynamically adding services. The users will be able to manipulate robots in the same way they use any Web service. In addition, robot software developers can reuse available services to design more complex composite services.

- **Reliability:** The system must be reliable in different perspective. First, it must be available such that it ensures continuous connectivity with users at anytime. In addition, it must provide consistent view of the robot status to the users. For example, the system should consistently report in real-time the list of connected robots and change the connectivity status each time a robot join or leave the cloud.

- **Modularity:** The system should be easily extensible by dynamically adding/removing components to/from the system. The modularity ensures the independence of the different modules which makes their integration more effective. This is very appropriate for service composition and orchestration to build more complex Web services for manipulating the robots. For instance, making experiments with a robot can be seen as a complex Web service composed of several other Web services including accessing robot, running a program, getting the list of nodes and topics, etc. The modularity has also the advantage of allowing software reuse.

- **Real-Time:** Once the user is connected to a particular robot, it is important that the system ensures small and controlled delays. Indeed, the user must be kept up-to-date with latest status updates of the robot for effective control and monitoring. Large delays and delay variations (jitter) will compromise

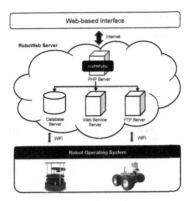

Fig. 1. High-Level System Architecture

the user experiments. Delays must be kept as low as possible to ensure interactivity between the user and the robot.

3.2 System Architecture Design

In this section, we describe the RoboWeb system architecture and discuss the design considerations. Figure 1 depicts a high-level overview of the system architecture. The bottom layer consists of the robotic ecosystem that comprises ROS-enabled robots, each of them runs its own ROS master node. Mobile robots are dotted with wireless communication capabilities allowing them to collaborate for performing certain missions on demand. the ROS platform is used for sensor data collection and streaming among the robot agents and the end-users (clients).

The top layer defines the Web interfaces for users to access and manipulate the robots remotely. We implemented a PHP library, called rosPHP, to act as an abstraction layer on top of ROS providing the required ROS functionalities to interact with ROS-enabled robots. The rosPHP layer allows the interaction between the end-users and the robots though SOAP Web services and provides several functionalities including connection to the Web server, getting the list of available ROS-enabled robots, getting ROS nodes and topics of selected robots, getting information about robots sensors, publishing and subscribing to a ROS topic, creating new ROS package, uploading, running and stopping ROS programs.

The core part of the system is the RoboWeb service broker. It basically include three main components: (1) the Web service server, which is required to deploy robotic Web services and respond to end-users requests. The Apache Axis Web server for development and deployment of SOAP Web services. (2) the back-end MySQL database that is used to store information about the whole cloud including robots, users, programs, reservations, experiments, etc. and (3) the FTP server, which is used to upload files, namely experiments output, user programs, and robot description files. The robot description files are XML files that contain meta-data about the robots and their sensors.

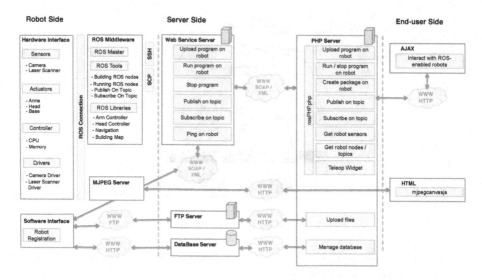

Fig. 2. Low-Level System Architecture: The figure presents four main parts of the RoboWeb System. The End-User side uses a AJAX interface to interact with ROS-enabled Robot through a PHP Server (rosPHP) the implements the core functionalities of ROS. The rosPHP server communication with the Web Service server that directly interfaces with ROS middleware installed on robots through SSH and SCP protocols to perform requested commands submitted by the user and ensure sending back responses to the end-user side.

Figure 2 presented a more detailed view of the system architecture and its subsystems.

The robot side of the system includes the hardware interface that consists of robot hardware resources (i.e. sensor, actuators, controllers) and their drivers. This interface is abstracted by the ROS middleware that provides a first level of virtualization to all robotic hardware resources. Indeed, any sensor or actuator data is provided by ROS as a a stream of data that can be manipulated by any client that subscribes to that data. ROS manages the hardware through ROS connection which provides tools and libraries required to control and manage hardware and software interfaces. The MJPEG server is defined as a ROS package that streams image topics captured from the robot camera ROS using the HTTP protocol, so that it can be displayed by any browser. The software interface is responsible for the robot auto-registration to the system. We developed a program that allows a robot to register to the RoboWeb system and publishes the services that it provides. In the server side, the Web service server interacts with the ROS middleware through the SSH secure communication protocol to execute commands or programs on the remote robot. On the other hand, it uses the Session Control Protocol (SCP) to transfer computer files between the server and to run program on the remote robot. We also consider the PHP server which essentially includes three main parts. The first part consists of the rosPHP library, which represents a PHP layer that defines ROS and network commands to be executed on the robot such as upload program to robot, run a ROS node on the robot, stop a ROS node, publish a ROS topic, create a ROS package, get robot sensor information, subscribe to a ROS topic and ping a robot, and tele-operate the robot. the rosPHP layer communicates with the Web service server via SOAP/XML protocol, and also define methods to access FTP and database servers via FTP and HTTP protocols.

The end-user side consists of the user-interface which uses AJAX to interact with PHP server. It also uses the *mjpegcanvasjs*, a JavaScript tool that allows the user to easily display, manage and modify ROS image streams received from MJPEG sever via HTTP.

4   Implementation and Deployment

4.1   Hardware and Software Suits

To demonstrate the feasibility of our architecture, we developed a complete prototype of the RoboWeb application and tested on a wireless local area network. The Web Service server was implemented on a computer laptop with Intel(R) Core(TM) i3 CPU, 4.00 Go RAM, and Ubuntu 12.04 OS, running Apache Axis (Apache eXtensible Interaction System) Web service framework for generating and deploying Web service applications; Apache Tomcat, which provides a Java HTTP web server environment for Java code (including Servlets and JSP) to run in; and Eclipse IDE for software development.

The front-end user interface provides an easy-to-use and intuitive GUI to interact with the robots living behind the cloud. It was implemented using: (*i.*) AJAX client side scripting technology for ensuring asynchronous interaction with the rosPHP server library that we developed. It provides the benefit of asynchronous communication with the server seamlessly in the background without interference with the display and the behavior of the web page; (*ii.*) HTML5 Web Workers technology to take benefit from its multi-threading capability in particular for subscribing to ROS topics; indeed, Web Workers technology allows the execute and run multiple JavaScript scripts in the background of a web page independently of other user-defined scripts, and enables to perform parallel and computationally expensive tasks without interrupting the user interface. This is particularly useful in our RoboWeb system as a robot may independently subscribe to or publish several ROS topics that must be handled with different threads in the user-interface; (*iii.*) mySQL triggers and procedures to manage the information and reservations of the robots; and (*iv.*) JQuery and CSS for the dynamicity and the design of the interface.

The back-end database was also implemented using the mySQL 5.5 server. The FTP server was set-up on the same computer laptop using the vsftpd 3.0 server (Very Secure FTP Daemon), which is an FTP server for Unix-like systems, and represents the default FTP server for the Ubuntu OS. Regarding the PHP server, we have installed PHP5 on the same computer laptop.

As for the robotics hardware, we tested our RoboWeb prototype with two ROS-enabled robots, namely the TurtleBot 2.0 robot and the Wifibot Lab V2 robot. Any other ROS-enabled robots can easily be added to the RoboWeb system as will be explained in the deployment subsection.

4.2   Deployment

In this subsection, we provide step-by-step guidelines on the deployment of the RoboWeb system through illustrative examples and we demonstrate how to use it for accessing and manipulating ROS-enabled robots.

The first step in deployment consists in setting-up and configuring the back-end system of the RoboWeb cloud, that is configuring the robots, running their ROS middleware and setting-up their networking configurations including the IP addresses, the IP port numbers, the IP Addresses of the ROS Masters and its port numbers. These settings are crucial for the ensuring the communication between the ROS-enabled robots and the system. Second, at its startup, the Web Service server will check and discover existing robots in the cloud automatically. Actually, once a robot joins the cloud, it uploads its description file on the FTP server. Then, it registers itself in the back-end database, or updates its status and IP address if it has already been registered. At this instance, the robots are considered as *active* and accessible to the end-user interface through the RoboWeb cloud. Finally, the robot invokes a web service that periodically tests its connectivity. This web service tests the robot connectivity every 30 seconds. If the robot disconnects or fails, the web service will attempt three times testing the robot connectivity: 180, 300 and 600 seconds later. If the robot remains still disconnected, the web service will deactivate the robot by updating its status in the database to be *inactive*, notify the administrator by email, and stop testing the robot connectivity. In what follows, we present the main functionalities at the user side.

1. **Register and authenticate:** First, the end-user is required to create an account to be authorized to access the robotic resources. Once the registration request is submitted and approved by the administrator, the end-user must authenticate to use the system functionalities. Non-authenticated users are only able to get information about active robots in the cloud. They are not allowed to reserve robots or perform experiments.

2. **Browse the list of active robots:** Once authenticated, the end-user is allowed to obtain and browse the list of active robots (i.e. already connected with the Web Service server) with information including the list of available ROS topics and ROS nodes, robot sensors (camera, laser data), IP address, and status. The top half of Figure 3 depicts the list of robot categories (TurtleBot 2.0, Wifobot Lab V2) supported by the RoboWeb robotic prototype.

   When the end-user selects a robot category, all active robots that belong to this category will be displayed. Then, the end-user can get information of a given robot including (1) robot description, (2) list of available ROS Nodes, and (3) list of available ROS Topics. The bottom half of Figure 3 shows the information about the selected robot. It is also possible for a user

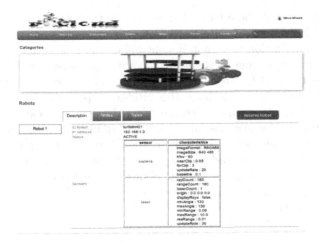

Fig. 3. Robot Description Interface

to look at the list of ROS topics and the list of ROS nodes of the selected robot, as illustrated in Figure 4. This interface allows the user to indentify the different ROS nodes and topics that he might need in his application and helps him choosing the most appropriate robot for his experiments before proceeding to the reservation.

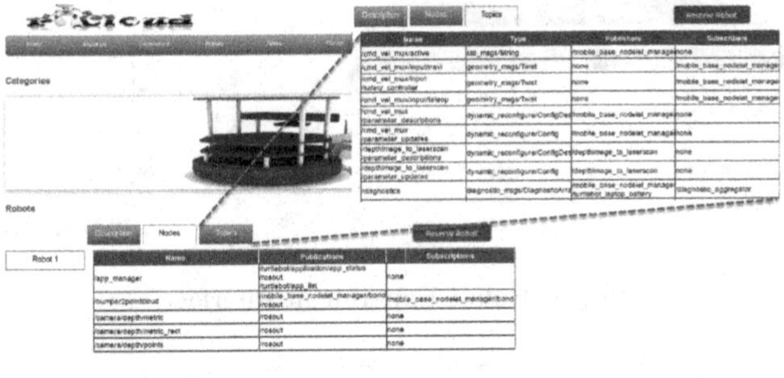

Fig. 4. List of Available ROS Nodes and ROS Topics in the Selected Robot

3. **Reserve Robot:** After browsing the list of robots and identifying currently active robots and their specifications, the end-user may reserve a robot to use for experimentation and/or remote manipulation. The reservation process consists in booking the requested robotic platform for a particular reservation date and time. The RoboWeb reservation system is able to check possible booking conflicts and only propose the user with available dates/times for the available active robots.

4. **Perform Experiment:** Once an authenticated user has successfully booked a robot, he will be allowed to access and use that reserved robot for running

his experiments at the allocated time slot. Authorized users are allowed to interact with and manipulate a given robot by uploading and running a ROS program, in addition to remotely controlling and monitoring it. For safety of execution, experiments should be run with the assistance of a local technical staff to avoid hazardous manipulation and control of the robot in the cyber-lab space. Figure 5 shows the "Robot Experiment Interface", which provides information concerning the selected robot, the booked period, the robot camera video streams, and the list of ROS topics. The Robot Experiment Interface also shows buttons to upload, run, and stop ROS programs on reserved robot. The end-user is allowed to publish and subscribe to any of the available ROS topics. He also allowed to send rospy commands (ROS Python) to control the robot. Execution results are displayed in the output area in real-time.

Fig. 5. Robot Experiment Interface

Fig. 6. System Fault-Tolerance: The figure shows an error message when the server stops working for any reason, warning the user and requesting him to contact the administrator

For maintaining connectivity with the server, the client system controls continuously whether the web server is working, and whether the reserved robot is still connected and active. The green light on the right side of the name of the reserved robot indicates that the robot is still active. When the connection is lost, the end-user will be updated by changing the connection color to the gray. Figure 6 displays the warning messages sent by the system to alert the end-user when a problem, with the web server or the robot, occurs.

5   Conclusion

In this paper, we presented RoboWeb, a SOAP-based service-oriented architecture that virtualizes robotic hardware and software resources and exposes them as services through the Web, contributing to the evolving concept of cloud robotics. The major contribution of this paper lies in the integration of different Web services technologies with the Robot Operating System (ROS) middleware to allow for different levels of abstraction (multi-layer architecture), ensuring more modularity and flexibility of the deployment. We have also demonstrated the feasibility and the added value of RoboWeb through a complete prototypic implementation.

Although we believe that this work provides a consistent step towards the future cloud robotics paradigm, we are currently planning and working on extending the RoboWeb system design and deployment in several perspectives. First, we aim at extending the deployment to the Internet rather than on a local area network. Proxy servers can be used for that purpose. Furthermore, we aim at looking into more depth into security issues, in particular, investigating potential attacks and threats that might compromise the robots' cloud operation, and undertake appropriate preventive measures. Finally, the RoboWeb system should allow the user to reserve and use more than one robot to be able to deploy multi-robot applications.

Acknowledgment. This work is supported by the iroboapp project "Design and Analysis of Intelligent Algorithms for Robotic Problems and Applications" [14] under the grant of the National Plan for Sciences, Technology and Innovation (NPSTI), managed by the Science and Technology Unit of Al-Imam Mohamed bin Saud University and by King AbdulAziz Center for Science and Technology (KACST).

The author would like to thank Fatma Ellouze for her excellent performance in this work in the context of her graduation project and her outstanding work in the implementation of the RoboWeb system.

Also, the author would like to thank Rihab Chaari, Dr. Slim Kallel and Dr. Wajdi Louati for the technical support they provided.

References

1. Chen, Y., Du, Z., García-Acosta, M.: Robot as a service in cloud computing. In: Fifth IEEE International Symposium on Service Oriented System Engineering. IEEE (2010)

2. Arumugam, R., Enti, V.R., Bingbing, L., Xiaojun, W., Baskaran, K., Konga, F.F., Meng, K.D., Kumar, S., Kit, G.W.: Davinci: A cloud computing framework for service robots. In: 2010 IEEE International Conference on Robotics and Automation (ICRA), pp. 3084–3089 (2010)
3. Waibel, M., Beetz, M., Civera, J., D' Andrea, R., Elfring, J., Galvez-Lopez, D., Haussermann, K., Janssen, R., Montiel, J.M.M., Perzylo, A., Schiele, B., Tenorth, M., Zweigle, O., van de Molengraft, R.: A world wide web of robots: Roboearth. IEEE Robotics and Automation Magazine (2011)
4. Hu, G., Tay, W.-P., Wen, Y.: Cloud robotics: architecture, challenges and applications. IEEE Network 26(3), 21–28 (2012)
5. Kamei, K., Nishio, S., Hagita, N., Sato, M.: Cloud networked robotics. IEEE Network 26(3), 28–34 (2012)
6. Lee, J.: Project report: web applications for robots using rosbridge (2012)
7. Osentoski, S., Pitzer, B., Crick, C., Graylin, J., Dong, S., Grollman, D., Suay, H.B., Jenkins, O.C.: Remote robotic laboratories for learning from demonstration. International Journal of Social Robotics, SORO, special issue on Learning from Demonstration (2012)
8. Yang, T.-H., Lee, W.-P.: A service-oriented framework for the development of home robots. International Journal of Advanced Robotic Systems (2013)
9. Kehoe, B., Matsukawa, A., Candido, S., Kuffner, J., Goldberg, K.: Cloud-based robot grasping with the google object recognition engine. In: 2013 IEEE International Conference on Robotics and Automation, ICRA (2013)
10. Quigley, M., Conley, K., Gerkey, B.P., Faust, J., Foote, T., Leibs, J., Wheeler, R., Ng, A.Y.: Ros: an open-source robot operating system. In: ICRA Workshop on Open Source Software (2009)
11. Du, Z., Yang, W., Chen, Y., Sun, X., Wang, X., Xu, C.: Design of a robot cloud center. In: 2011 10th International Symposium on Autonomous Decentralized Systems (ISADS), pp. 269–275 (2011)
12. Kato, Y., Izui, T., Murakawa, Y., Okabayashi, K., Ueki, M., Tsuchiya, Y., Narita, M.: Research and development environments for robot services and its implementation. In: 2011 IEEE/SICE International Symposium on System Integration (SII), pp. 306–311 (2011)
13. Osentoski, S., Jay, G., Crick, C., Pitzer, B., DuHadway, C., Jenkins, O.C.: Robots as web services: Reproducible experimentation and application development using rosjs (2011)
14. iroboapp: Design and analysis of intelligent algorithms for robotic problems and applications, http://www.iroboapp.org

Towards Code Safety with High Performance

Ghazaleh Nazarian[1], Luigi Carro[2], and Georgi N. Gaydadjiev[3,1]

[1] Faculty of Electrical Engineering, Mathematics and Computer Science
Delft University of Technology, Mekelweg 4, 2628 CD Delft, The Netherlands
g.nazarian@tudelft.nl
[2] Instituto de Informatica, Universidade Federal do Rio Grande do Sul, Av. Bento
Gonçalves, 9500,Porto Alegre, Brazil
carro@inf.ufrgs.br
[3] Dept. of Computer Science and Engineering, Chalmers University of Technology,
Rannvagen 6, Goteburg, Sweden
georgig@chalmers.se

Abstract. Reliability is a major issue for safety-critical embedded
systems such as biomedical implants. In such systems, hardware fault
tolerance techniques are usually not available in off-the-shelf processors,
because of the intrinsic energy costs of hardware duplication or triplica-
tion. As an alternative, software schemes based on compiler transformations are used for error detection and recovery. A common software error
class caused by hardware transient faults is Control-Flow Errors (CFEs).
In this paper we demonstrate how a new technique based on software
instrumentation can benefit from loop-unrolling, with huge impact on
control-flow reliability. We show the impact of loop-unrolling on fault-
coverage and performance of these schemes. Thanks to the proposed approach, significant fault-coverage concerning CFE can be obtained with
no extra costs, and even faster than other available techniques with the
same fault-coverage level.

1 Introduction

Traditionally the most important concern in digital systems design is performance. On the other hand, with technology advances, the ongoing trends of
shrinking feature sizes and increasing chip density have made processors more
susceptible to transient faults [1]. As a result, reliability is emerging as another
important design criterion especially for safety-critical embedded systems such
as biomedical implants. In these systems, operating on batteries, another very
important criterion is the overall energy consumption. There is a large body
of research on hardware optimizations for performance, reliability and power-
consumption [2] [3] [4]. Given the energy constraints, hardware optimizations
can not be used for off-the-shelf processors in many systems. Software optimizations are alternative techniques for reliability without requiring special hardware.
Software reliability optimizations add extra code to detect and correct errors
during program execution, caused by transient hardware faults.

E. Maehle et al. (Eds.): ARCS 2014, LNCS 8350, pp. 209–220, 2014.

Hardware faults may cause two types of errors in program execution: data and control-flow errors. Experiments on the influence of heavy-ion fault injection on program behavior shows that more than half of the injected faults cause Control-Flow Error (CFE) [5]. Other works show that about 75% of injected data errors are masked [6] [7] [8]. Based on these statistics, CFE is a major reason for system breakdown and safety-critical systems require a dedicated reliability optimization for detecting and correcting this class of errors. Software optimizations for CFE detection associate unique signatures with branch-free sections of the code, which are referred as Basic Blocks (B-blocks) [9] [10]. At compile time, the code is instrumented with *set* and *test* assertions. *Set* assertions, used in all B-blocks, update the runtime signature. *Test* assertions, added at predefined program locations, compare the runtime signature with the associated signatures to verify correct execution. The added assertions cause extra performance and energy overheads. The performance overhead of CFE detection methods depends on the category of the CFE detection. Methods from path-based category have lower fault-coverage and lower overhead, while methods in the predecessor/successor-based category have high fault-coverage and high overheads [11].

The target of this paper is safety-critical systems with high performance and low energy requirements. In such systems, both optimizations for improving performance and reliability are required. The challenge which remains is to understand which error detection/recovery method is efficient to be used with performance-oriented optimizations, in order to provide high performance and reliability with low energy-consumption. From reliability-optimization aspect, this challenge is satisfied if employing the reliability optimization together with a performance-oriented optimization does not degrade the fault-coverage.

Among the CFE detection methods we investigate the impact of loop unrolling on two methods; Control-flow Correcting Assertion (CCA) [10] and Selective Control-Flow Checking (SCFC) [11]. SCFC is a novel hybrid method with the lowest possible overheads and moderate fault coverage [11]. SCFC is chosen for our investigation, due to the fact that it selects the optimum program points to add assertions by analyzing the Control Flow Graph (CFG) topology at compile time. Therefore, the performance and energy overheads are minimized without degrading fault-coverage significantly. Since SCFC instrumentation is done with the knowledge of the CFG topology, it is expected that using SCFC together with compiler optimizations that change this topology (like loop unrolling) does not degrade the fault coverage. The other method (CCA [10]) belongs to predecessor/successor-based category with the highest fault coverage. It is important to note that high-coverage CFE detections (such as CCA) do not analyze the CFG topology before adding assertions. Hence, most compiler optimizations (which are mainly loop-related) go against either fault-coverage or performance in these approaches. On the contrary, thanks to its topology analysis, SCFC can benefit from compiler transformations that change the CFG topology.

In this paper we present a case study of the previous concept, showing that a traditional compiler technique like loop-unrolling can improve SCFC performance while sustaining high fault coverage. For this study workloads are chosen from a benchmark suite containing safety-critical code for biomedical implants. The main contributions of this paper are:

- Achieving higher performance and reliability using SCFC (for CFE detection) together with loop unrolling (for performance-improvements);
- Improving fault coverage of SCFC by additional 9.75% on average;
- Analysis of the obtained results based on the workloads CFG.

The remainder of this paper is organized as follows: Section 2 gives an overview of software optimizations targeting reliability and performance. Section 3 briefly illustrates the two studied CFE detection methods with an example. In this section also the effect of loop unrolling on the studied methods is analytically investigated. In Section 4, the experimental setup and obtained results are given. In this section we show SCFC benefits from loop unrolling in terms of fault-coverage and performance. Finally, the conclusions are given in Section 5.

2 Related Work

There are several software optimization methods to improve reliability by instrumenting programs with additional code to check run-time program execution. EDDI [12] is a method to detect data errors which checks the consistency between duplicated instructions. However due to the major influence of CFE in modern digital systems malfunctioning, we aim at detection methods targeting this important class of errors. Several software optimization methods proposed for CFE detection are: CCA [10], ECCA [13], CFCSS [9], YACCA [14], CEDA [15], ACFC [16], Abstract Control Signatures (ACS) [6], SCFC [11] and SWIFT [17]. SWIFT is a hybrid method combining CFCSS for CFE and EDDI for data error detection.

In all the CFE detection methods a unique signature is associated to each B-block. At run-time *set* assertions update *Runtime Signature* (RS) to the current B-block signature and *test* assertions check the correctness of the RS content to validate control-flow correctness. *Set* assertions are added to all B-blocks to update RS along the control-flow path. However, the locations where *test* assertions are added, depend on the CFE detection category. The two CFE detection categories, depicted in Figure 1 are *path-asserting* and *predecessor/successor-asserting* methods. A path-asserting method adds *test* in one B-block per control-flow path[1] to assert correct path execution. Predecessor/Successor-asserting methods add *test* in all B-blocks to check if the previous (or next) B-block in the execution flow is the correct predecessor (or successor). The difference between these two categories is in the number of added *test* assertions in the program. Predecessor/Successor-asserting methods add more *tests*, therefore has higher

---

[1] A *path* is group of B-blocks executed in an uninterrupted sequence.

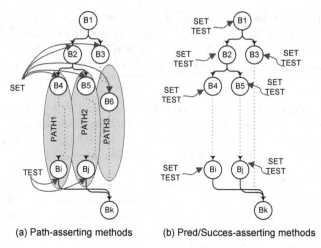

(a) Path-asserting methods   (b) Pred/Succes-asserting methods

Fig. 1. Two categories of SM techniques

overheads and also potentially higher fault-coverage. Path-asserting methods add less *test* assertions, have less overhead but lower fault-coverage.

CFCSS, ECCA, CEDA, YACCA and CCA are all a predecessor/successor-asserting methods with high fault coverage and high overhead. Among this group CCA has the simplest *set/test* assertions and no extra CF-parameters. ACFC is a path-based method that adds *tests* to the last B-Block of the loops and the exit B-Block of the program. ACFC does not add *tests* at the end of paths which are formed due to conditional branches. As a consequence, it is efficient only in programs with symmetric CFG topology. If a program is not symmetric due to unbalanced conditional statements (an *if* without an *else* counterpart), ACFC adds dummy *elses* to balance the CFG and then instrument it. This causes extra branches and is the major reason of overhead in ACFC. ACS is also a path-based method, since it adds one *test* assertion for group of B-Blocks in single-entry-multiple-exit regions. ACS offers a coarse grain CFE detection, useful in commodity systems which require high performance while 100% fault-coverage is not demanded as in safety-critical systems. Both methods are in the path-based category, have simple and low-cost assertions.

SCFC is a hybrid method. It uses CFG analysis information and adds low-cost *test* assertions to the last B-Block of the identified control-flow paths, including the paths resulted from conditional statements. B-blocks that are not part of a control-flow path (at compile-time it is not clear if the B-block is executed with group of other B-blocks at run-time or not), are called lonely-blocks. SCFC does not leave these blocks un-detected, it adds a *predecessor-test* assertions to them. Since SCFC adds *test* also to the conditional paths (as opposed to ACFC), it is efficient even in programs with un-balanced asymmetric CFG topology. Compared to ACS, SCFC has two differences: 1) it defines finer grain paths; and 2) it guards lonely-blocks with *predecessor-test* assertions. As a result, it provides higher fault coverage. High level of fault coverage makes SCFC more suitable for safety-critical systems.

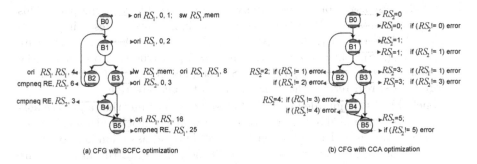

Fig. 2. CFG optimized for CFE detection

The authors of [18], have investigated the impact of different compiler optimizations on the fault-recovery ability of ACCE [19]. ACCE is a recovery method which uses CEDA [15] for CFE detection. The result of this investigation shows that several compiler optimizations can increase the fault recovery rate. It is also demonstrated that there is no specific optimization that can increase ACCE fault coverage and this is the structure of the workloads which influences how optimizations impact the recovery rate. Regarding today's safety-critical systems requirements, there is a need for high performance and reliability at the same time. Compiler-based code transformations for increasing performance reduce the number of executed instructions, and increase parallelism level and memory locality in high-performance superscalar, vector, and parallel processors [20]. Among the discussed methods in [20] loop-unrolling is a widely-used method to increase instruction-level parallelism, applicable for most of the workloads. Loop-unrolling changes CFG topology and B-block sizes. Since SCFC analyzes CFG topology and based on the obtained results adds assertions to the program, loop-unrolling can be used before SCFC optimization to improve performance while preserving high fault coverage.

3   The Impact of Loop Unrolling on SCFC and CCA Optimizations

In this section, first we give a brief explanation over the mechanism of the hybrid CFE detection (SCFC) and a method from predecessor/successor-asserting category (CCA) with an illustrative example. CCA is chosen as the representative of high-coverage CFE detection methods due to its simple *set* and *test* assertions and higher coverage compared to other methods in the category. After the methods explanation, we discuss the influence of loop-unrolling on fault coverage of SCFC and CCA.

Figure 2.a. shows an example CFG subgraph instrumented with SCFC. SCFC adds two assertion types based on the CFG analysis:

1. B-blocks residing in control-flow paths are instrumented with low-cost path-based assertions, meaning that each B-block in the path has a *set* assertion

and the *test* assertion is added only to the last B-block of the path. This *set* assertion is an OR instruction with an immediate representing the B-block MASK (ori RS_1, RS_1, MASK), which updates path-runtime-signature contents (RS_1). The *test* assertion is cmpneq instruction to compare the contents of RS_1 with the path CONST (cmpneq RE, RS_1, CONST). RE is a restricted register that holds the results of fault detection.

2. Lonely-blocks are guarded with *predecessor-test*, meaning that a *predecessor-set* assertion is added to the predecessor of the lonely-block and a *predecessor-test* assertion is added to the lonely-block. This *set* assertion is also an OR instruction, but it updates the contents of the predecessor-runtime-signature (RS_2) to the signature of the predecessor B-block ($oriRS_2, 0, Sig_{pre}$). The *test* assertion is an instruction comparing RS_2 contents with the predecessor signature ($cmpneqRE, RS_2, Sig_{pre}$). If there is an inconsistency RE is written.

In the subgraph depicted in Figure 2, SCFC defines {B1, B2} and {B0, B3, B5} as control-flow paths and B4 as a lonely-block. Respectively, it instruments the B-blocks in the control-flow paths and the lonely-block with corresponding assertions, as shown in Figure 2.a.

Figure 2.b. shows the same CFG instrumented with CCA assertions. CCA adds a pair of set RS_1 in the end of the predecessor B-block and test RS_1 at the beginning of the current B-block to check the predecessor correctness. It also adds a pair of set RS_2 at the beginning of the B-block and test RS_2 to the end of the B-block for detecting erroneous jumps to/from mid of the B-block. In case inconsistencies are detected an error recovery routine will be called. However B-blocks with multiple predecessors can not be guarded with the first pair of assertion ($set/test\ RS_1$). In the depicted CFG, B1 and B5 are not guarded with RS_1 checking.

Loop unrolling may change CFG topology, B-blocks number and their sizes. The effect of unrolling loops on the CFG depends on the loop that is unrolled: if it is *while* or *for* loop; if it is a nested loop or there is a conditional statement in the loop-body. Figure 3 shows different CFGs before and after unroll. Unrolling simple for-loops, without conditional-statements or other loop-constructs in the body, does not change the CFG topology as depicted in Figure 3.a. In this case the unrolled CFG has the same B-blocks numbers and only the number of instructions in the unrolled B-block (B2 in the figure) is increased. On the other hand, the CFG of for-loops with conditional-statements (or a loop-constructs) in the body, changes after unrolling. Figure 3. b. shows how the CFG of such a loop changes after unrolling with increased number of B-blocks. Unrolling while-loops requires checking the loop-condition before loop body repetition and *break* in case the condition does not hold. The *break* statements cause extra branches in the unrolled CFG (as shown with **bold arrows** in Figure 3). Figure 3.c. shows that, opposed to for-loops, unrolling even a simple while-loop changes the CFG and the total B-blocks number.

Change of CFG after loop-unrolling affects CFE detection fault coverage. As discussed above CCA is weak in fault detection of B-blocks with multiple

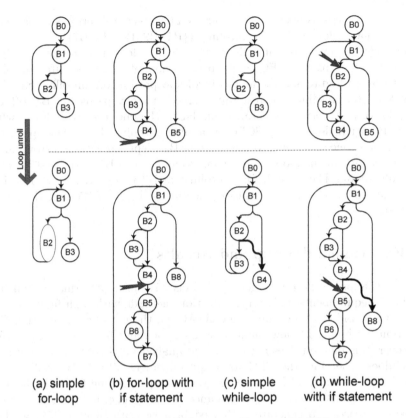

(a) simple for-loop   (b) for-loop with if statement   (c) simple while-loop   (d) while-loop with if statement

Fig. 3. Impact of for-loop unrolling on the CFG

predecessors. Therefore, if the resultant CFG after unroll has more number of such B-blocks, CCA fault coverage may decrease. In Figure 3.(b) and (d), it is shown that unrolling loops with a conditional statement in the body, adds the number of B-blocks with multiple predecessors in the resultant CFG. This is the case also in nested loops, when the out-most loop is unrolled. In these cases CCA fault coverage decreases. On the other hand, SCFC analyzes the newly formed CFG after unrolling and groups most of the multiple-predecessor B-blocks to the new set of control-flow paths.

SCFC has a higher fault-coverage when CFG has a bigger control-flow path in the loops than smaller ones. Since SCFC resets the path-runtime-signature in the first block of the control-flow path (RS1 in Figure 2.a), having a bigger loop-control-flow path with less number of loop-iterations helps to detect more number of erroneous branches to the loop-control-flow path. As an example, the control-flow path of the loop in Figure 3.b, before unrolling is {B1, B2, B4}. After unrolling this control-flow path expands to {B1, B2, B4, B5, B7}. An erroneous branch to the end of B4 (depicted by an arrow in Figure 3.b), is not detected by SCFC in the loop-control-flow path before unrolling ({B1, B2, B4}). This is due to the fact that the path-runtime-signature (RS_1), is reset in the beginning of B1 and this error is masked. However, SCFC detects this erroneous branch in the loop-control-flow path after unrolling ({B1, B2, B4, B5, B7}).

Contrary to for-loops, unrolling while-loops does not result in bigger loop-control-flow path. SCFC fault coverage in not increased after unrolling while-loops. In Figure 3.d, the loop-control-flow path before unrolling has three B-blocks. After unrolling, the resultant loop-control-flow paths are {B1, B2, B4} and {B5, B7}. An erroneous branch similar to the one discussed above, which targets B4,is not detected by SCFC even after unrolling the while-loop. In Figure 3.d, an erroneous branch to the begin of B2 (depicted with an arrow) in the second iteration of the loop, is equivalent to an error in B5 at the first iteration of unrolled-loop. The error before unrolling in B2 is detected by SCFC, But, SCFC can not detect the erroneous branch to the begin of B5 after the loop is unrolled.

4   Experimental Setup and Results

Since in this paper we are targeting systems with high performance and high reliability requirements, only CFE detection methods with high fault-coverage level (SCFC and CCA) are investigated. ACFC, the path-based-asserting CFE detection method, adds low number of assertions and has low fault-coverage. Moreover, this method does not define and analyze CFG control-flow paths, as SCFC does. Therefore the CFG topology refinement after loop-unrolling does not solve the problem of low fault-coverage. Loop unrolling favors both SCFC and CCA methods in terms of performance, as the level of instruction-level parallelism increases. To generate optimized binaries with SCFC/CCA, we have used CoSy compiler-development framework [21]. This framework contains different modules (so called engines) responsible for common compilation tasks, e.g, scheduling, etc. SCFC/CCA are implemented as a new engine and added to the compiler. We show how loop unrolling influences SCFC and CCA fault-coverages. In this section first the used workloads in our experiments, the error model and the error injection frame-work for evaluating the fault-coverages are introduced. Next, the obtained results are illustrated and analyzed.

workloads: We have selected ImpBench benchmark suite as a representative for applications which require high reliability and performance. ImpBench is a benchmark suite with applications typical for biomedical implants.

Control-Flow Error Model: Errors at software level occur due to hardware transient faults caused by electro-magnetic radiation or wire crosstalk. The impact of transient hardware faults at software control flow can be categorized in two CFE types based on the reason of the occurrence:

- CFEs that occur due to a fault in the opcode of a non-branch instruction and conversion to a branch instruction. The consequence of this type of CFE is an erroneous jump from the middle of a B-block to the end of the same B-block or to another B-block in the CFG. This type of fault is referred to as FT1;

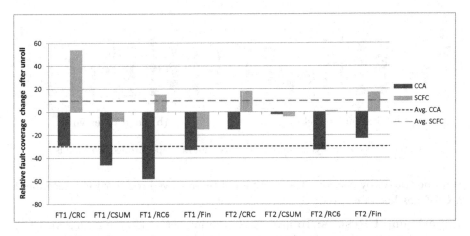

Fig. 4. Loop-unrolling impact on fault coverage

- CFEs which happen due to a fault in the operand bits of a branch instruction. This CFE type causes an erroneous jump from the end of a B-block to a random location. In the rest of the paper this type is referred to as FT2.

Faults which cause a branch instruction change to a non-branch will either behave as FT2 or may cause a data error and not a CFE. Data errors should be detected with another group of detection methods as discussed in section 2

Error Injection: In order to evaluate the impact of loop unrolling on SCFC and CCA fault coverage, we have used an error-injection mechanism that injects the two CFE types discussed above. We have emulated FT1 and FT2, using a special error-injector instruction and a Linear-Feedback-Shift-Register (LFSR) which are implemented in the simulator. The error-injector instruction is added in the beginning of the program-under-test along with a random value (generated by RANDOM linux command) as its operand. The random value is used as the LFSR seed with $x^{32}+x^{31}+x^{29}+x+1$ polynomial. The LFSR with this polynomial generate pseudo random numbers [22] and we use it to generate faulty branch targets. The random value also determines the trigger time of the error. After the number of cycles specified by the trigger time has passed, an error is generated.

For generating FT1, the first fetched non-branch instruction after the trigger time is converted to a branch instruction with a random value as its operand. This is done by modifying the corresponding opcode bits of the register between *Fetch* and *Decode* pipeline stages. The random value of the operand is the LFSR register value at that moment. An FT2 error is generated, for the first fetched branch-instruction after the trigger time, by changing the operand bits of the register between *Fetch* and *Decode* to a random value. The random value for branch operand is provided by the LFSR.

Error Detection Mechanism: In order to detect the errors, one of the registers in the register file is reserved for the *test* assertions. In case a control-flow error is detected by *test* assertions, this register is written. After the simulator generated

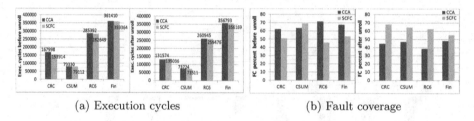

(a) Execution cycles   (b) Fault coverage

Fig. 5. Execution cycles and fault coverage in loop-unrolled workloads

runtime traces, by checking the contents of the reserved register we determine if a CFE has been occurred.

Experimental Results: To investigate the impact of loop unrolling on CCA and SCFC fault-coverage, we have executed four sets of simulations for four versions of workloads binaries. The different versions of binaries are generated with four versions of optimized compilers: 1) with SCFC but without loop unrolling; 2) with SCFC and with loop unrolling; 3) with CCA but without loop unrolling and 4) with CCA and loop unrolling. The generated workload binaries are evaluated using Synopsys Processor Designer cycle-accurate simulator [23]. Each set of simulation run, consists of 1000 runs with one error injected in each run. The obtained fault-coverage results from running the binaries without loop-unrolling, are used as the baseline to investigate the improvement or degradation of CCA and SCFC fault-coverages after loop-unrolling.

The impact of loop unrolling on SCFC and CCA fault-coverage is illustrated in the diagram of Figure 4. The diagram shows fault-coverage improvement or loss due to loop unrolling for the two error types (FT1 and FT2). On average fault-coverage of SCFC is improved by 9.75%, while CCA fault coverage is decreased by 29.87%. The main reason of fault-coverage improvement in SCFC is due to CFG analysis prior to instrumentation. Loop unrolling restructures workloads CFG topology. SCFC takes this restructuring into account, forms new control-flow paths and adds required number of assertions. However CCA, does not adapt to the new topology and instruments the code with the same number of assertions before unrolling. The peculiar cases where SCFC fault-coverage after unrolling has degraded is for CSUM workload. This workload has two while-loops, that after unrolling have smaller control-flow paths. As discussed in section 3, this condition is not favorable for SCFC and degrades its fault coverage.

The plot in Figure 5.a. shows the total execution-cycles for SCFC and CCA before and after loop-unrolling. As the data in the diagram of execution-cycles after loop-unroll shows, in three example workloads SCFC has less number of execution-cycles than CCA. The only case which SCFC causes higher execution-cycles than CCA is for CRC. This is due to the fact that a high percentage of B-blocks of this workload have multiple-predecessors. CCA does not instrument these blocks with inter-block *set/test* assertions, while SCFC does not leave any B-block without being checked. As a consequence SCFC causes higher execution-cycles, but also higher fault coverage after loop-unroll, as illustrated in Figure 5.b. High fault-coverage level of SCFC, when loop unrolling is used (for instruction-level parallelism), makes SCFC a better method for CFE detection than CCA for safety-critical systems with high performance requirement.

5   Conclusions and Future Work

In this paper the impact of loop unrolling on a new control-flow error detection method, SCFC, is investigated.The results are compared with one of the traditional detections schemes with the highest fault-coverage. Comparing results show that SCFC, thanks to its control-flow graph analysis, can benefit from traditional compiler optimizations as loop unrolling, both in terms of performance and fault coverage. Other techniques with similar fault coverage do not allow such optimization, which are crucial for current day processors. The average fault coverage improvement of SCFC with loop-unrolling compared to a version without loop-unrolling by 9.75%, shows that SCFC is a suitable control-flow error detection method for safety-critical systems with high-performance requirements. Moreover, it shows that this technique can be applied in modern processors that can exploit instruction-level parallelism, hence providing high fault-coverage and performance at the same time. As future work, we investigate the impact of other loop-transforming compiler optimizations on SCFC method. It is expected that compiler transformations which simplify the control-flow graph topology can improve SCFC performance and fault-coverage.

References

1. Zhu, D.: Energy management for real-time embedded systems with reliability requirements. In: Proceedings of International Conference on Computer-Aided Design, ICCAD 2006, pp. 528–534 (November 2006)
2. Ganesh, T.S., et al.: Seu mitigation techniques for microprocessor control logic. In: Proceedings of the Sixth European Dependable Computing Conference (EDCC 2006), pp. 77–86 (2006)
3. Mahmood, A., McCluskey, E.J.: Concurrent error detection using watchdog processors-a survey. IEEE Trans. on Computers, 160–174 (1988)
4. Saxena, N., McCluskey, E.J.: Dependable adaptive computing systems the roar project. In: Proceedings of International Conference on Systems, Man, and Cybernetics, pp. 2172–2177 (1998)
5. Gunneflo, U., Karlsson, J., Torin, J.: Evaluation of error detection schemes using fault injection by heavy-ion radiation. In: Proceedings of Nineteenth International Symposium on Fault-Tolerant Computing, FTCS-19, pp. 340–347 (June 1989)
6. Khudia, D.S., Mahlke, S.: Low cost control flow protection using abstract control signatures. In: Proceedings of LCTES, pp. 3–12 (June 2013)
7. Feng, S., Gupta, S., Ansari, A., Mahlke, S.: Shoestring: Probabilistic soft-error reliability on the cheap. In: Proceedings of ASPLOS (2010)
8. Wang, N.J., Quek, J., Rafacz, T.M., Patel, S.J.: Characterizing the effects of transient faults on a high-performance processor pipeline. In: Proceedings of DSN (June 2004)

9. Oh, N., Shirvani, P.P., McCluskey, E.J.: Control flow checking by software signatures. IEEE Trans. on Reliability 51(1), 111–122 (2000)

10. Kanawati, G.A., Nair, V.S.S., Krishnamurthy, N., Abraham, J.A.: Evaluation of integrated system-level checks for on-line error detection. In: Proceedings of IEEE International Computer Performance and Dependability Symposium, pp. 292–301. IEEE (September 1996)

11. Nazarian, G., Seepers, R.M., Strydis, C., Gaydadjiev, G.N.: Compiler-aided methodology for low overhead on-line testing. In: International Conference on Embedded Computer Systems: Architectures, Modeling, and Simulation (SAMOS XIII), pp. 219–226 (July 2013)

12. Oh, N., Shirvani, P.P., McCluskey, E.: Error detection by duplicated instructions in super-scalar processors. IEEE Trans. on Reliability, 63–75 (March 2002)

13. Alkhalifa, Z., Nair, V.S., Krishnamurthy, N., Abraham, J.: Design and evaluation of system-level checks for on-line control flow error detection. IEEE Trans. on Parallel and Distributed Systems 10(6), 627–641 (1999)

14. Goloubeva, O., Rebaudengo, M., Reorda, M.S., Violante, M.: Soft-error detection using control flow assertions. In: 18th IEEE International Symposium on Defect and Fault Tolerance in VLSI Systems, pp. 581–588. IEEE (November 2003)

15. Vemu, R., Abraham, J.: Ceda: Control-flow error detection using assertions. IEEE Trans. on Computers 90(9), 1233–1245 (2011)

16. Venkatasubramanian, R., Hayes, J.P., Murray, B.T.: Low-cost on-line fault detection using control flow assertions. In: 9th IEEE On-Line Testing Symposium, pp. 137–143. IEEE (July 2003)

17. Reis, G.A., et al.: Swift: software implemented fault tolerance. In: Proceedings of International Symposium on Code Generation and Optimization, CGO, pp. 243–254 (March 2005)

18. Parizi, R.B., Ferreira, R.R., Carro, L., Moreira, Á.F.: Compiler optimizations do impact the reliability of control-flow radiation hardened embedded software. In: Schirner, G., Götz, M., Rettberg, A., Zanella, M.C., Rammig, F.J. (eds.) IESS 2013. IFIP AICT, vol. 403, pp. 49–60. Springer, Heidelberg (2013)

19. Vemu, R., Gurumurthy, S., Abraham, J.: Acce: Automatic correction of control-flow errors. In: Int. Test Conference, pp. 1–10 (2007)

20. Bacon, D.F., Graham, S.L., Sharp, O.J.: Compiler transformations for high-performance computing. ACM Trans. Computing Surveys 26(4), 345–420 (1994)

21. Cosy compiler, http://www.ace.nl/compiler/cosy

22. George, M., Alfke, P.: Linear feedback shift registers in virtex devices (2007), http://www.xilinx.com

23. Synopsys processor designer, http://www.synopsys.com/Systems/BlockDesign/processorDev/Pages/default.aspx

Detecting Compromised Programs
for Embedded System Applications

Xiaojun Zhai[1], Kofi Appiah[1], Shoaib Ehsan[1], Wah M Cheung[1], Gareth Howells[2],
Huosheng Hu[1], Dongbing Gu[1], and Klaus McDonald-Maier[1]

[1] School of Computer Science & Electronic Engineering
University of Essex, Colchester, UK
{xzhai,kappiah,sehsan,wmcheu,hhu,dgu,kdm}@essex.ac.uk
[2] School of Engineering and Digital Arts
University of Kent
Canterbury, UK
W.G.J.Howells@kent.ac.uk

Abstract. This paper proposes an approach for detecting compromised programs by analysing suitable features from an embedded system. Features used in this paper are the performance variance and actual program counter values of the embedded processor extracted during program execution. "Cycles per Instruction" is used as pre-processing block before the features are classified using a Self-Organizing Map. Experimental results demonstrate the validity of the proposed approach on detecting some common changes such as deletion, insertion and substitution of programs. Overall, correct detection rate for our system is above 90.9% for tested programs.

Keywords: ICmetrics, Self-Organising Map (SOM), embedded system security.

1 Introduction

As embedded systems involve various aspects of our everyday lives, they are often needed to process sensitive information or perform critical functions, which make security an important concern in embedded computer architecture design [1]. The rapid growth of embedded systems has transformed the way we create, destroy, share, process and manage information. However, this has also paved the way for unauthorised access, fraud and other related crimes [2]. Security has been extensively explored in the context of general purpose computing and communications systems, such as cryptographic algorithms and security protocols [3]. Such security measures typically provide a basis for securing embedded system rather than enabling a system's overall security. On the other hand, as embedded systems are often specific to a certain function, the resources and cost are very limited by the strict performance and power constraints. Consequently, it is a challenge to increase overall dependability, integrity and robust security of embedded systems [4].

E. Maehle et al. (Eds.): ARCS 2014, LNCS 8350, pp. 221–232, 2014.

Identification and security of these embedded systems are emerging as an important concern in embedded computer architecture design. Mechanisms to protect the embedded system can be either included in the hardware architecture or at software level. Physical Unclonable Function (PUF) [5] or hardware intrinsic security [6], have been proposed as physically more secure alternative to storing secrets in a digital memory [7]. The core idea behind these approaches is to use the manufacturing process variation to identify the integrated circuits, which offers a higher level of security against physical level attacks. However, they are limited by environmental variance such as changes in temperature, user interactions and software. There is much existing work focusing on detecting software failure, tampering and malicious codes in embedded systems [1, 4, 8]. These approaches require storing sensitive data in the system as "valid" samples or template. For example, a basic-block control flow graph (CFG) is usually stored and used to examine the running program.

Currently, researchers are working on alternative solutions to the above problems in the fields of digital forensics and machine learning [9]. As electronic devices and components cannot have exactly the same frequency response and latency due to tolerances in production and the different designs employed by various manufacturers, it is possible to find unique features or identifiers from the electronic devices [9]. In order to recognise the features, various machine learning algorithms can also be applied. Based on the above ideas, a new concept termed ICmetrics (Integrated Circuit metrics) was introduced [10]. Embedded systems typically consist of hardware and application specific software, and are applied in a specific environment. These could result in the embedded system performing uniquely to the others. Consequently, the structure, characteristic and behaviour of an embedded system can also be used to identify the devices. Fig.1 exhibits a typical embedded system and ICmetrics system.

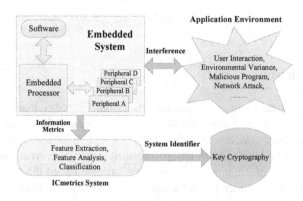

Fig. 1. A typical embedded system and ICmetrics system

In Fig. 1, the embedded system can be affected by many factors, for example, compromised software, unauthorised access, environment changing, internal structure failure and malicious code. All these effects could change the behaviour or characteristic of the embedded system significantly. Since the ICmetrics system is continually monitoring the information metric, and behaviours derived from the embedded system change over time as well, a different system identifier could be generated. As a result of this, a different encryption key will be generated by the key cryptography mechanism [11], using a two phase approach to deal with training and recall. As the ICmetrics system only relies on the properties and features of the system, the system identifier (i.e. basic number or encryption key) can be regenerated on demand and there is no requirement to store it locally. The major advantage of the ICmetrics system is no user data or template is required to be stored, which is essential for applications that have no direct interaction with human operators. Thus, the ICmetrics can improve both security and dependability based on exploitation of the system's unique behaviour.

The information metrics used in the ICmetrics system can be collected from any aspect of the embedded system, for example, memory usage, program monitoring, processor caches, and register status checking. In this paper, we limit the focus on monitoring the system processor's status while running various programs. A method for detecting compromised programs is proposed. The method extracts suitable features from the embedded system (i.e. the performance variance and program counter (PC) register of the embedded processor), enabling it to identify the running programs using Self-Organising Map (SOM) classifier [12]. The experimental results demonstrate the effectiveness of the proposed method for identifying compromised programs. The performance variance and PC status can be one of the information metrics for the ICmetrics system.

The remainder of this paper is organised as follows. A survey of related work is presented in Section 2. The proposed algorithm is introduced in Section 3. The experimental setup and the implementation results are discussed in Section 4. Finally, the conclusions are presented in Section 5.

2   Related Work

As most information is being digitized to facilitate quick access, digital privacy is becoming even more important in protecting personal information [13]. Arora et al [1] addressed secure program execution by focusing on the specific problem of ensuring that the program does not deviate from its intended behaviour. Similar to [1], Rahmatian et al [4] used a CFG to detect intrusion for secured embedded systems by detecting behavioural differences between the correct system and malware. An attack is detected if the system call sequence deviates from the known sequence. Yang et al [14] presents a very interesting approach for detecting digital audio forgeries mainly in MP3. Using a passive approach, they are able to detect doctored MP3 audio by checking frame offsets.

Information hiding can be used in authentication, copyright management as well as digital forensics [15]. Swaminathan et al [15] proposed an enhanced computer system performance with information hiding in the compiled program binaries. The system wide performance is improved by providing additional information to the processor without changing the instruction set architecture. In [16] Boufounos and Rana demonstrate with the use of signal processing and machine learning techniques, to securely determine whether two signals are similar to each other. They also show how to utilize an embedding scheme for privacy-preserving nearest neighbour search by presenting protocols for clustering and authenticating applications.

ICmetrics can be defined as a unique characteristic that a program possesses when running on a particular embedded device and can be used to identify the program and hardware. In this paper we use Cycle per Instruction (CPI) to extract corresponding PC values, and use it as ICmetric for program identification. Using an unsupervised SOM to reduce the dimensionality of PC values, we introduce an offset rule similar to that presented in [14] to detect compromised programs rather than detecting digital audio forgeries. Thus using machine learning techniques [16], we are able to determine whether two PC values are similar to each other, with the use of the program binaries [15] and no prior knowledge of the source code. The following section describes our system to detect compromised programmes in details.

3   Methods for Detecting Compromised Programs

In this section, we first provide an overview of the proposed methods for detecting compromised programs, and then details of the proposed method are introduced.

3.1   Overall System Architecture

In computer systems, a program normally consists of three structure levels: (1) function call level, as represented by function call relationship; (2) internal control flow for each function, represented by a basic-block CFG; (3) instruction stream within each CFG [1]. A program is comprised of a number of micro operations, which depend on the instruction sets and the exact processor architecture that are used in the embedded system. The number of clock cycles for each instruction depends on the used hardware architecture and type of instruction, for example, most of instructions only require one clock cycle to be executed in modern pipelined processer architecture, but some instructions require multi-cycle to be executed, as they need access to memory during processing (e.g. Load, Store and Jump). In particularly, these multi-cycle instructions indicate where the functions call or the condition branch is [4]. Consequently, we can approximately detect the function call or condition branch based on the variance of the processor's performance. In addition, the value of PC register shows the instruction stream of a program, which is also a suitable source for monitoring changes at the instruction level.

Based on the above principle, through monitoring the processor's performance, we detect changes in the function call and CFG, and then analyse the PC values within each CFG. Finally, an overall evaluation could indicate whether the program is compromised or not. In the proposed work, we measure the average CPI as the parameter of a processor's performance. Fig. 2 shows a block diagram of the proposed program monitoring system.

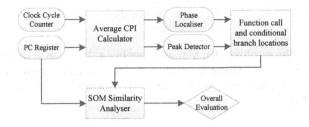

Fig. 2. Overall block diagram of the proposed monitoring system

In Fig. 2, phase localiser and peak point detector blocks are used to obtain the function call and conditional branch location information from average CPI profile respectively, and then the obtained information will be used to extract features for the SOM classifier. The final evaluation is based on the results of the SOM classifier.

3.2   CPI Analysis

CPI indicates the complexity of instructions executed within a particular period of time. The average CPI of a processor can be calculated as described in [17]. Fig. 3 shows an average CPI profile while a program is running in an ARM cortex-M3 processor based embedded platform, where I and f_{max} are 2^{11} and 120 MHz respectively.

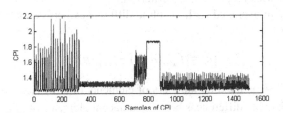

Fig. 3. Example of average CPI diagram

As can be seen from Fig. 3, the program mainly consists of five phases, and there are also many variances (i.e. peaks) within each phase. In the following sections, we introduce a method to obtain the position information of the phases and peaks.

Phase Localiser Block
In the phase localiser block, there are mainly two sub-blocks: mean filter and critical point localiser. The mean filter is first used to smooth the original CPI diagram, the critical point localiser is then used to localise the positions of each phase.

Mean filter
A 1×w rectangular window is used as a mask in the mean filter, the local average value within the mask is then calculated. Let $f(n)$ denote the CPI value at position n which is always the centre point of a rectangular window B with size 1×w. The window mean value $f_{mean}(n)$ is calculated by (1):

$$f_{mean}(n) = \sum_{n \in B} f(n) / w \qquad (1)$$

Fig. 4 shows the resulting diagram after applying the mean filter on the original CPI diagram (i.e. Fig. 3), where w is set to '5'. As can be seen from Fig. 4, the variances within each phase have been significantly suppressed, and the boundaries of each phase still stay intact.

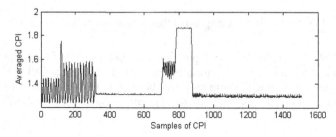

Fig. 4. Resulting CPI diagram after applying the mean filter

Critical point localiser

As the values of two adjacent points at the boundary are normally significantly different, the proposed method is to localise the high variance points, and then select the best candidates based on pre-defined criterion.

Let f_{mean} denote averaged CPI, absolute differences between adjacent elements of f_{mean} can then be calculated by:

$$d(n) = \left| f_{mean}(n+1) - f_{mean}(n) \right| \qquad (2)$$

where $1 \leq n < N$, N is the total numbers of elements in array f_{mean}, $d(n)$ is n^{th} element in an array of absolute differences between adjacent elements of $f_{mean}(n)$.

A threshold t_1 is first used to select the high variance elements from array d, where the indices of the elements are greater than t_1 they are stored in array d_1. After that, absolute differences between adjacent elements of d_1 are calculated to form d_2. Finally, a threshold t_2 is used to select the boundary candidates, where elements greater than t_2 are selected as the candidates. Values of t_1 and t_2 are fixed based on experimental results. In this work, t_1 and t_2 are set to 0.03 and 9 respectively. Fig. 5 shows resulting diagram after applying the critical point localiser on Fig.4.

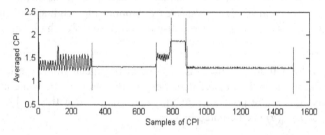

Fig. 5. Resulting diagram after applying the critical point localizer

Peak detector block

In order to obtain positions of peaks and valleys, we apply the peak detector on array d rather than the original array f_{mean}. Pseudo-codes for detecting the peaks are summarised as follows:

```
Peak detection procedure:
Input: d_i is an array of absolute differences between ad-
jacent elements of f_mean in the i^th phase.
Output: P = {p_1, p_2, p_3, ..., p_i} where p_i is a set of locations
for the i^th phase.
for all samples in d_i do
    if d_i(n - 1) < d_i(n) and d_i(n) > d_i(n + 1) then
        d_i'(j) = d_i(n); /* record the amplitude in array d_i'(j) */
    end
end
t_i=mean(d_i'(j));  /*t is mean of all the elements in d_i'*/
for all samples in d_i' do
    if d_i'(j) > t then
        p_i = j;  /*mark j^th element as a peak*/
    end
end
```

Fig. 6 shows resulting diagram after applying the peak detector on array d.

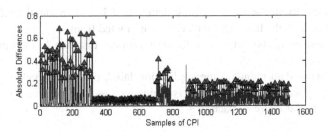

Fig. 6. Diagram following the application of the peak detector

Similarity Analyser

The similarity analyser has three different parts, each with a measure to ascertain the originality of the program in execution. The three parts are the phase, peak and SOM analysers. The first part is used to verify if the number of known phases is the same as the number of phases in the executed program. Any mismatch shows that the number of function calls differ, signifying an insertion or deletion. The second part compares the number of identified peaks within each phase. It must be noted that any difference in the number of peaks does not necessarily mean the program is compromised, but rather a variation in CPI. The first two parts of the analyser becomes useful when the system has completed a cycle. The final part of the analyser uses the SOM to measure similarity between known programs and programs currently executed.

The basic principle of the SOM is to adjust the weight vectors until the neurons represent the input data, while using a topological neighbourhood update rule to ensure that similar prototypes occupy nearby positions on the topological map. PC values extracted from the program execution trace, corresponding to the peaks in the trace are used as inputs to the SOM during training and testing. For a given network with k neurons and N-dimensional input vector $\mathbf{K^i}$, the distance from the jth neuron with weight vector w_j ($j<k$) is given by

$$D_j^2 = \sum_{l=1}^{N} \left(K_l^i - w_{jl} \right)^2 \tag{3}$$

where w_{jl} is the lth component of weight vector w_j. The vector components of the winning neuron w_k with minimum distance D_k are updated as follows, where $\eta \in (0,1)$ is the learning rate.

$$\Delta w_k = \eta \left(K^i - w_k \right) \tag{4}$$

Updates are only carried out during the training phase. Additionally, for every neuron in the network we maintain two extra parameters; the minimum and maximum distances of all input vectors associated with any particular neuron.

After training, the next step is to associate each of the network neurons with the corresponding program or sub-program. In this work, we use Vector Quantization (VQ) [12] to assign labels to the trained neurons in the network as follows:

- Assign labels to all the input training data. The label is an identifier for the program from which the training data has been extracted from.
- Find the neuron in the network with the minimum distance to the labelled input data.
- For each input data maintain the application label, the corresponding neuron and the distance measured. The distance is maintained as a tie breaker for applications that share similar address space.

For each network neuron, we estimate the number of programs that are associated with that neuron. If only one program is associated with a neuron and the number of data points exceeds 5% of the total number of program data points, the neuron is exclusively assigned to that very program. For all programs with more than 5% of data points associated with a neuron, we create a codebook with an entry for the neuron, and the corresponding programs, each with its distance range (i.e. minimum distance and maximum distance).

4   Experimental Results

An embedded system based on a STMicroelectronics STM32F207IG microcontroller equipped with an ARM 32-bit Cortex-M3 processor is used in the proposed work [18]. A combination of KEIL µVision IDE, and ULINKpro Debug and Trace Unit [19] is used to download the program and trace the instructions executed in the microcontroller. High-speed data and instruction trace are streamed directly to the host computer allowing off-line analysis of the program behaviour [19]. MATLAB is used to implement the proposed method prior to hardware implementation. It should be noted that our experimental platform limits the complexity of test programs, as it comes with only 128KB of on-chip RAM and 2MB of external SRAM, for which only 1MB is usable when the tracing port is enabled. This limitation falls within the scope of our initial embedded architecture, expected to have minimal memory, power and computational resources. The concept presented here is very scalable; as the available resources increase the complexity of applications can also be increased.

As our initial focus is dedicated and constrained embedded systems, five algorithms from the automotive package of the MiBench benchmark suite [20] are selected: angle conversion (AC); bit count (BC); cubic function (CF); random numbers (RN); and square roots (SR). These five algorithms are mixed together as a single program, and this program is treated as original. We also propose five further compromised programs formed by various combinations of the five algorithms. In each combination AC, BC, CF, RN, and SR are executed twice. In addition to the above, we also use an "unknown" algorithm "Fibonacci Series (FS)" to replace AC, BC, CF, RN, and SR to represent another five compromised programs for testing. Since the FS algorithm consists of some similar sub-functions to the known algorithms, this experimental setup is more suitable for evaluating the proposed system. At the beginning of the test, we run the original program five times separately in the embedded platform, and all the program execution trace profiles are stored into five different files respectively. One of the files (i.e. the training file) is used for training the SOM classifier and the remainder are used for testing.

During training, PC values from the "training file" are used as input to the SOM. The size of the training vectors is 2048, taken from 2048 PC values for each peak in the training file. The vector values are then normalised before feeding them into the SOM. The epoch use for training is set to 1000, after which VQ is used to assign labels to the neurons. The outputs of the training are network weights, a record of each phase, the corresponding neuron(s), and associated minimum and maximum distance for the phase. In these experiments the network size has been fixed to 20 each of length 2048. For testing, each of the test files (27 files in total) is fed into the trained network to generate individual output files. The output after testing is the peak

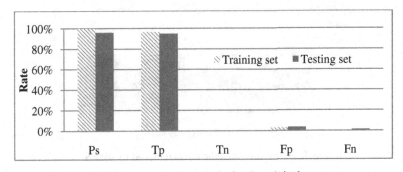

Fig. 7. Training and testing results for the original program

similarity (P_s), the correct detection rate (true positive (T_p) and true negative (T_n)) representing the correct detection rate of the SOM for known testing programs and unknown testing programs respectively, rate of misclassified unknown testing programs (false positive (F_p)) and rate of programs misclassified as compromised (false negative (F_n)). Fig. 7 shows the training and testing results for the original program.

Table 1. Outputs of SOM using compromised testing programs

	P_s (%)		T_p (%)		T_n (%)		F_p (%)		F_n (%)	
	$T_1{}^a$	$T_2{}^b$	T_1	T_2	T_1	T_2	T_1	T_2	T_1	T_2
AC	98.0	98.0	86.5	82.7	0	0	3.9	5.8	9.6	11.5
BC	95.8	94.4	86.7	86.8	0	0	6.7	2.9	6.7	10.3
CF/FS	90.9	0	40.0	0	0	50.0	0	50.0	60.0	0
RN	40.0	80.0	87.5	75.0	0	0	0	0	12.5	25.0
SR	98.7	94.7	68.8	73.8	0	0	1.3	1.3	29.9	25.0

a. Without unknown algorithm; b. With unknown algorithm

As shown in Fig. 7, the training and testing results have very similar performance, but P_s for a particular algorithm may vary when it is executed at different times. This is because CPI does not remain exactly the same as the original value in the training file. In Table I, RN has been repeated twice in T_1 and we replaced CF with FS representing the unknown algorithm in T_2. P_s of 40% in Table I shows RN has the least peak similarity compare to the other algorithms, suggesting RN has been compromised. However, the result from the T_p (87.5%) shows that the algorithm is known to the SOM. Overall, the correct detection rate for our system is above 90.9% for uncompromised programs. P_s of 0% in Table I shows that FS is completely different from CF in the original training file. The result for T_p (0%) in Table I shows that FS is unknown to the SOM. T_n (50%) means that 50% of codes are unknown to the SOM and F_p (50%) means that 50% of codes are known to the SOM but they appeared in the wrong section. As an unknown program is introduced, the overall SOM recognition rate for each algorithm is reduced, which indicates the original program has been compromised. In our experiments, the threshold for detecting a compromised program is set to 50%. Hence a program is treated as compromised if T_n is greater than 50%. Fig. 8 shows the PC profile when the CF is replaced by the FS.

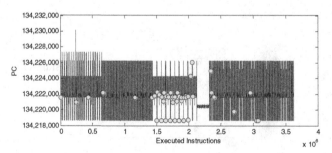

Fig. 8. PC profile when the CF is replaced by the FS

In Fig. 8, the yellow circles indicate selected peaks from compromised part of the executed intrusions. As can be seen from the figure, most of the circles are concentrated at FS section, with the very few sparsely distributed over the remaining programs, contributing to the marginal error.

5   Conclusion

In this paper, we have presented an approach for detecting compromised programs by analysing CPI and PC from an embedded system. Through monitoring the processor's CPI, we detect changes in the function call and CFG, and then analyse the PC values within each CFG using SOM. The results achieved show that the proposed algorithm can be used to detect the changes in a program, and the information metrics can further be generated based on the outputs from the SOM. For example, different basic numbers could be generated based on the results of SOM, as a result of this, different encryption keys can be generated by the key cryptography mechanism, using the recall phase. Since the main aim of this research work is to implement a real-time security solution for complex embedded computer architectures, more evaluation on realistic attacks for the proposed algorithms will further be investigated. Moreover, the proposed algorithm can be used in combination with other ICmetric approaches to evaluate commercial embedded system benchmarks. For evaluation parameters of real-time detection system, the proposed algorithm can also be implemented with a soft-core processor on FPGA as part of an on-line protection system. The online implementation will have the capability of extracting execution trace from customised tracing interfaces directly located on the processor, determine the behaviour in real-time, and subsequently halting the program to prevent any harmful effect on the embedded system architecture.

Acknowledgment. The authors gratefully acknowledge the support of the EU ERDF Interreg IVa 2 Mers Seas Zeeën Cross-border Cooperation Programme – SYSIASS project: Autonomous and Intelligent Healthcare System (project's website http://www.sysiass.eu/).

References

1. Arora, D., Ravi, S., Raghunathan, A., Jha, N.K.: Secure embedded processing through hardware-assisted run-time monitoring. In: Proceedings Design, Automation and Test in Europe, pp. 178–183 (2005)
2. F-Secure Corporation: F-Secure reports amount of malware grew by 100% during 2007, Helsinki, Finland (2007)
3. Dongara, P., Vijaykumar, T.N.: Accelerating private-key cryptography via multithreading on symmetric multiprocessors. In: IEEE International Symposium on Performance Analysis of Systems and Software, pp. 58–69 (2003)
4. Rahmatian, M., Kooti, H., Harris, I.G., Bozorgzadeh, E.: Hardware-Assisted Detection of Malicious Software in Embedded Systems. IEEE Embedded Systems Letters 4, 94–97 (2012)

5. Suh, G.E., Devadas, S.: Physical Unclonable Functions for Device Authentication and Secret Key Generation. In: 44th ACM/IEEE Design Automation Conference, pp. 9–14 (2007)

6. Handschuh, H., Schrijen, G.-J., Tuyls, P.: Hardware Intrinsic Security from Physically Unclonable Functions. In: Sadeghi, A.-R., Naccache, D. (eds.) Towards Hardware-Intrinsic Security, pp. 39–53. Springer, Heidelberg (2010)

7. Hospodar, G., Maes, R., Verbauwhede, I.: Machine learning attacks on 65nm Arbiter PUFs: Accurate modeling poses strict bounds on usability. In: IEEE International Workshop on Information Forensics and Security (WIFS), pp. 37–42 (2012)

8. Arora, D., Ravi, S., Raghunathan, A., Jha, N.K.: Secure embedded processing through hardware-assisted run-time monitoring. In: Proceedings of Design, Automation and Test in Europe, vol. 171, pp. 178–183 (2005)

9. Hanilci, C., Ertas, F., Ertas, T., Eskidere, O.: Recognition of Brand and Models of Cell-Phones From Recorded Speech Signals. IEEE Transactions on Information Forensics and Security 7, 625–634 (2012)

10. Kovalchuk, Y., McDonald-Maier, K.D., Howells, G.: Overview of ICmetrics technology-security infrastructure for autonomous and intelligent healthcare system. International Journal of u- and e- Sevice, Science and Technology 4, 49–60 (2011)

11. Howells, G., Papoutsis, E., Hopkins, A., McDonald-Maier, K.: Normalizing Discrete Circuit Features with Statistically Independent values for incorporation within a highly Secure Encryption System. In: Second NASA/ESA Conference on Adaptive Hardware and Systems, pp. 97–102 (2007)

12. Kohonen, T.: Learning vector quantization. In: Michael, A.A. (ed.) The Handbook of Brain Theory and Neural Networks, pp. 537–540. MIT Press (1998)

13. Deng, M., Wuyts, K., Scandariato, R., Preneel, B., Joosen, W.: A privacy threat analysis framework: supporting the elicitation and fulfillment of privacy requirements. Requirements Eng. 16, 3–32 (2011)

14. Yang, R., Qu, Z., Huang, J.: Detecting digital audio forgeries by checking frame offsets. In: Proceedings of the 10th ACM Workshop on Multimedia and Security, pp. 21–26. ACM, Oxford (2008)

15. Swaminathan, A., Mao, Y., Wu, M., Kailas, K.: Data Hiding in Compiled Program Binaries for Enhancing Computer System Performance. In: Barni, M., Herrera-Joancomartí, J., Katzenbeisser, S., Pérez-González, F. (eds.) IH 2005. LNCS, vol. 3727, pp. 357–371. Springer, Heidelberg (2005)

16. Boufounos, P., Rane, S.: Secure binary embeddings for privacy preserving nearest neighbors. In: IEEE International Workshop on Information Forensics and Security (WIFS), pp. 1–6 (2011)

17. Annavaram, M., Rakvic, R., Polito, M., Bouguet, J., Hankins, R., Davies, B.: The fuzzy correlation between code and performance predictability. In: The 37th International Symposium on Microarchitecture (MICRO), pp. 93–104 (2004)

18. STMicroelectronics. STM32F207G DATA Sheet, http://www.st.com/ (accessed on January 2013)

19. KEIL. Keil uVision IDE Data Sheet, http://www.keil.com/uvision/ (accessed on January 2013)

20. Guthaus, M.R., Ringenberg, J.S., Ernst, D., Austin, T.M., Mudge, T., Brown, R.B.: MiBench: A free, commercially representative embedded benchmark suite. In: IEEE International Workshop on Workload Characterization, pp. 3–14 (2001)

Independent Kernel/Process Checkpointing on Non-Volatile Main Memory for Quick Kernel Rejuvenation

Shuichi Oikawa

Division of Information Engineering, Faculty of Engineering,
Information and Systems, University of Tsukuba
Tsukuba, Ibaraki, Japan

Abstract. This paper presents a quick operating system kernel rejuvenation technique based on the integrated management of the main memory and a file system on non-volatile (NV) memory. The proposed technique independently takes and restores the checkpoints of the kernel and processes in order to accelerate the kernel rejuvenation. We implemented its prototype in Linux, and performed evaluation experiments on a system emulator. The results show the significant reduction of the time required for kernel rejuvenation.

1 Introduction

Software rejuvenation [1] is a proactive technique that copes with software aging. Since software aging tends to occur in large and complex software systems, the operating system (OS) kernel is one of such typical systems; thus, the kernel rejuvenation can improve the reliability of systems [2]. The kernel rejuvenation is, however, typically realized on virtualized environments because various optimizations are possible in order to reduce downtime of systems. Therefore, rebooting the kernel was an only choice to realize the kernel rejuvenation on smaller non-virtualized systems. Rebooting the kernel, however, is a time consuming task, and it makes downtime of such systems long.

In these days, byte addressable non-volatile (NV) memory technologies, such as STT-RAM, PCM, and ReRAM, are being actively researched. Because they are byte addressable, they can be used as main memory by directly connecting them to CPUs [3]. Because they are non-volatile, they can also be used as storage devices [4]. Therefore, the main memory and file system management can be integrated, and the integration enables NV memory to be used as both the main memory and storage. Our approach of such integration constructs a file system on NV memory, and its blocks are allocated for the use of the main memory [5]. This approach enables a tight integration by making the memory allocator directly consult the file system in order to obtain requested memory pages on demand. The file system searches free pages and marks them allocated. Freed pages are returned to the file system.

E. Maehle et al. (Eds.): ARCS 2014, LNCS 8350, pp. 233–244, 2014.

This paper presents a quick kernel rejuvenation technique based on our integrated management of the main memory and a file system on byte addressable NV memory. The proposed technique independently takes and restores the checkpoints of the kernel and user processes in order to accelerate the rejuvenation. It utilizes the integrated management in the two ways. First, the kernel can be quickly rejuvenated by restoring only the execution image of the kernel because NV memory can be excluded from the checkpoint. Second, the NV memory pages allocated for a user process are instantly converted to a checkpoint file without copying. Therefore, the total cost to restart a system can be significantly reduced. We implemented a prototype of the proposed technique in Linux, and performed evaluation experiments on a system emulator. The results show the significant reduction of the time required for rejuvenation.

The proposed technique can also be used for a replacement of the current hibernation mechanism, which requires saving and restoring the whole volatile memory. It makes it unnecessary to save the kernel portion of the memory, and the kernel is rejuvenated after system resumption. It is also possible to make system resumption even faster by selectively restoring user processes on demand.

The rest of this paper is organized as follows. Section 2 describes the background and the related work. Section 3 describes the target system structure that is based on NV main memory. Section 4 presents the design and implementation. Section 5 shows the experiment results. Finally, Section 6 concludes this paper. Unless otherwise specified, NV memory mentioned in this paper is byte addressable.

2   Background and Related Work

2.1   New Non-Volatile Memory Technologies

New NV memory technologies, such as PCM, MRAM, and STT-RAM, enable persistent data store without power supply. Since these technologies use resistance values rather than electric charge, their values are persistent without continuous power supply. PCM technology is based on a chalcogenide material, which takes the two states, amorphous and crystalline. Because their resistance values are different, they can encode binary information. Since PCM requires the material state being changed, changing its value takes longer and also its lifetime is limited. MRAM technology is based on a magnetic tunneling junction (MTJ), which consists of two ferromagnetic layers and one tunnel barrier layer. One of ferromagnetic layers of can change its magnetic direction. Because their resistance values of different directions are different, they can encode binary information. STT-RAM is a new type of MRAM, of which performance of STT-RAM is comparable to DRAM, and there is no need to treat it differently [6]. While MRAM and STT-RAM have better characteristics than PCM in order to be used for main memory, they are less dense; thus, their capacity tends to be less than PCM. Since the researchers and manufacturers of NV memory claims that scaling DRAM will end soon because of fundamental technology limit, such as leakage and refresh dynamic power, NV memory became a candidate that can replace or be used along with DRAM.

The researches on their use for either main memory or secondary storage have been conducted actively but independently. Because these NV memory technologies are byte addressable and can achieve access speed comparable to DRAM, their use for main memory has been studied. The development of PCM matured before MRAM and STT-RAM, it was first considered to be the most close to replace DRAM; thus, there were the active researches conducted to utilize PCM as main memory [3]. Since these were the researches on the computer architecture, the operating system (OS) takes only a minor role [7]. There were also the researches that construct file systems on NV memory by taking advantage of its byte addressability and larger capacity [4].

2.2   Checkpointing

Checkpointing was developed as a technique for rollback recovery. The state of an executing program is saved in persistent storage. After a failure, the program can be restarted from the saved state.

Checkpointing is useful also for software rejuvenation in the two ways. First, checkpointing can accelerate software rejuvenation by restarting a program from its clean state. Booting a complex program, such as the OS kernel and database systems, takes time. It takes less time to restore its state that was saved soon after its booting, and such a state is clean to make it rejuvenated. Second, checkpointing enables the continuation of an executing program, of which execution environment depends on the software that requires rejuvenation. While such a program also needs to be rebooted without checkpointing, checkpointing enables its continuous execution with interruption caused by the rejuvenation of its underlying software.

Dong, et. al. [8] proposed a utilization of PCM as a device to save a checkpoint image in it. This work assumes that PCM chips stacked on top of DRAM chips and that the data in DRAM can be copied directly to PCM within the same memory module. It employs the existing method to select the data to copy from DRAM to PCM. Li, et. al. [9] proposed a fault-tolerance process abstraction based on NV memory, called NV-process. While NV-process requires the significantly different management of user processes and memory pages, our technique is simple and more applicable to the existing systems. Moreover, NV-process does not discuss anything to shorten the time for the kernel rejuvenation.

2.3   Integrated Main Memory and File System Management

The integrated main memory and file system management is the core mechanism of our work, and is described in Section 3.

As its related work, there are only few papers that describe the integration of main memory and storage. Bailey, et. al. [10] discusses various possibilities, including the integration of main memory and storage and the aspects of execution models, made possible by employing NV memory as main memory.

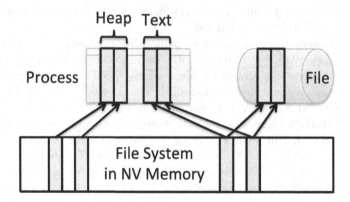

Fig. 1. A system that integrates NV main memory and a file system

Jung, et. al. [11] describes the policy and possible effect of the integration, but does not mention any of software rejuvenation. It is important to mention neither of them realized the integration.

3   System Based on NV Main Memory

This section describes the background of the work presented in this paper. Firstly, the target system structure is described. Next, the virtual memory system architecture is described. Finally, the integration method of main memory and file system management is described.

3.1   Target System Structure

Since there is no publicly available system that employs NV memory as its main memory, we need to construct a reasonable target system structure. In this paper, we assume that 1) DRAM and NV memory constitute the main memory of a system, and 2) DRAM and NV memory are placed in the same physical address space. DRAM and NV memory are connected to the memory bus(ses) of CPUs, and they are mapped in the same physical address space; thus, they can be accessed in the same way with appropriate physical addresses, and there is no distinction between them from the OS kernel.

Our approach to use NV memory integrates the main memory and storage management; thus, NV memory takes the roles of both the main memory and storage. The integration method utilizes a file system constructed on NV memory. The file system is used to store directories and files, and these contents persist across the termination and rebooting of the OS kernel. The free blocks of the file system are allocated for main memory while a system is running. They are returned to the file system when a system terminates. Figure 1 depicts such integration of the main memory and storage management.

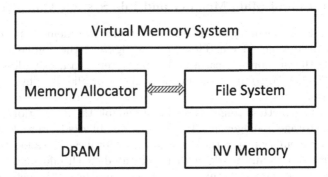

Fig. 2. Virtual memory system architecture and its relationships with the memory allocator and a file system

On the target system structure, of which memory consists of DRAM and NV memory, the kernel is loaded on DRAM and manages the whole DRAM by its memory allocator. This is mainly because the memory management in the kernel heavily depends on the memory allocator for its flexibility. NV memory is used for user processes. Memory requests from user processes are per page. Such requests match the per block allocation from a file system.

We consider this structure is reasonable when our primary target systems are clients devices, such as note PCs, tablets, and smart phones. Since these client devices do not require a large amount of storage spaces, NV memory suffices the needs of storage.

3.2   Virtual Memory System

The virtual memory system of the Linux kernel is built upon the memory allocator and file systems, and they are tightly integrated for efficiency. Figure 2 depicts the architecture. Traditionally, the memory allocator manages DRAM, and file systems manage storage. Since our target system employs NV memory for storage, a file system is used to manage NV memory. The virtual memory system uses the memory allocator to allocate physical memory pages from DRAM. It then maps the allocated DRAM pages in virtual address spaces, and finally they become accessible from processes.

The virtual memory system can use XIP[1]-enabled file systems, such as Ext2 and PRAMFS [12]. When they are used, files can be directly mapped in user process address spaces. Since the physical memory pages of the files are mapped through the virtual memory system, no copying of pages occurs. We use the XIP feature to map files on NV memory to avoid unnecessary copying.

---

[1] XIP stands for eXecution In Place.

3.3   Integration of Main Memory and File System Management

In order to use NV memory as main memory, physical memory pages need to be allocated from a file system. Therefore, in Figure 2, the double arrowed line that connects the memory allocator and a file system is a missing link. The link needs to be connected to make the memory allocator allocate physical memory pages from a file system.

The integration method connects the link to enable the integration of the main memory and storage management. It allocates free blocks from a file system for the use of main memory just as those are allocated for files. The allocation is done by finding free blocks and marking them allocated. Such information is stored in the management data structures of a file system; thus, this method requires the *direct* manipulation of those data structures, and the additional code for the allocation and freeing needs to be implemented. The integration method was implemented in Ext2 and PRAMFS. Its details are described elsewhere [5].

4   Design and Implementation

This section describes a quick kernel rejuvenation technique. In order to take advantage of the integrated management of the main memory and a file system, the proposed technique consists of two methods, one for the kernel and the other for user processes. While both of the methods are based on the checkpoint/restart system, they take different approaches in accord with the natures of the kernel and user processes. The combination of the different approaches enables the significant reduction of the total cost of the kernel rejuvenation.

4.1   Kernel Rejuvenation

On our target system structure, of which memory consists of DRAM and NV memory, the kernel is loaded on DRAM and manages the whole DRAM by its memory allocator. The size of DRAM can be small because DRAM is used to store the kernel's internal data structures but not user processes. NV memory is used for the memory allocation of user processes, and the XIP feature of a file system on NV memory reduces the necessity of page cache significantly.

Since the size of DRAM is small on our target system and the kernel resides on DRAM, the cost to copy the whole DRAM is small. Therefore, we take an approach to copy the whole DRAM in order to checkpoint and to restore the kernel. The whole DRAM data is copied to NV memory to checkpoint the kernel, and the copy is restored to DRAM to rejuvenate the kernel.

Before checkpointing the kernel, the devices of a system need to bet set to the known states, so that the kernel can resume the devices when rejuvenated. The Linux kernel provides the suspend/resume feature of devices as a part of its power management subsystem. This feature is used to set the devices in the quiescent states and to resume them.

4.2   User Process Checkpoint/Restart

NV memory is used for the memory allocation of user processes; thus, the blocks of a file system created on NV memory are allocated and mapped in the virtual address spaces of user processes. While these blocks are not referenced from any files, they are a part of the file system; thus, they can become a part of files by having files reference to them.

The proposed approach for the checkpoint/restart of a user process has these allocated blocks instantly converted to a file without copying. A process that needs to be restarted after kernel rejuvenation takes a checkpoint, and saves it in a file. The checkpoint file is created from the blocks allocated for the process. The references to these allocated block are added to the checkpoint file in order to convert them to the file. Such conversion does not require allocating new blocks and copying the data to these blocks. Only the management data structures inside the kernel need to be additionally saved in the checkpoint file. Therefore, creating a checkpoint of a user process can be finished quickly.

The restart of a process from a checkpoint does not require copying the data, either. The blocks saved in the checkpoint file are directly mapped in the virtual address space of the restarted process; thus, they are referenced from the appropriate page table entries of the process. When the checkpoint file is used just once to restart a process, the blocks of the file can be overwritten. If a process may be restarted multiple times from the same checkpoint file, the data of the checkpoint file needs to be preserved. In this case, the copy-on-write (COW) is applied to the mapped blocks.

Figure 3 depicts the checkpoint/restart of a user process by the proposed system. The figure shows that the blocks allocated for a process directly become a part of the checkpoint file, and also that the the blocks of the file are directly mapped in a process. Except for the management data structures inside the kernel, the execution image of a process can reside on NV memory as a file.

4.3   Putting Pieces Together

The proposed technique independently takes and restores the checkpoints of the kernel and processes in order to accelerate the kernel rejuvenation. The checkpoint of the kernel is taken at the boot time because the kernel rejuvenation is our objective. In order to skip over a time consuming boot process but to keep the checkpoint consistent with the file system on NV memory, the checkpoint should be taken before mounting the file system. When the kernel is rejuvenated by restoring the checkpoint, the kernel mounts the file system; thus, the data of the file system can be preserved across the kernel rejuvenation.

In order to continue the processing of user processes after the kernel rejuvenation, the checkpoints of processes are taken just before the rejuvenation. The checkpoint files are stored in the file system on NV memory. After the kernel is rejuvenated and the file system is mounted, the checkpoint files become accessible. Because the data of the file system is preserved across the kernel rejuvenation, the checkpoint files created before the rejuvenation are the latest

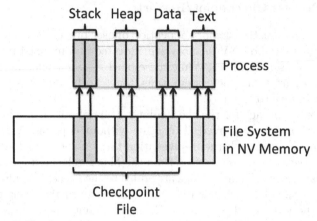

Stack Heap Data Text

Process

File System
in NV Memory

Checkpoint
File

Fig. 3. Checkpoint/restart of a user process by the proposed system

ones. User processes are resumed from these checkpoint files. Therefore, they can continue the work across the rejuvenation.

Checkpoint/restart systems handle user process states, such as a process id, opened file descriptors, signal handlers, and so on, managed inside the kernel. They usually implement kernel modules that retrieve and restore these states. The amount of data required to save these states is much smaller than a user process image, the existing mechanism is sufficient enough.

5   Evaluation

This section first describes the evaluation method and then shows the experiment results.

5.1   Evaluation Method

We employed the QEMU system emulator to construct the target system as described in Section 3.1. The evaluation results presented below do not take into account the difference of access latencies between DRAM and NV memory because of the two reasons. First, this paper focuses on an application of the integrated main memory and file system management to software rejuvenation. Second, NV memory technologies are still under active development, and it is possible that some of them, such as STT-RAM and MRAM, will perform comparably to DRAM [6].

The version of QEMU used for the evaluation is 1.0.1, and QEMU emulates x86_64. It was modified to emulate NV memory that persists its contents across termination and rebooting of the emulator. A file is used for the persistence of NV memory. The file is mapped into the physical address space emulated by QEMU. The experiments were performed on QEMU invoked with the following options:

```
% qemu -icount 0 -m 128 -nvmemory \
  file=nvmm.img,physaddr=0x100000000
```

With the above options, QEMU is invoked with 128MB DRAM along with NV memory mapped from 0x100000000 of the physical address. The size of the file emulating NV memory (nvmm.img) is 4GB. While the size of DRAM is passed to the Linux kernel through BIOS, the information of NV memory is not passed in order to make their management separate.

The evaluation of execution costs needs to measure execution times. Times counted by the interrupts from a timer device are not accurate enough on system emulators. Instead, the number of executed instructions is used as the measure of execution costs. Our past work [13] shows that the number of executed instructions strongly correlates with the execution cost of mobile processors, such as Intel Atom, which are our target systems; thus, it is adequate to use the number of executed instructions for the evaluation of execution costs. The -icount 0 option of QEMU lets the TSC (time stamp counter) register count the number of executed instructions. The RDTSC instruction reads the value of TSC.

The Linux kernel version 3.4 and BLCR version 0.8.5 [14] were modified as described in Section 3.3 and 4. We employed PRAMFS as its file system.

5.2   Quick Rejuvenation Experiment

We performed an experiment that evaluates the proposed quick rejuvenation in two steps because the rejuvenation of a system including user processes is not automated yet. First, we measured the numbers of the instructions for the boot and rejuvenation of the kernel. Second, we measured the numbers of the instructions for the checkpoint/restart of a user process using the existing and proposed methods. Finally, we calculated the total rejuvenation costs by the existing and proposed methods from these numbers.

Table 1 shows the numbers of the instructions measured for the boot and rejuvenation of the kernel. The number of instructions for the kernel boot is calculated from the values of the TSC at the beginning of start_kernel() and just before opening the console in kernel_init(). start_kernel() is the first function written in the C language that starts the boot process, and kernel_init() is almost the last step of the boot process that mounts the root file system. The number of instructions for the kernel rejuvenation includes all the necessary steps required for the rejuvenation including the restoration of the memory image, the register contents, and the device states.

The experiment results show that the kernel rejuvenation is x10 faster than the kernel boot. The restoration of the device states takes approximately 20% of the number of instructions for the target emulator system, of which configuration is relatively simple. Since real hardware systems have more complex configuration, the cost for the restoration of the device states may increase for them.

Table 1. The numbers of instructions for the kernel boot and rejuvenation

Method	Instruction count
Kernel Boot	570,187,040
Rejuvenation	55,120,925

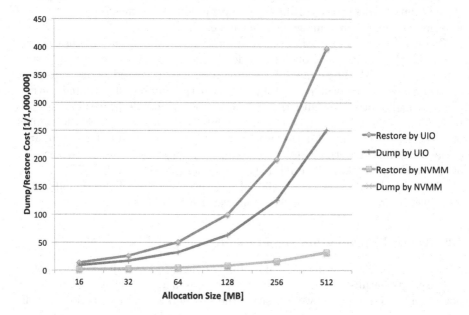

Fig. 4. Comparison of the checkpoint and restart costs of a user process on QEMU

Figure 4 and 5 show the checkpoint and restart costs and the calculated rejuvenation costs by the existing and proposed methods, respectively. The allocation size is the memory size allocated by a user process. Boot+UIO shows the cumulative cost of the kernel boot and the checkpoint/restart of a user process by the existing method that copies the data between a process and a file. Quick Rejuvenation shows the cumulative cost of the kernel rejuvenation and the checkpoint/restart of a user process by the proposed method that preserves and restores the pages of a user process without copying.

The results show the significance of the proposed method. The proposed method is x10 faster than the existing method for all the allocation sizes of a user process. While the cost for the existing method increases sharply as the allocation size of a user process increases, the cost for the proposed method increases only gently. Therefore, the proposed method works significantly better than the existing method for user processes of various allocation sizes.

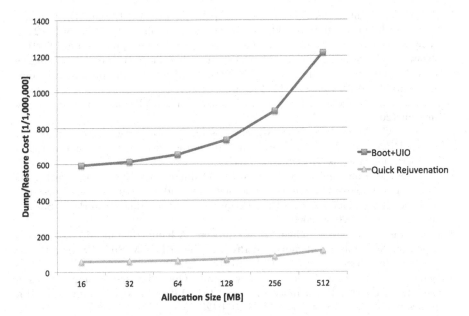

Fig. 5. Comparison of the cumulative costs for the rejuvenation of system on QEMU

6   Summary

This paper presented a quick software rejuvenation technique based on the integrated management of the main memory and a file system on NV memory. By having NV memory dedicated to the memory allocation for user processes, the kernel image can be quickly restored independently from NV memory. By converting the blocks allocated for a user process to a file, it becomes possible to take its checkpoint and to restore it without copying data. The proposed technique was implemented in Linux, and the evaluation results showed the significant reduction of the time required for rejuvenation.

References

1. Huang, Y., Kintala, C., Kolettis, N., Fulton, N.: Software Rejuvenation: Analysis, Module and Applications. In: Proc. of Int'l Symp. Fault-Tolerant Computing, pp. 381–391 (1995)
2. Baker, M., Sullivan, M.: The Recovery Box: Using Fast Recovery to Provide High Availability in the UNIX Environment. In: Proc. of the USENIX Conference, pp. 31–44 (1992)
3. Lee, B.C., Ipek, E., Mutlu, O., Burger, D.: Architecting phase change memory as a scalable dram alternative. In: Proc. of the 36th International Symposium on Computer Architecture (ISCA 2009), pp. 2–13 (2009)

4. Condit, J., Nightingale, E.B., Frost, C., Ipek, E., Lee, B., Burger, D., Coetzee, D.: Better I/O through byte-addressable, persistent memory. In: Proc. of the 22nd Symposium on Operating Systems Principles (SOSP 2009), pp. 133–146 (2009)

5. Oikawa, S.: Integrating Memory Management with a File System on a Non-Volatile Main Memory System. In: Proc. of the 28th ACM Symposium on Applied Computing (SAC 2013), pp. 1589–1594 (2013)

6. Park, S.W.: Overcoming the Scaling Problem for NAND Flash. Flash Memory Summit (2012)

7. Mogul, J.C., Argollo, E., Shah, M., Faraboschi, P.: Operating system support for NVM+DRAM hybrid main memory. In: Proc. of the 12th Conference on Hot Topics in Operating Systems, HotOS 2009 (2009)

8. Dong, X., Muralimanohar, N., Jouppi, N., Kaufmann, R., Xie, Y.: Leveraging 3D PCRAM technologies to reduce checkpoint overhead for future exascale systems. In: Proc. of the Conference on High Performance Computing Networking, Storage and Analysis, SC 2009 (2009)

9. Li, X., Lu, K., Wang, X., Zhou, X.: NV-process: A Fault-Tolerance Process Model Based on Non-Volatile Memory. In: Proc. of the 3rd ACM SIGOPS Asia-Pacific Workshop on Systems, APSys 2012 (2012)

10. Bailey, K., Ceze, L., Gribble, S.D., Levy, H.M.: Operating system implications of fast, cheap, non-volatile memory. In: Proc. of the 13th USENIX Conference on Hot Topics in Operating Systems, HotOS 2011 (2011)

11. Jung, J.-Y., Cho, S.: Dynamic co-management of persistent RAM main memory and storage resources. In: Proc. of the 8th ACM International Conference on Computing Frontiers, CF 2011 (2011)

12. Protected and Persistent RAM Filesystem (2012), http://pramfs.sourceforge.net/

13. Oikawa, S., Miki, S.: File-based Memory Management for Non-Volatile Main Memory. In: Proc. of the 37th IEEE Annual International Computers, Software & Applications Conference (COMPSAC 2013), pp. 559–568 (2013)

14. Hargrove, P., Duell, J.: Berkeley Lab Checkpoint/Restart (BLCR) for Linux Clusters. In: Proc. of Scientific Discovery through Advanced Computing (SciDAC), pp. 494–499 (2006)

Author Index